797,885 Books

are available to read at

www.ForgottenBooks.com

Forgotten Books' App
Available for mobile, tablet & eReader

ISBN 978-1-330-86652-8
PIBN 10115778

HOW TO PREPARE
ESSAYS, LECTURES, ARTICLES,
BOOKS, SPEECHES
AND LETTERS

WITH HINTS ON WRITING FOR THE PRESS

BY

EUSTACE H. MILES, M.A.

FORMERLY SCHOLAR OF KING'S COLLEGE, AND HONOURS COACH IN ESSAY-WRITING
AT CAMBRIDGE UNIVERSITY

THIRD IMPRESSION

RIVINGTONS

34, *KING STREET, COVENT GARDEN*
LONDON
1905

CONTENTS

PART III.

How to Express Ideas : Style.

PART IV.

How to Teach, Learn, and Practise Composition: with General Hints.

Part V.

Hints on Writing for the Press, Speaking, and Letter-Writing.

Part VI.

Advantages of this System, with Answers to Objections.

Appendix.

PREFACE

MANY who themselves can easily write excellent Articles or make excellent Speeches, by the light of nature, will utterly fail to teach beginners the art of Writing or Speaking. Indeed, some of the very greatest Essayists have made quite ridiculous attempts to explain how 'Style' can be acquired, or even what it really *is*.

An illustration from elsewhere may show the true reason for this failure. A player of Billiards sees Roberts making one of his large breaks, or a player ·of Lawn Tennis sees Doherty make a beautiful stroke from the back of the court; or else perhaps it is Latham who is playing Tennis or Rackets, or it may be some celebrated Cricketer or Rower or Fencer or Boxer. But, whoever it may be, if he does his work *well*, then that work will look very easy. The admirer now goes home and tries to imitate what he has seen the skilled player do; in the next game which he plays he tries to reproduce the stroke, but fails lamentably. Why is this? Probably it is chiefly because he does some *part or parts* of the action wrongly.

A good stroke at Billiards, for example, is a very *complex* thing. It cannot be perfect unless each part of the stroke be perfect in itself; and unless, at the same time, each part be perfectly combined with the other parts. There must be not only perfect parts but also perfect co-operation or co-ordination of the parts.

The one chance of improvement for an average individual is to find out what these parts are, and then to master them one by one. He must analyse the whole stroke, and must not attempt to do it as if it were a single unit. It is true that the born player, by the light of genius, does the whole stroke *as* a whole stroke, and perhaps is not aware that it *can* be divided into parts: he may even deny it. None the less it has often been proved that it *can* be divided into parts, and that to master each part separately is a much easier process than to master the whole at once. It is not going too far to say that for average people to master the whole stroke at once is an absolute impossibility.

Unfortunately, however, a great deal of our teaching is in the hands of those who do things instinctively and by the light of nature. They themselves do the whole thing as a whole, all together, and in a single action, and they may do the thing very well indeed. But, because they do it in this way themselves, it does not in the least follow that this is the best way for others to learn to do it. They themselves are geniuses, and therefore exceptions: most of those who are to be taught are not geniuses but average people, or people below the average. They have to move step by step and with effort over the ground which the genius covers with a flying leap.

And this applies also to Essay-Writing and Speaking. They are very complicated processes, and must be practised and conquered *part by part*, before the various parts can be successfully combined together, and before Essay-Writing and Speaking can be done as single processes.

Let me take another comparison. Supposing you had to build a house, and only had a pile of bricks, or perhaps only rough-hewn stones of various sizes. How would you set about building your house? We will suppose that you can already put bricks in a line, and even put mortar between them, or arrange rough-hewn stones so that they could make a single wall. Now, in building a house, will you begin by making a room? No, perhaps you will first get a full list of rooms, etc., and then choose just those which you want. Otherwise, you will probably forget some important room, or you might even forget the staircase. Secondly you will decide on the size and positions of the various rooms: you will assign to the chief rooms the largest size and the best positions, and you will decide the shape of the rooms also. Now you might begin to build, for now you have your plan mapped out. Now, also, it would be time to attend to the mortar. Last of all, there might come the furnishing. But it is obvious that you could not build a house well or easily, unless you had had *practice in each one of these departments*, in deciding on the rooms, in arranging them, in planning them, in building them, and in furnishing them. Each part would have to be studied by itself, and it is well known that there are specialists who give up their lives to one or two of these several departments, or even to a sub-division of one of them.

An Essay or a Speech is not less complicated than

this. I will assume that you have the Words already, and the power to fit them into Sentences. You have the bricks and a certain kind of mortar. It now remains for you to do the rest of the work part by part. E.g. you will have to *Collect* and make a list of your Ideas (Headings and Sub-Headings) for the Essay or Speech. You will have to *Select*, deciding which are to be used and which are not. You will have to *Arrange* the selected Headings. And then you will have to *Express* them—in itself not a simple task.

Let me take just one of the branches of *Expression* alone, and you can then realise how complicated is the process of Essay-writing or Speaking. You have an Idea which you feel ought to be *Emphasised*, because it is so important. Now how can you emphasise it? Of course you can underline it, or you can repeat it, perhaps changing the words. Well and good : these are quite legitimate means, though there are some who do not allow underlining. But what other means can you use? When I wished just now to emphasise the difficulty and complexity of most of the things that geniuses do so easily, I emphasised it by a Comparison or Illustration, namely that of building a house. It is the same with Essay-Writing and Speaking. This is one of the most useful means of Emphasising, and is really (see p. 284) a form of Repetition. By a Comparison we repeat the Idea under a slight disguise. And why did I particularly choose the building of a house, or the playing of a game? I did so because I thought that it would be easier to understand, and I thought also that it would be more interesting. Another means of Emphasis (see p. 291) would be Contrast. Black stands out far more emphatically if there is a background of white. Freedom is far more emphatically described if there is the contrast of slavery ; and so on. And there are many other means of Emphasising, which will be shown in their proper place (p. 281). The above will be sufficient for the present purpose. The lesson surely is that to emphasise, in this way, an Idea which is felt to be important, is not an automatic process to most people ; it is not done instinctively, and by the light of nature. They may feel that the Idea *ought* to be Emphasised, but they do not know the means. And they obviously ought to practise this art of Emphasising by itself, as a separate Exercise, centring and focussing their attention on this alone.

My method will therefore be to take each part of the process of Essay-Writing or Speaking, since it *is* a complicated process, and to see how each of the parts can be mastered by itself. I shall go upon the principle upon which the Romans went in their conquests, viz. ' DIVIDE ET IMPERA ', ' Isolate what you have to master, and master it part by part'. And, besides this, make certain of what you have already mastered, before you proceed to fresh attacks.

For I do not think that the reason why so many people fail to write good Essays or to make good Speeches is so much that they are barren of Ideas, or that their Grammar is bad, or even that their Expression is very bad ; I think their chief fault is that *they try to do all at once that of which they cannot yet do any single part well,* even by itself. I often noticed that most Candidates in Examinations used to begin to write their Essays at once. They never realised that their minds were thereby being distracted and divided among many different processes, each of which is particularly hard even when taken alone. For all at once their minds are being called upon to Collect Ideas, to Select and decide which are important, etc., to Arrange the Selected Ideas, and to Express them. To try all this as a single action is most extraordinarily unscientific, even if a few brilliant geniuses here and there have succeeded in the attempt.

As I said above, few things are more lamentable than the attempts of many good Writers to say what good Writing is. It helps the learner very little to be told that good Writing can be known by its indefinable charm! The real truth is that good Writers seldom know how it is that they write well: they have not analysed the Art of Writing. With myself it has been very different. I have had to teach myself most of what I know. At School, there were few who wrote worse Essays than I did. Since then I have learnt a great deal from various books, and have learnt a great deal more by experiments, and by attempts at teaching others.

The process by which I arrived at the conclusions which are given in this Book might be interesting to the reader.

I first of all began with Games, and at Games I failed to improve, in spite of training and practice. Eventually I discovered the reason why, and I found that it would be almost impossible to improve without studying a Game *part by part.* I found that what I had considered to be a simple action was really an action consisting of perhaps ten or fifteen parts ;* all those parts I now began to master separately, and I improved far more than I had thought possible. It then occurred to me that this same Method might be applied to the learning and teaching of other things besides Games : I tried to apply it to various subjects, e.g. History, and Philology. The different Principles, by which each part might be mastered, I have attempted to work out by making experiments, by reading Books, by listening to advice, and by trying to teach and lecture, and by writing down my ideas on paper and taking notes of the different results from time to time.

Essay-writing is one of the last things which I have tried to teach at Cambridge, and it only occurred to me to do so when I saw what a great need there was for some such teaching. For here every Examination now has an Essay in it. At Oxford the Essay has been insisted on for a longer period.

I found that the books on the subject were mostly by geniuses and not by patient plodders like myself; not only were they far too detailed to begin with, but they did not go to the root of the matter. I found also that those who were supposed to teach the subject would occasionally ask, 'How *can* one set about teaching Essays?' Indeed I once heard a well-known Essay-

* See "Lessons in Lawn Tennis" (Upcott Gill).

writer say that Essay-Writing could not possibly be
taught; for he said he himself had tried to teach it.
And of course it is probably true that perfect Essay-
Writing cannot be entirely taught. But it occurred to
me that in a subject like this there must be some way
of *improving* people, not indeed up to the point of perfection, but yet considerably.

I therefore tried to divide the subject into its various
parts, asking myself what an Essay-writer ought to do
first of all, what should be the first part that he should
attack; and it occurred to me that the Collection of
Ideas or Headings should come first, somewhat as in
the house the list of rooms should come first. Then
these Ideas should be examined, so that the important
Ideas might be selected, and the rest of the Scheme
should be made, including the Sub-Headings to these
Main Headings. The Ideas should be Arranged, and a
general Outline of the Essay should be made, somewhat as one would make an outline of a Drawing or of
a Map, before one proceeded to fill in the details.

But I found that to Collect the Ideas was by no
means a simple task. The English education does not
encourage learners to think. They are generally told to
reproduce the ideas of others, and, unless the question
comes straight out of the Text-book, they often find
themselves quite unable to answer it. On examining
the Essays of various pupils I found that they had been
Collecting together in their Essays only half the facts
or illustrations which they really knew all the time. It
became then a problem, 'How could the Headings for

an Essay be Collected?' And I began to make various *Lists* which might apply to *many kinds or types* of Essays. These Lists will be found e.g. on pages 83 and 92. I have called them 'General Lists'. If the reader, for instance, had to give a survey of England as it is to-day, he would find it very hard to think of Headings; but if he had a General List of Headings, if he had before him all the chief topics, then he would find it very fairly easy to Select what he wanted. So I made a certain number of general Lists which would apply to *most* Essays.

Then came the difficulty of learning these Lists, and to meet this I have suggested that, when once the Lists have been mastered and understood, they might be learnt by means of Rhymes.

The process of Arranging these Headings I also found very difficult, and my chief help was to get hold of two or three different Principles, which will be explained on page 172 foll., and to use the Card-System (p. 186).

But 'Style' was the hardest part of all. I knew that certain Writers were good Writers, and had a good Style; but I found it extraordinarily hard to analyse that Style. Why should such-and-such a piece be good English and good Style, and another piece quite the reverse? The greatest help here (see p. 212) I got from the New Testament.

I thus arrived at the results which I give in this Book. And it seemed to me a great advantage, in a complex subject like this, to divide it into its component parts, and then to see how each part can be practised by itself, and how each mistake can be analysed by the learner, for himself, and can then be corrected. This appears to me to be the only scientific way of teaching the average learner. *It is of little use to show him the perfect model without analysing it,* and making him see exactly where it differs from the imperfect attempt. It follows therefore that the Book is not intended for the genius, who does the whole thing correctly as a whole, and not only correctly but also without conscious effort. That is to say, it is not for him unless he wishes to teach others. If he *does* wish to teach others, then even *he* might find this Book of some help. For instance, if a learner says to him 'How shall I emphasise this idea?', the genius-writer will probably be entirely at a loss: he will be unable to understand the state of mind of anyone who feels a difficulty here. He himself does the thing unconsciously and automatically: he 'knoweth not how'.

The Book is meant for those who themselves intend to write Books, either in Prose or in Poetry, or Articles, or Essays, or who wish to prepare Speeches of various kinds (whether they be after-dinner Speeches, or Speeches in the House, or at Meetings, or at Debates), or Lectures, or Sermons. Even Conversation and ordinary Letters will be helped by the method which I outline. For Examiners, for Teachers, for Learners, for Critics, I believe the suggestions may be of value. There are a great many, for instance, who are under the delusion that it is 'economy' to write everything huddled together on a small piece of paper; a good deal of failure in Writing is due to this false economy. Paper is becoming cheaper and cheaper, and, the more liberally it is used, the better the results are likely to be.

Above all, the Book is intended for beginners, for average people, and for those who are below the average. As I have meant it to suit all readers, I have approached the same idea from many points of view. For instance, when I have treated of Comparisons, I have not only treated them under various Headings, e.g. under 'the means of Interesting the readers', 'the means of making a thing Clear', or 'the means of introducing Variety', or 'the means of Emphasising', etc, under all of which Headings Comparisons should come; but I have also *collected, in a special Chapter* on Comparisons, these various functions which are theirs. Besides this, I have suggested special *Exercises* on Comparisons, and have called attention to some of the commonest *Faults* with respect to them.

I believe that, if the Principles of Learning *this* subject are once mastered, they will be found useful in learning almost any other subject. I have certainly found them of great value in helping the Memory, and in helping the teaching of History, Philology, Prose-Compositions, Verse-Compositions, and numerous other subjects. If this is so in reality, it would be a great help for teaching and learning generally, and it would show that many (if not all) subjects can to some extent be learnt and taught according to a single method ; in which method not the least important factor would be the practising of the various processes singly, so that the whole attention may be concentrated and focussed on each one process independently)

I should like to express here my thanks for the great care which has been taken in the printing of this work. Of course some errors must have escaped notice, and I shall be glad to have them pointed out. In fact, any suggestions will be very welcome.

KING'S COLLEGE, CAMBRIDGE 1899.

Part I.

B

PART I. INTRODUCTION AND SUMMARY.

[When the Book is being read for the first time, Chapter IV. might be omitted.]

CHAPTER I. ADVANTAGES OF BEING ABLE TO WRITE AND SPEAK WELL.

FOR the advantages of preparing Compositions and Speeches by the system suggested in this Book, I must refer to Chapter LXXIV. (p. 397). Here I shall speak chiefly of the general advantages of being able to Write well and to Speak well.

One of the tendencies of English education is to make the learner absorb a number of facts without ever thinking over them or using them. Now the preparing of Compositions and Speeches should make him think over and review his mental stock-in-trade from time to time, and should encourage him to add to this stock, that is, to read, listen, ask questions, and meditate. It should also give him greater activity in putting his stock-in-trade to some use : otherwise the masses of materials might either lie uncultivated, or might at any rate be very difficult to utilise.

Besides this, the preparing of Compositions and Speeches should encourage business-like qualities : not only should it train people into the habit of going straight to the point, but in many ways it should save time and exertion. Time and exertion are not absolutely the same as money, but still he who saves time and saves exertion has more chance of saving and making money.

Another faculty which is very much wanting in England is the faculty of speaking well and *readily* and without nervousness. In many American Schools, the children are taught to make speeches at a moment's notice. In England, people are not wont to have their Ideas ready collected or ready arranged, and, when suddenly called upon to speak, they have to give most of their attention to the collecting and arranging of the Ideas; the result of it is that they often express these Ideas not only without Rhythm, but even without Grammar. For, if they have to think of *what* they are to say, viz. the Subject-Matter, they cannot possibly give their full attention to *how* they are to say it, viz. the Expression and Style.

Essay-writing and Speaking, so far as the actual Writing and Speaking are concerned, will force students to give *definite shape to their Ideas :* how little we can tell whether we *really* understand a given Idea or not, until we have tried to put it in words, to describe it to someone else.

The immediate advantages of being able to write Books, etc., are almost too obvious to need mention. With regard to the writing of Books in modern times, two considerations might be passed by unless attention were called to them. In the first place, there is far more division of labour in the writing of Books: so that, even if a person cannot write a whole Book, that person may nevertheless be able to do some *part* of the work. At present we hear chiefly of Index-Makers and of people who prepare Summaries, but one day we may find the work of Book-writing subdivided to such an extent that some people will be able to Collect Ideas, other people will be able to Arrange them, and other people will Express them in good language. Others again will Criticise, and will polish up the work as a complete whole.

The second consideration is that, if a person cannot write a Book, at any rate he or she may be able to write an *Article ;* for day by day Articles are becoming more common than Books. Essays (see the Preface) have lately been introduced universally into Cambridge Examinations, and more and more attention is being paid to them. But, quite apart from this 'Scholastic' movement, and the increase of Essay-writing in Schools, the number of *Magazines* is growing larger every year, and those who can write Articles for them are in a position to earn quite a large income. The Articles are paid for at different rates, but, allowing about 2 or 3 guineas for an ordinary Article of 3000 words, the reader can easily see how many Articles it would take to make an income of, say, two hundred and fifty a year ; it would mean about 80 to 120 Articles. If a Writer of fair ability practised each part of the art of Essay-writing quite separately, then he should soon be able to write an ordinary Article in a single day.

Yet another point is to be noticed. Those who cannot write whole Articles can at least write *Paragraphs.* The number of Newspapers is increasing, and every Newspaper wants many Paragraphs on many topics. He who practises Collecting and Arranging and Expressing Ideas can write a readable and interesting Paragraph in a very few minutes. Such papers as the "Daily Mail" pay well for interesting Paragraphs, and here again quite a respectable income might be earned.

But the preparing of Essays, Speeches, etc., should have far more widely reaching effects than these. Perhaps as much as anything else it should tend to encourage honesty and *fairness and open-mindedness*. Until a person prepares an Essay or Speech with a view to showing it or imparting it to others, he probably does not realise a quarter of the Ideas which the subject may suggest. When, however, he has forced himself to detect fallacies in his own views, then his power of seeing both sides of a question and, with an impartial and unbiassed candour, showing them to others also, will grow almost beyond belief. By exposing fallacies, he will develope his reasoning powers wonderfully.

This does not merely affect arguments and writings : it affects the whole of life. One is perpetually being brought face to face with some *custom*, and, unless one has practised fair and open reasoning, and has learnt to see both sides of a question, one is apt to follow blindly as a slave of Custom, and so to be doing something altogether wrong, even when this 'something' be injurious or dishonest. The man who has discussed all kinds of questions with himself, not as a partisan, but as a searcher after truth (as the Essayist should be), will not tamely allow himself to obey others implicitly : his whole life will be more and more guided by Reason, and less and less by Custom.

And this does not concern himself alone : he will be able not only to judge better for himself, but also to *help others* to judge better for *themselves*.

This will be especially the case in Teaching. In fact, we might say that Teaching is quite impossible unless the Teacher has those qualities and advantages which should come from the preparing of Essays and Speeches. Among such qualities would be *prompt Reasoning* and the rapid Collection of Ideas (which will encourage and will in turn be helped by wide reading and careful thought and discussion), the Selecting and 'Proportioning' of Ideas (which will force the Writer to ask himself what is important and what is not). Then again there will be the Arranging of Ideas, and the Connecting of one Idea with another, and this will be a great help for the *Memory*. Besides this, the Ideas and their Expression will become far *clearer;* and a person will be able almost unconsciously to think of a good Comparison or Contrast when he wishes to explain something or to Emphasise it. In working out these Comparisons and Contrasts, he cannot fail to increase his *Sympathy* with the readers and with people in general; for he will be bound to ask himself 'What interests the reader?' and 'What Motives can I appeal to?'

This power of interesting others, and of persuading them and convincing them, is essential to Teaching in the wider sense, i.e. influencing others by anything that we say.

One or two details may be mentioned in conclusion.

The Practice of Rhythm must have some effect upon the mind itself, though the exact effect is not yet known; but a quality which it may perhaps help considerably is general Neatness.

So far we have spoken especially of the Effects upon the intellect and character, but there still remains one more effect, namely, the effect it has in giving *pleasure* to others as well as to oneself. Among the greatest of pleasures, and among the purest, is that of helping others; and, quite apart from this, a vast deal of pleasure can come from the mere reading of a number of good Ideas well arranged and well expressed.

The satisfaction which such a piece of reading may give both to the Writer and to the reader must not be left out of account. It is only recently that people have investigated the effect of pleasurable feelings upon the whole body and upon its power for work; and nowadays, before subjects are recommended for study, it ought first to be asked whether these subjects are likely to be not only interesting but also pleasant. With regard to Essay-Writing and Speaking, one may safely say that, when once the first drudgery is over, they are certain to be both interesting and pleasant.

And, however good may be the effects of Writing well and Speaking well, they will become still better if these arts are learnt and practised in the right way instead of being left 'to get themselves taught'.

CHAPTER II. COMMON TYPES OF SUBJECTS FOR COMPOSITIONS.

I SHALL here mention and give examples of only one or two of the commonest types of Essay-Subjects: the reader can easily add other examples and other types from his own experience or imagination.

I.

1. A very usual type of subject is that which involves as it were a bird's-eye view of things in general. 'Rome under the Empire', or 'London to-day', or a Comparison between the two, would be specimens. The Writer is at a loss to know what to mention and what to omit: if he only had a complete List of Headings, then he would be better able to select. This Essay, then, may be called a Period-Essay, as it involves an all-round review of a Period (e.g. its Government, Religion, Education, and Commerce). See p. 83.

2. But an all-round review of a Period is needed for many other Essay-Subjects besides this. ' The *Results* of Democracy (e.g. in England)', or, in fact, the Results of many things, need this review also. Otherwise, how can we tell *where* Democracy's Results are to be looked for, or what they are? The Results may extend to all sorts of spheres, and, unless we *do* review the Period, we shall be in danger of passing by some sphere of the very greatest importance.

3. 'The *Causes* of England's Success' will also need this all-round review. For what sphere may not have had its influence (e.g. Geography, Government, Religion, or Commerce)? And, unless we look everywhere, we shall almost certainly omit some powerful Cause.

So Causes of events, or of phenomena, as a rule demand the Period-Headings also.

4. And this will apply also to Essays on *Hindrances*. 'What are the Obstacles to a union with America (Russia, France, etc.)?'

So far, then, these Headings are required for an Essay on a Period, for an Essay on two or more Periods compared and contrasted, for an Essay on Results, and for an Essay on Causes, or on Hindrances. Is there any other subject where they are required?

5. 'The *Sphere* of Government-control' (what it is and what it should be): this, again, needs the List of Headings. 'Does Government control, or ought it to control, *a, b, c, d*, . . . ?' and so on : those are the questions which we must answer.

6. '*War*', '*Colonisation*', '*Slavery*'—these are topics often set in Essay-papers. How shall we deal with words so vague? Well here again we must call the Period-Headings into play when we consider Causes, Hindrances, and Effects : though other Headings are needed also, as we shall see directly.

7. '*Ignorance is bliss*': this may be called the 'Proverb-Essay', or the Dictum-Essay. But what kind of 'Ignorance' is meant? Ignorance in Government, in Religion, or in Commerce? All these departments of life, and many others, will furnish us with materials and examples for or against the Dictum. What other departments? Those which are in the Period-Headings.

8. A *Person* is to be the theme? Then we must consider (among other things) what caused him to be as he was, what hindered him, what Effects he produced, and what his Sphere of activity was. And here once more we need to pass the Headings in quick review before us.

For the other Headings needed for such an Essay, see below (p. 92).

9. An Essay on *Tennyson*, or some Author. Here, at last, we seem to be free. But here we are dealing with a Person, and we need to review his Period, if we would get at the Causes and Hindrances and Effects. And then, what did he write about? Shall we not need the Period-Headings here also? Was it about Virtue, or Intellect, or Religion, or what?

Thus all the above Essays might be classed together as involving a survey of the departments of life, i.e. as involving a survey of what we call the Period-Headings. But this is not all that they involve.

The Essay on *an Author* would have these Headings, in so far as the Author is considered as a Person. His Works demand them too: the Instances (i.e. a List of his Works), Causes and Hindrances, Description, Effects, etc., must all be considered.

II.

a. When we have an Essay on a wide subject like '*Democracy*', or 'Colonisation', or 'War', we need another set of Headings as well. These are given on p. 92, and include 'Concrete Instances', 'Causes', 'Hindrances', 'Description', and 'Effects'. We should also have 'Evidences', 'Comparisons', and 'Contrasts'.

The 'Description' itself has many 'Sub-Headings', as we shall see on p. 92.

These might be called General Essay-Headings: and almost every Essay involves the use of them.

β. The Essay on *a Person* (e.g. Napoleon) would include Instances (i.e. the events of his life), Causes and Hindrances of his development, Description of Character, Sphere of Activity, etc. (see p. 97), Effects, and so on.

For other subjects, the reader is referred to such Books as 'Pros and Cons' (Swan Sonnenschein), and to p. 133 (below).

The common types, therefore, though at first sight they may seem to be very numerous, can mostly be classed together under the Formula of 'Essays which require some or many or most of the Period-Headings, and some or many or most of the General Essay-Headings (Instances, Causes, Effects, etc.)'.

Lighter Articles and Speeches will often bring into play these General Essay-Headings (p. 92), and may even be much improved by a rapid glance through the Period-Headings (p. 83). But as a rule these, together with Descriptions (e.g. of scenery), will not require such Lists. There will not be the same need to search for the Ideas themselves: the problem will generally be how to Select, Arrange, and Express Ideas.

CHAPTER III. THE CHOICE OF A SUBJECT.

As I have said elsewhere, a Choice of subjects is not always allowed to learners, who are often all told to write an Essay on one set Subject, whether they know anything about it or not. In such a case Choice is out of the question. It may be suggested to Teachers that they should allow a Choice wherever it is possible. Either they might allow a Choice of one out of four subjects, or they might allow an absolutely free Choice within certain limits. I have found a very good plan to be to set three or four subjects of various kinds, and to ask for *Schemes* of *all* the subjects, and for any single subject as an Essay also.

One high authority says emphatically that, whenever there is a Choice of subjects, the Essayist should choose the one about which he already knows least. This is singularly bad advice for Examination purposes. Far better advice would be, "Choose and practise your weakest subjects on ordinary occasions, but in Examinations, where a great deal may depend upon success, choose the subject which you can do best". In the same way, in Games, I should recommend anyone to practise his weakest strokes in Practice-Games, etc., but in Matches to use his best strokes.

Apart from this, it may often be useful to choose that subject which is not only interesting at the present moment, but which might be useful in after-life, according to the career to which one is looking forward.

The Interest of the Writer must make a great deal of difference to his Essay or Speech, and it is astonishing that Schoolmasters so seldom practise boys in Essay-Writing or Speaking on subjects about which they are really keen. I know of one small School where a general paper is set, for very short Essays, and, out of about fifteen questions, there is scarcely one in which nearly all the boys would not feel interested. The subjects are Games, Bicycling, Stamp-collecting, in fact almost anything which boys care about. But this School is an exception. There is generally a vague idea that such things are 'trivial' or 'frivolous'. How little do those who say such things understand the Schoolboy's mind. A game of Football 'frivolous'! I dread to think of what our Nation would be like if for our Games we substituted the ponderous Gymnastic system, the "March at the word of command". There can be no harm in setting these subjects, and, so far as Expression is concerned, they are better practice than anything else, because the Essay-Writer or Speaker has to devote less of his attention to the thinking out of the Ideas themselves. He understands them better, that is to say if he is really a boy.

Besides this, it is also necessary to choose a subject in which you can interest the readers or hearers. It is not enough that the subject should interest the Writer or Speaker. It is for this reason that many Books and Articles are rejected by Publishers and Editors. The subjects are thought either to be non-popular or at any rate to have been treated in a non-popular manner.

In addition to the Choice of a subject, there is also *the Choice of treatment:* the same subject, treated in a different way, may be (to all intents and purposes) a new subject. For this, see Originality (p. 219). The Writer might first consider a subject (e.g. Ancient *Slavery*) generally, by the General Headings on p. 92 ; then he might consider some *one* Heading as an Essay all by itself, e.g. Results (good and bad, for the Slaves and for others), or Comparisons and Contrasts (with modern Servants, etc.).

To sum up, then : in so far as you can, choose such a subject, and such a way of treating it, as shall interest not only yourself but also your audience.

CHAPTER IV. DIFFERENCES BETWEEN VARIOUS CLASSES OF COMPOSITIONS.

Note.—This Chapter may be omitted (or left till the end) when the Book is being read for the first time.

In this Book I have tried to treat the different classes of Compositions and Speeches together, i.e. to give advice which may apply to all of them collectively. But there is a great deal which can only apply to some one branch of Composition by itself. For instance, Chapter LXXIII. will only apply to Letter-writing.

The differences between Books and Letters, to take the two extremes, are very great; and yet the classes pass into one another by almost imperceptible stages. It is not a great step from the Book to the long Essay, from the long Essay to the short and lighter Essay, from the lighter Essay to the still lighter Article, from the Article to the serious Letter, and from the serious Letter to the ordinary Letter.

Again, with regard to Speaking, it is not a great step from the series of Lectures (which may correspond to the single Book), to the single Lecture or Speech, and from that, through the Debate, to the ordinary Conversation.

But these various classes of Writings and Speeches may differ very considerably from one another, for instance in their Arrangement of Ideas. In a Speech, especially before a popular audience, there must be so much more *variety*, so much more *humour*, and so much more *repetition*, than in a serious Lecture to a number of specialists.

A great deal will depend on the *length* of the Composition, and a great deal on who the *readers or hearers* are. Of course it is generally safest to address the stupidest, with occasional words here and there for those who are more intelligent, φωναέντα ξυνετοῖσι. The Author, again, may be addressing simply the people of his own times or the people of future times as well, and he may be addressing only his hearers or readers or the very severest critics as well. Much also will depend on his *Aim or Aims* (see p. 48), and upon whether he wishes to treat the subject seriously or lightly. For it must be remembered that a serious method of treatment is not always suited to a serious subject. A Paper like " Punch" has taught many lessons which rabid fanatics have utterly failed to teach.

Then again, an Essay* or Speech may be what is called *Partisan*-Work, or it may be what might be called *Fair-Play* for both sides.

A great deal more than one would think will depend on whether the Composition is to be *Spoken or ' Written'*, and, if 'Written', whether it will be read in Writing or in Type-writing or in Printing. And even the kind of Writing or Type-writing or Printing may be a very considerable consideration.

One difference between Writing and Speaking I have

---

* An Essay has been defined as an attempt, a tentative suggestion, rather than a complete treatise. Such was its early sense, and many Essays and Articles would still rank as tentative ; but a large number are far more than this—they are more or less exhaustive monographs.

never yet seen mentioned, except in reference to Poetry: it is that Writing is hampered by *lines*.   The eye has to pass from the end of one line to the beginning of the next, and the breaks and delays, though inappreciable as individual breaks and delays, are in their sum-total stupendous.   For the delays generally involve a break in the thought itself—a break inconceivably minute, yet (like the Atom of the Atomic Theory) none the less real and actual.

For many of the other characteristics of Speaking as opposed to Writing, I must refer to p. 384.   Here I need only allude to one or two more of them.

If a Speech or Composition is to be spoken and *heard*, then there is a chance of Illustrations from the sur-roundings, or from Maps or Diagrams, or by some other means (for instance, Plans drawn on a Black-board).   But, even with these helps, what is Spoken must be made very much *clearer* than what is Written, for this reason. The listener who does not understand a thing cannot possibly turn back, as the reader can, and go through the sentence over again.   If the sentence is not under-stood directly it is said, either it will not be understood at all, or the hearer, in puzzling it out, will lose the sentences which immediately follow.   Indeed he may lose the whole thread.

Now, as it is hard to be sure that any given sentence will be clear to all or even to most of the hearers, it will often be safer to repeat the Idea, to approach it from different points of view (see p. 181), and not to try to pack as many Ideas as possible into as small a Composition as possible, as Books and Articles often do, and do quite rightly; one will have to *Repeat* (see p. 270), and (see pp. 281, 291) to give *Comparisons and Contrasts*.

This will serve another purpose besides ensuring Clearness. It will Emphasise the important Ideas, and it will keep up the Interest.

But on the other hand, in spite of the Repetitions and Comparisons and Contrasts etc., the Spoken Composition should be *shorter* than the Written Composition. The reader can put aside a Book when he is tired, saying to himself " I will finish it off some other time"; but the hearer cannot do this; and thousands of clergymen whose Sermon might be mastered if it were in print, and if people could plod through it a little bit at a time, can only succeed in keeping the attention of their *hearers* for a quarter of an hour at a time; the other quarter of an hour or more is worse than useless: it is exasperating.

Since, therefore, that which is Spoken must have more Repetition and Variety, and must be shorter, than that which is Written (and which can therefore be studied at leisure), that which is Spoken must of necessity have fewer Ideas.

In Composition, the nearest thing to Speaking is Letter-writing; ordinary Letters one seldom reads more than once. Ordinary Letters, then, must be almost as clear and unmistakable as Speeches.

It is this need of absolute Clearness which *makes Speaking of inestimable value for Essay-Writing*. There are a great many Teachers who do too much 'Reading' and too little Speaking. I have known Lecturers who have practically never Spoken (except in the sense of reading out Lectures from Notes); they have generally failed as Lecturers.

At the beginning of Essay-Writing one should try to Write something which can be both heard and read;

this is a very safe rule.   For a Writer is apt to be obscure and dull, and a Speaker is apt to be diffuse and careless, relying too much on gesture, stress, and tone.

In all the different classes of Composition, a good many conditions have to be taken into account.   First of all, come the place and the surroundings—there is a difference between Speaking in a building and Speaking in the open air, between Speaking where Illustrations are ready to hand and Speaking where there is no chance of Illustrations.   It is, by the way, a most singular thing that open-air preachers so seldom make any allusions to their surroundings : they do not realise (as Jesus did) that the things which can be seen around them ought to be used as Comparisons and Contrasts.

The time also has to be taken into account, and, in Writing, the number of words.   The usual number of words for an Article in a Review will be three thousand.

The subject also will make a great deal of difference, and besides this the amount of work which has been already done on the subject by others.

A Debate again will be quite different from any other form of Composition, and will require more readiness.

We may now briefly summarise the different classes of Compositions, and the reader will see for himself that there must be many varieties in the method of treatment, although a number of general rules apply to all of them alike, such as " Collect the Headings ; then Select some ; then Underline the important Headings ; then Arrange ; then Express ; and lastly put aside, and Revise, and read out loud, so as to correct the Rhythm."

First of all will come the Book. The Summary of the Book may correspond very closely to an Essay or an Article. Or the Essay or Article may be compared with a Section of the Book, or with a Chapter of the Book. Here then we have a Book and an Essay, and we see what their relation is: a Book may be like a long Essay, or like a number of Essays on one subject.

Both the Book and the Essay will have Paragraphs; and Paragraphs themselves can form a separate class of Composition, as an Editor of a Newspaper or Magazine knows better than anyone.

A Paragraph again consists of Sentences, and even a Sentence may be a separate form of Composition. And the Sentence itself may consist of Clauses, and these Clauses will consist of Words.

Now of all the above Compositions, whether they be Books or Essays or Articles or Paragraphs, the more one divides up and splits up (within certain limits), the clearer the work is likely to be. As a model of a bad Writer in this respect we may take Professor Freeman, whose Paragraphs last sometimes for a page and a half, or even for several pages. Milton, in his History of England, is even worse.

A Letter differs from the above Compositions in certain respects, although it resembles them in others; it also should be subdivided into Paragraphs, and a new subject should begin a new Paragraph. See further p. 390 foll.

As to Speeches, Lectures, Sermons, etc., a serious or long Speech or Lecture or Sermon may be compared with the Summary of a Book, or with a Section or Chapter of a Book, or with an Essay or Article.

Supposing we had a Debate, we might compare the Debate to a Section or Chapter of a Book (or to an Essay) which answered or supported a Section or Chapter of another Book (or another Essay).

With a Paragraph, in Writing, we may compare some of the Speeches which are made after dinner, or (by verbose individuals) in the course of an ordinary Conversation.   As a rule, however, our Speaking takes the form of Conversation, i e. we Speak in Sentences rather than in Paragraphs.   In Literature this is not nearly so common as might be desired; a great deal can be learnt from Dialogues or Conversations, since people would read them as a change from the stereotyped Essay.

CHAPTER V. DIFFERENT WAYS OF LEARNING.

OF the different ways of practising the art of Teaching and Learning, and of practising Composition and Speaking I shall treat later on (in Chapters LXIV.–LXXI.). Here I wish to speak rather more about the general Principles of the art of Learning *anything*.

There are numbers of ways of Learning, and there are numbers of Teachers or Theorists who understand one way only. Some say we can only learn to do a thing by doing it; others say we can only learn to do a thing by reading Books on the subject; and so on. But, as a matter of fact, no one single method of Learning can be sufficient for anyone unless he be a genius. This, then, is the first fallacy which we expose, that there is only one way of Learning, and that all other ways are useless.

A second fallacy is that Learning is merely sucking-in, as it were, that is to say merely reading or listening; true Learning is a great deal besides this.

The Learner must not only suck-in and absorb, but must absorb with an *open mind*. Open-mindedness is a quality sadly undeveloped in England, whereas in America it is encouraged with great care. The Learner, then, should listen or read with an open mind, studying not only in order to absorb but also in order to understand thoroughly, and to *criticise* and test, and finally to adopt or reject according to the results. Afterwards he should make a *record* (see p. 354) of what he has learnt, and should meditate over it. He should ask about the various difficulties or doubtful problems, consulting not only actual people, but also Books and Dictionaries, which will tell him what he wants, perhaps more quickly, but anyhow more patiently.

And not only should he absorb, and think over, and criticise what he has listened to and what he has read, but he should also apply it and put it into practice in the right way.

He should ask for criticism from others; but, if he is unwilling or unable to do this, he should at any rate criticise himself, either by looking at his work after an interval, or by comparing it with some pattern.

But of all methods of Learning none is better than the attempt *to teach others:* of this I shall speak below.

It is important to learn as much and at the same time as little as possible. Do not learn twenty different instances all by themselves, if you can learn *one* single instance and the principles which it illustrates, and then apply these principles to other instances also. For example, in Essay-Writing, the Writer will find that, in treating the Ideas or Headings, certain principles such as Clearness, Appropriateness, Variety, Connexion, and Proportion, all have to be considered. A good model would show him all these principles. He will find that these same principles will apply to the Expression of Ideas. He will therefore be saving time if he learns them thoroughly once for all, and does not have to learn them twice.

A few details about Learning may be suggested here.

1. The Attention should be concentrated on the subject, and this needs an exertion of the will. This in its turn must be much easier for you if you enjoy good *health*, and if you take an *interest* in the subject, and if you can introduce some Variety into it (see p. 251).

2. Of course you must also *understand* the subject and realise it, and a great help to this will be to *begin with what is known* and familiar and easy, and to proceed from this to what is unknown and less familiar and and more difficult. Comparisons and Contrasts will be a great aid. Indeed, without these a proper Interest in the subject, or even a proper understanding of the subject, is almost impossible.

3. Throughout the processes of Learning you should *observe and make Notes*. This applies equally whether you are Reading (p. 352) or whether you are Listening (p. 358). Throughout Learning you should ask *Questions*, either of yourself or of others (by word or by letter, or by consulting Books and Articles). •

4. You should also keep in your *Memory* what you have learnt, storing it partly in your mind, and partly in Notes and Note-books.

5. What you have learnt you should not merely remember, but you should also think about and *digest*, and this is best done by putting the Ideas into practice, and by exercising yourself in the various departments of Essay-Writing, one by one; e.g. see p. 361.

6. Always invite *Criticism;* and do not be afraid of criticising others. There is no reason to criticise them in public: you can keep your work in that department absolutely private, and it is generally better to do so.

7. As to *Teaching others*, you can either actually teach them by words, or by Letters, Articles, etc., or you can teach them in imagination. If you imagined yourself to have an audience, or a Class of pupils, you would take more pains in the preparation than if you were preparing things merely for yourself. And, whether you are Writing or Speaking, the general principle to remember is that you must appeal, in nearly everything you say, to the very stupidest people possible. You may take it for granted, in Teaching, that, if the stupidest understand your meaning, then those who are less stupid will understand it also, and the clever cannot possibly fail to do so.

Teaching is one of the best means of Learning, not only because it forces one to prepare one's work carefully, and to be criticised whether one wishes it or not, but also because it gives one a sense of responsibility: it reminds one that one is no longer working for self alone.

8. Throughout Teaching and Learning one should go over the old work constantly, and not merely put it aside and never look at it again; and one should also use Cards (p. 186) or keep Note-books in which to write down from time to time, and to rearrange, various hints as to faults, improvements, and lines of research.

CHAPTER VI. **SUMMARY OF THE BOOK, WITH A RHYME.**

IN this Chapter I shall try to summarise the main part of this work, so that those who have not the time or the inclination to go right through it may at any rate grasp the general plan of it, and may be able to refer to any particular Chapter or page for further information on any particular topic.

After showing (on p. 3 foll.) how important and *advantageous* it is to be able to Write fairly well and to Speak fairly well, and after making one or two suggestions as to the *Choice* of a Subject, I shall point out (p. 37 foll.) some of the General *Principles* of Composition, such as Appropriateness. What may be almost perfect in one Essay or in one Paragraph or in one Sentence may be quite out of place, quite bad, in another. Even a slang word may be the only possible word in a certain Context. 'Variety' (pp. 42, 251) will be another General Principle.

Then, on p. 44 foll., I shall try to give the *Chief Faults* in Composition. The reader will see that the list is long: and that, if he merely tries to write whole Essays all at one 'sitting', he is little likely to escape them all.

So the chief *Difficulty* in Composition, at least as it is usually attempted, is that[a large number of hard things have to be done all at once, in any *one* of these the Writer or Speaker is apt to be making mistakes. The difficulties would be much lessened if these things were collected together in a list, and if each Writer or Speaker found out which were *his* difficulties or faults, and if he then practised special Exercises in order to overcome them one by one. For I have tried to make it clear that difficulties are due not only to the complexity of the subject but still more to the attempts which have been made to teach it all together, as a single process. For there may be mistakes in one or many or even all of the following Headings—to select a few out of many :—Collection of Ideas or Headings, Selection, Underlining, Arranging, Illustrating and Contrasting, Clearness, Brevity, Vigour and Emphasis, Interest, Variety, Rhythm, Grammar, Vocabulary, Punctuation, etc. It was hard to break the faggots when they were in a bundle, but it was easy to break them when they were taken one by one.

Next (on p. 48) I have said a few words about the *Aims and Motives* of Writers and Speakers, for this has to be considered throughout Composition. Everything must be appropriate to the Aim of the Writer or Speaker, as well as appropriate to the subject, and to the readers or hearers. In fact, there would be almost innumerable ways of doing a Composition on one single subject, according to the different Aims and audiences that one had in view.

In PART II., I treat of the *Ideas and Headings*, showing that these have to be Collected, Selected, Underlined, and Arranged, and that Illustrations and Contrasts have to be found, before one can begin to express them. PART II., therefore, has very little to do with Expression or Style, though it is impossible to avoid this branch altogether.

On p. 57 foll. I give one or two bad Schemes of Essays, and then I point out what are the commonest faults in Schemes of Essays generally. These faults are faults in the Headings (for instance in their Arrangement) quite apart from their Expression.

After this, on p. 60, I try to show *what the Ideas and Headings ought to be*, that is to say the ideal. For example, they ought to be complete (for the special purpose), they ought to be well proportioned, and appropriate to the Aim and subject and audience, they ought to be wholesome, interesting, and suggestive, and fair and unbiassed, and they ought to have other good qualities besides.

Then comes the great difficulty, namely, the *Collection* of Headings and Sub-Headings. And after general advice on this subject (see p. 63), I have mentioned those Headings which are most often *omitted*, such as Evidences, Fallacies, Objections, Comparisons, Contrasts, Causes, Effects, etc.: see p. 71.

In order to give the reader some chance of having a good Collection of Headings, and less chance of omitting the important Headings, I have offered (e g. on pp. 83, 92) a few *General Lists*, which are not quite complete but yet approach to completeness; two of these Lists will be found sufficient for most purposes. One of these is called the List of Period-Headings, such as Geography, Religion, Education, Commerce, War, etc. (see p. 83); the other is called the List of General Headings, and includes Instances, Causes and Hindrances, Effects, Aims, etc.: this latter List will be found on p. 92.

Having explained (p. 73) what are all the various uses to which the Headings can be put, I have proceeded (p. 87) to suggest how the Lists may be learnt; for it will be worth while to learn these Lists, and to learn them in the right way. This will make them still more useful.

Having shown what are the main Headings for various Essays, I go on (p. 95) to the *Sub-Headings* for various Essays; and I finish up with Headings for an Essay on a Person (p. 96), on an Author (p. 129), and Headings for Literary Criticism. After this (p. 133) follow Topics for Composition, and the skeleton of an Essay on 'Progress'.

Some of the Headings are so important that they demand special Chapters to themselves. Among these are :—

Authorities and their Faults (p. 139);
Other Evidences (p. 145);
Fallacies (p. 150);
Definitions (p. 159);
Parallels and Comparisons (p. 162 : cp. p. 281);
Contrasts (p. 291);
Quotations (p. 163).

So much for the Collection of Headings.

We now come to the task of *Selecting* those which we want, and *Rejecting* those which we do not want; and Chapter XXXI. (p. 166) explains why we should select certain Headings : for instance they may be Important, or Interesting.

The Headings, having been Selected, must now be '*Proportioned*' (p. 170). This is best done by *Under-lining*. In other words, we must decide which are to be Emphasised very much, and which are to be

Emphasised rather less, and which are to be thrown into the background.

Next, the Headings must of course be *Arranged* (p. 172). There are various principles, which are explained on p. 178, and these will settle our Arrangement; but the greatest help towards the mechanical work of Arranging will be the "*Card-System*". This is described in Chapter XXXIV. (p. 186), and its advantages are shown in Chapter XXXV. (p. 192), where the saving of time and energy, and the improvement in the results, and various other merits, are briefly touched on.

PART III. (p. 202 foll.) concerns the *Expression of Ideas and Style*. It presupposes that the Ideas or Headings have already been Collected, Selected, Underlined, and Arranged, and perhaps written out in a Scheme, and that they are now ready to be Expressed.

The reader will doubtless be amazed at the amount of time which has to be spent before he arrives at the stage of Expressing his Ideas at all. But, the more he examines the subject, and the more he goes by his personal experience, the more he will find it worth while to spend time on, and to practise carefully,[this first department of Composition, as opposed to the mere Expression.] Indeed one might almost say that, if this first department has been thoroughly well done, that is to say, if the Scheme of Headings and Sub-Headings has been well prepared, the Expression will be a comparatively easy matter.

Chapter XXXVI. (p. 202) will give *General Hints* on Expression, and Chapter XXXVII. (p. 205) will point out the chief *Difficulties and Faults* in Expression.

The reader will then be told how to find out for himself the chief Characteristics of any Author's

Expression and Style. He will see a familiar passage from the New Testament (p. 212) taken and *analysed;* and, having learnt this, he will have at his fingers' ends instances of nearly all the most desirable characteristics of Expression. And he may find it worth while to consider (see p. 219) how far he should try to *imitate* the Style of any one person.

Then follow Chapters on Originality (p. 219), Force (p. 222), Clearness and Simplicity—a most essential consideration (p. 227), Brevity and Economy (p. 238), Appropriateness, and Unity (p. 243), Variety (p. 251), and Interest and Suggestiveness (p. 255).

In this last Chapter he will see how important it is to [study the audience or reader, quite apart from the likings of the Writer himself. The great mass of Writers and Speakers forget to study those to whom they are Writing or Speaking, and the result is that they fail, not only to be clear, but also to be interesting and suggestive; they go too fast or too slow or in the wrong lines altogether.]

Interest is required especially in the Beginning, or rather in the Beginnings: for instance, in the Beginning not only of the Essay but also (cp. p. 311) of the Paragraph.

Chapter XLVIII. deals with *Connexion and Cohesion*, and the previous Chapter (p. 261) with *Endings*, which should as a rule be Impressive. There follows a most important matter for consideration, namely (*Force and*) *Emphasis*. The two are nearly the same, but I have attempted to treat them in separate Chapters. The various *Means of Emphasis* are described (p. 270) and special Exercises are suggested, for instance special Exercises on Comparisons (p. 289), and Contrasts (p. 295); these

Comparisons and Contrasts serve so many purposes that they demand whole sections to themselves : their uses will be found on pp. 281, 291.

No less important than Emphasis is the *Absence of Emphasis* (p. 278). It is of little use to make a statement emphatic, if you make all the other statements emphatic also ; there is a great art in throwing these into the background.

After the Comparisons and Contrasts there follow (p. 296 foll.) the uses of *Questions* and *other Rhetorical Devices ;* but these will be found in more detail in other Books.

Chapter LVI. deals with *Rhythm*, of which the importance is very great ; but it is suggested that Rhythm should not be considered till the end of an Essay. It is true that it should be constantly practised as a special Exercise, but it should not be allowed to engross the mind, when the mind should be considering the more weighty matters, such as Clearness and Interest.

After this we have a few words on Chapters (p. 308), Paragraphs (p. 310), and Sentences (p. 315).

Then follows quite a brief section on *Grammar or Syntax :* the cause of most mistakes in Grammar is pointed out, and a safe rule is given on p. 320.

A safe rule is also given, on p. 324, as to the choice of *Vocabulary.*

After some notes on *Writing, Spelling, and Punctuation,* this Part of the work finishes with a few lines (p. 330) on the art of *Revising* an Essay, a most necessary art, but one that is very little studied or put into practice.

PART IV. gives notes on how to *Correct* Compositions (p. 335), pointing out especially how each fault should be traced back to its cause and classified, e.g.

D

"Such and such a fault is one of Obscurity". The Exercise to get rid of this fault is, let us say, to turn passages into simple English : see p. 232.

Of the three Chapters that follow, the first is ' *How to Teach Composition*'. Here especial attention is called to the Part-by-Part System ; *the Aims of Teaching* are explained (p. 345) in order to show that it is worth while spending a great deal of time in laying the foundations accurately and firmly, since so much of the whole future life will depend on these foundations.

Very much the same advice, but adapted to the point of view of the learner, is given in Chapter LXVII. (p. 347) : the learner is there told *How to Practise.* There are also suggestions on *How to Read Books and Articles, etc.* (p. 352), and on *How to Learn from Lectures and Speeches* (p. 358). In these two latter sections it is as well to emphasise the general advice, " Try a thing for yourself before you go to anything or anyone for information." You should try (if there is time) to work out the subject beforehand ; and then, after you have read or listened to the information, you should note it down in a special Note-book, and if possible make certain of understanding it, of remembering it, and of using it.

General Hints and Helps are added in Chapter LXX.

PART V. (p. 367 foll.) is more special, giving *Hints on Writing for the Press*, including the Correction of Proofs and Index-Making, and giving advice as to how to apply to Publishers and Editors.

As Chapter LXXI. deals only with *Writing*, so Chapter LXXII. deals only with *Speaking*, and Chapter LXXIII. only with *Letter-Writing*.

In PART VI. (p. 397 foll.) I have suggested the *advantages of this whole System*, especially the System of practising all subjects *Part by Part*, by means of special Exercises, instead of trying to learn the subject all together by a single Process. This is in Chapter LXXIV.; the next Chapter supplements it by giving the *Objections* to such a system as mine, and answers to these Objections.

Last of all, an Appendix offers a list of useful Books.

General Hints on Preparing Essays etc., in Rhyme.

Don't write, but first think- out your aims,
your public, and the topic's claims.

———

Define by Contrasts, Illustrations,
Examples, and Exaggerations.

———

Use General Lists, Objections state
and meet : but don't exaggerate.

———

Collect Main-Headings ; then collect
Sub-Headings ; underline, reject.
Arrange beginnings, end, and sections,
to show proportion and connexions.
Revise ; write out ; wait ; read, reclaim
th' obscure, harsh, ill-adapted, tame.

CHAPTER VII. SOME GENERAL PRINCIPLES OF COMPOSITION.

IN learning any subject, after one has viewed it as a whole, it is necessary to take it to pieces and analyse it, and to consider each one of its parts or departments. There are many reasons why this should be the best way for average learners, even if the genius manages to produce successful results without any such labour. Yet even *he* will find that the labour of analysing and of practising Part-by-Part has not been thrown away, if he ever has to teach others.

In going through the various parts or departments of Writing and Speaking, it will be of the greatest help and also of the greatest interest to find any Principles which apply more or less to all of them, or to many of them. *I* Are there any such Principles that apply, for example, to Essay-Writing in its different departments? to the Collection and Selection and Underlining and Arranging and Expressing of the Headings and Sub-Headings?

One of such underlying Principles certainly is *Unity*. Now this word may convey very little meaning to anybody but a specialist, and yet it is a most important Principle or Law. It is easier to look at 'Unity' from another point of view, viz. as a kind of Economy, that is to say, the giving up and discarding of what is unnecessary ; this is not the whole of 'Unity', but it is the

most essential part of it.   We have to throw aside and
keep out whatever is superfluous, whether it be in Words
or Clauses or Sentences or even whole Paragraphs, that
is to say, whole Ideas; in a Book, it may be even
necessary to the 'Unity' to cut out a whole Chapter.

We might possibly define the 'Unity' of the Composition by saying that one ought to be able to sum up
the whole in a single word or a single sentence, and that
one ought to go through the whole without being able
to cut out anything as spoiling the particular effect
intended.   But the 'Unity' of a Composition as a
whole is a very hard thing to define at all satisfactorily : obviously the Composition should have one
main subject, one leading and guiding Idea, though
that Idea may be looked at from very many points
of view, and though many Ideas may be introduced
which do not *seem* to belong to the subject and yet
serve to illustrate it.

As an instance, let us take a passage on p. 212.   One
would say that rain and storm had very little to do
with a description of a person who was really good ;
nevertheless they come into one of the most admirable
descriptions which we can find anywhere in Literature.
They are described as beating against a house, and
in the one instance as having no effect on it but in
the other instance as bringing it to its fall.   They are
details, but they serve to make Clear and to Emphasise
the main Idea.

No Writer seems to be going off the point, and to
be violating the Law of 'Unity' and Economy, more
than Carlyle does.   As we read his " Frederick the
Great ", the characters at first appear to us to have no
more connexion with one another than the characters

in a Harlequinade, yet, before the book is done, we see that they all throw some light upon the life and times of Frederick the Great : that is to say, they do not violate the Law of 'Unity'.

For 'Unity' is indeed something beyond mere Economy. We can divide up the whole into its various parts, and say that the whole consists of A, B, C, D, and E. But we cannot be safe in saying that the whole is no more than a series of parts $(A + B + C + D + E)$; for each part exists not only by itself but exists also to throw light on all the other parts, and in turn to be lighted up by them. This therefore will be another sign of 'Unity', not merely that there is nothing unnecessary in any part, but also that each part has some connexion with the other parts and could not be removed without the other parts losing something.

Within the 'Unity' of Composition as a whole, there is a 'Unity' of each part : each Section or Paragraph must have its 'Unity', each Sentence within the Paragraph, and we might almost say each Clause within the Sentence.

The principle of Economy must not be carried too far in any of these parts. *Clearness* and Definiteness, and what may be called Simplicity, are not to be sacrificed for the sake of Unity. We must leave definite and clear Ideas in the reader's mind. This applies not only to the Composition as a whole but also to every Section, Chapter, and Paragraph, to every Sentence, and to every Clause. Moreover there is this to be remembered : we must not judge of the Clearness of any one part by itself : the rest of the parts are expected to throw light on it ; otherwise many Sentences would be quite indefensible, but, as it is, they quite justify themselves because they say, "We are perfectly clear if you consider us not by ourselves but in our context".

In other words, besides the Principle of ' Unity', and the Principle of Clearness, there is a third Principle, viz. *Co-operation*. Each part, whether it be a Section or a Paragraph or a Sentence or a Clause or a Word, must be as far as possible perfect in itself and yet must be practically *dependent* on other parts, just as they must be dependent on it. We shall see that, as Civilisation advances, people become more and more dependent upon one another; and we may say that, the more one nation comes to depend on other nations, the more likely there is to be Co-operation in the world, and hence something approaching to universal perfection.

It follows from this that each part of the Composition, as well as the whole Essay, must be appropriate to its special purpose, while the whole Composition must be appropriate to and adapted to the aim of the Writer, to the subject, and to the people for whom he is writing : this applies equally to every part of an Essay. The Ideas, their Selection, their Emphasis, their Arrangement, and their Expression, must all depend upon the *Fitness for the particular conditions*. It is most important to realise that this Law of Fitness pervades almost the whole of Composition, so that what may be excellent in itself, or excellent in a certain context, will be even extremely bad in another context. What may be nourishing food for a person in the prime of life may actually kill an infant. On the other hand, the running about for hours together, which is so good for the boy, would be impossible for an old man, and

might even kill him. Hence each part of the Composition, the Section, the Paragraph, the Sentence, and
the Word, must not be judged by itself, as people are
wont to judge texts from the Old or the New Testament, but in the light of this question : " Is it appropriate to this particular Composition, to the particular
subject and aim of the Writer or Speaker, and to the
particular readers or hearers, and the particular place
in the Composition itself?"

There is yet another Principle, which might come
under the Heading of Appropriateness, and that is
'*Proportion*'. A Paragraph, which would be excellent
in one Essay, may be quite out of place in another, for
there it would perhaps emphasise some Idea which in
this Essay was not of the least importance ; or, vice versâ,
a Paragraph, which passed over some unimportant
Idea with a few light words in one Essay, might be out
of place in another Essay where the Idea *was* of importance. Hence in every part of Composition every
part must be in proportion to its importance. This
is most clear when we come to consider the length of
a Paragraph. It is a *general* rule that an important
Idea should have a long Paragraph: the 'bulk', or 'mass',
of the Paragraph (as Prof. Barrett Wendell aptly calls it)
should usually mark out the Idea as one of weight.

The Beginning and the Ending are most important,
not only for the Essay itself, but for every Section, and
Paragraph, and Sentence. As a rule the Beginning
should be interesting, and the Ending impressive ; but,
within the Essay, the Beginning and the Ending may
both be used as links to connect the different parts
together.

The Law of *Connexion* is scarcely less important

than any of the above; it might come with the Law of Unity and the Law of Co-operation, but still there is a distinction. It would be possible to have an Essay of which each part contributed something to the general effect, and yet this Essay might be wanting in Connexion. For, supposing we took the various Headings and wrote them down on Cards, and then shuffled these Cards, the different parts would still have the Principle of Unity and Co-operation (to a certain extent), and yet would be utterly wanting in Connexion, at any rate in so far as Connexion depends on the right Order and Arrangement.

Throughout the Composition, and all its parts, the *Order* and Arrangement are of great moment. Not only is it required that each *Word*, for example, shall be well chosen and appropriate: each Word must also be in its right place. For the particular purpose it should be just here or just there.

Last of all one cannot imagine Appropriateness (to the particular subject, the particular purpose, and the particular 'audience' of the Writer), or Arrangement, without a great deal of *Variety:* the Law of Variety, therefore, will be the next Law we shall mention.

Almost everywhere in life there is felt from time to time a need of change, and this applies to every department of Composition and Speaking: there must not be monotony in the Arrangement of Ideas, in the Comparisons and Contrasts, in the length of the Paragraphs, of the Sentences, of the Words, in the Construction, in the Rhythm, and so on. There must be Variety.

But the Variety must not be unnecessary. It must be within due bounds; it must be appropriate and adapted to the readers, etc. Variety is one of the chief means of securing Clearness, Interest and Attention, and Emphasis.

Another Law that goes through the whole of Composition, from the Ideas (Headings and Sub-Headings) down to the individual Words and the Punctuation, is *Clearness*.

Such other Principles as *Interest* and Suggestiveness, and (especially in the Endings) *Impressiveness*, apply to a great many departments (e.g. the Headings and Sub-Headings, the Comparisons, etc.), but can hardly be called 'Principles of universal application'.

We cannot say that any one of the above Laws is more important than any other, for no single one of these Laws stands by itself; here one will yield to another, and elsewhere this other will have to yield to the first. In a perfect Essay, the Laws would be found never to go against one another; each apparent exception to one Law would eventually be found to come under some higher Law. Perhaps the highest Law of all, if one *had* to choose some one out of the list, would be the Law of Appropriateness.

CHAPTER VIII. DIFFICULTIES AND FAULTS IN COMPOSITION, WITH A SAMPLE SCHOOLBOY-ESSAY (ANALYSED).

An Essay is set on "Tyrants". A boy sends in an exercise which is perhaps very bad in its Expression and Style; there are mistakes in Punctuation (p. 328), in Vocabulary (p. 324), in Grammar (p. 320); there is often a want of Rhythm, of Clearness, of Interest, of Variety, and so on. But this need not trouble us just yet. Here we need only notice the Ideas. We analyse the Essay, and find some such Ideas as this.

1. Tyrants unpopular;
2. spend money of poor;
3. but often successful in war;
4. cruel;
5. often short reign;
6. some patriotic.

Now here are Ideas which are

a. very meagre, compared with what the boy knows and could easily work out : *e.g.* he has omitted—

Evidences (very important here);
Causes of rise of Tyrants;
Obstacles to rise and to tenure of power;
etc.

β. all on the same level of Importance, like a picture with its background as distinct and detailed as its foreground;

γ. badly arranged; for here we have

1. a point against Tyrants;
2. do.;
3. a point for them;
4. a point against;
5. a characteristic, not necessarily for or against;
6. a point for them.

The Ideas are not arranged and grouped under Main Headings.

Why are there so many faults?

As in Games, so in Composition, one of the great difficulties of a learner is that his Teacher is very often one who does his work without knowing how. It is 'natural' to the Teacher to do the work well, but he is unconscious of the processes which are being gone through very quickly in his own mind; and the result is that he thinks the work is simple and easy, merely because it is very simple and easy to *him*. He cannot put himself into the position of the learner to whom the work is very complicated and very difficult.

The result of it may be that he tells the learner to "write an Essay", to "be natural", to "do nothing consciously", to "sit down and not think what he shall write". The learner writes an Essay, or what he calls an Essay; it is then corrected, and the next week the learner writes another Essay. By repetition and practice of a kind he improves *up to a certain point:* for example, he becomes able to get through the Essay more *quickly* and *easily;* but there are too many faults to be corrected at once, there is too much to be thought of at once, in the process of Essay-writing; and perhaps there is not one single part that he knows how to do correctly even by itself. How much more must he fail when he attempts to combine the various parts together in a single process. That the average learner should succeed without having acquired each part laboriously and carefully by itself is almost an impossibility.

Not one single part has been clearly taught him, still less has any single part been practised in the right way. When the individual faults have been pointed out, they have probably been pointed out merely as individual faults; the general principle has not been pointed out at all. The boy has not been told exactly *how and why* his particular fault was a fault, and how his particular class of fault might have been avoided, and might best be got rid of for the future.

Once again, though he may have done hundreds of Essays, yet he may not have gathered any general lesson which may apply to all Essays, or at any rate to all Essays of a certain class. He may have done an Essay on 'The Age of Pericles', another on 'The Age of Alexander the Great', another on 'The Age of Cato', another on 'The Age of Augustus', another on 'The Age of Charlemagne', another on 'The Age of Napoleon', and so on. Each, however, may have been done as if it had nothing in common with any of the other Ages; he may never have been told that in each Essay there will be *very much the same Headings* to be considered, for instance, War, Justice, Finance, Government, Religion, Literature, and so on. He has been doing as utterly separate topics those which were really connected by many points of similarity.

The same will apply to his Essays on Individuals, such as Epaminondas, Philip of Macedon, Tarquin, Caesar, Seneca, etc. He may have done many such Essays without being told that in all such instances it is necessary to consider very much the same Headings, such as (see p. 92) Evidences, Parallels and Contrasts, Effects, Aims, Changes, and so on.

He may be, and is almost certain to be, in a hurry to begin, and very reluctant to spend time on a practice which cannot be without a certain amount of drudgery.

As he does his Essay, he will probably 'economise' paper, cramping on a single page, filled with many additions and corrections, what ought to have been spread over many pages, and so he may have to rewrite a good deal of what he does.

He will forget to take into account that he will have various readers, some ignorant and unliterary, others lazy and unenthusiastic, others scholarly and severe, and others (like most women) demanding *personal* items and details.

And thus he may choose quite the wrong method of treating the subject. The chief faults will correspond to the pieces of advice which are given below. The learner may have made no Scheme of his Essay at all (see p. 56), or (p. 57) he may have made a bad Scheme.

As to his Ideas, see page 54. He may have omitted Comparisons and Contrasts, as well as a great deal that he really knows. He may have used no common sense; his Beginning may be uninteresting; his changes from one topic to another may be jerky; and there may be no proper Proportion of the Ideas, which appear in his Essay as if they were all equally important or unimportant; he may give Quotations which he has not properly 'digested'.

In Style and Expression (see p. 205), his Paragraphs may be too long; his work may be full of Abstract phrases and far from clear; he may have no Rhythm; and, in brief, his Style may be full of faults.

It is to remove these difficulties and to correct these faults that the following pages are written.

CHAPTER IX. AIMS AND MOTIVES OF WRITERS AND SPEAKERS.

ON p. 102 we shall consider the Aims and Motives which lead men to act in certain ways. We shall notice how the Motives were liable

 to *change* from time to time (p. 102),

 to be *mixed:* often, the more Motives there are,
  the more incentive there is to action.

Similarly, the Speaker may speak and the Writer may write with one or more of the following Aims in view, or his Aims may differ at different times.

His Aim may be

 to interest his audience, even if his ultimate
  Aim is

 to get for himself money or fame, etc. (or to
  escape poverty or obscurity, etc., p. 103);

 to please his audience, by amusing them or
  flattering them;

 to excite their reason ('For heaven's sake *do*
  use your reason,' said Demosthenes); and
  so to convince them,

 to persuade them, or to dissuade them, or to
  correct some false opinions.

  We might include here the desire to elicit
  independent thought, e.g. by suggesting a
  problem to be worked out;

 to describe something, so that the reader or hearer
  may see what the Writer or Speaker sees,

to instruct them and improve them, and to
benefit their
    body (e.g. health),
    intellect,
    character and morals ;
to glorify some people, or to defend them, and
perhaps to vilify and to blame others.

It is most important to know, as far as you possibly
can, what your Aims are in Writing or Speaking on
any given occasion. For not only is this a part of your
'Duty towards Yourself,' but it should actually influence
the whole of your Composition. You should adapt and
fit everything to your Aim—after making sure that your
Aim is not low.

PART II.

PART II. IDEAS : HOW TO COLLECT, SELECT,
UNDERLINE, AND ARRANGE
HEADINGS, AND SUB-HEAD-
INGS.

CHAPTER X. BAD SCHEMES FOR COMPOSITIONS, AND FAULTS OF THE IDEAS AND HEADINGS.

THE chief faults in Essay-writing have been already touched on (p. 54). Here we need only repeat, in more detail, the chief faults in the Ideas or Headings of an ordinary Essay or Speech.

(1) The Headings are *incomplete*. Nine Essays out of ten omit the Evidences, which (see p. 147) should never be omitted, the exposing of Fallacies (p. 150), and, in a Period, the Period before (p. 126) and the Period afterwards (p. 125), and (p. 110) the consideration of all the various Classes. Essays, again, generally omit Illustrations and Analogies (p. 281), and Contrasts.

(2) A good many of the Ideas in average Essays are *off the point;* the Writer begins all right but is apt to fly off at a tangent.

(3) Some of the Ideas are untrue: this may be from ignorance, or it may be from carelessness about the Evidences.

And here we may class those Ideas which are *unfair* and biassed (p. 141), and also Fallacies (p. 150). We find that a great many of the Ideas are *illogical:* these may be classed under the heading of Fallacies.

(4) In Books (rather than in Articles and Essays) we too often find Ideas which are not exactly untrue, but are *unwholsesome;* many modern Novels are remarkable for their unwholesomeness.

(5) A good deal may be quite true, and quite whole-some, and quite fair, and to a certain extent appropriate to the subject ; but still it may be quite *uninteresting* to the readers or hearers. In Books by specialists we generally find much which has very great merits, and is not so much unintelligible as uninteresting to the general public. We do not doubt that it is interesting to the Writer, but that is an entirely different matter.

(6) We have mentioned, above, that most Essays are wanting in Comparisons and Contrasts. This a grievous deficiency for many reasons (see p. 281).

(7) The Ideas may also be wanting in *Proportion* (p. 170). They may all appear as equally important, or the unimportant may be emphasised.

(8) They may be wanting in *Connexion* and Cohesion (p. 263).

(9) They may be *unoriginal* and copied direct from some Authority; on this point see p. 163 foll.

(10) The Scheme of the Essay may have been bad: and this suggests a whole host of considerations (see p. 57).

(11) Last of all, the Essay may be to some extent interesting, but it may not be fertile in *suggestions.* We shall see, on p. 357, that the best Books and Articles to read are those which suggest most to the reader, those which make him think most; one often comes across Writings which do not encourage one to think in the very least; rather, they seem to paralyse one's power of thinking. I make a habit of classifying Books in my mind according to the amount of new Ideas and new lines of thought that they have suggested, quite apart from the Arrangement of Ideas or the way in which the Ideas are Expressed. Among such Books,

those by Froebel, Buckle, Seeley, and Herbert Spencer, come in the very front rank.

I wish to end this Chapter with two remarks on Schemes or Plans for Essays, Speeches, etc.

1. Many a Composition has been a failure because it has had no Scheme : it has been like a house (possibly a beautiful house) built on sand, or, rather, like a house built without scaffolding.

2. Other Compositions have failed because their Scheme has been faulty. The following Diagrams will give a few specimens of faulty Schemes.

....
....
....
....
....
....
....
....
....

and so on.

DIAGRAM I.

Scheme No. I is bad, because it is so cramped : there is little chance of additions or serious alterations, and there is little or no chance of re-arrangement. The Ideas are not clear : they do not give a bird's-eye view of the topic. False Economy of paper is perhaps the chief cause of error : I say false, because paper is of far less importance than time, mental labour, and a satisfactory result, to say nothing of eyesight.

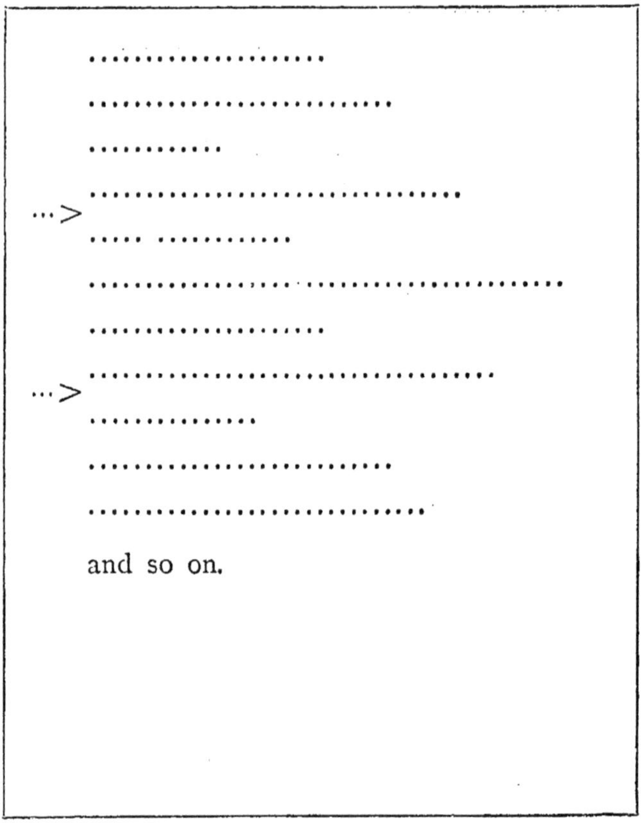

DIAGRAM II.

Diagram II gives a somewhat better Scheme, because it has Margins, in which additions and corrections can be written. But these additions are clumsy, and, besides, re-arrangement would be very difficult.

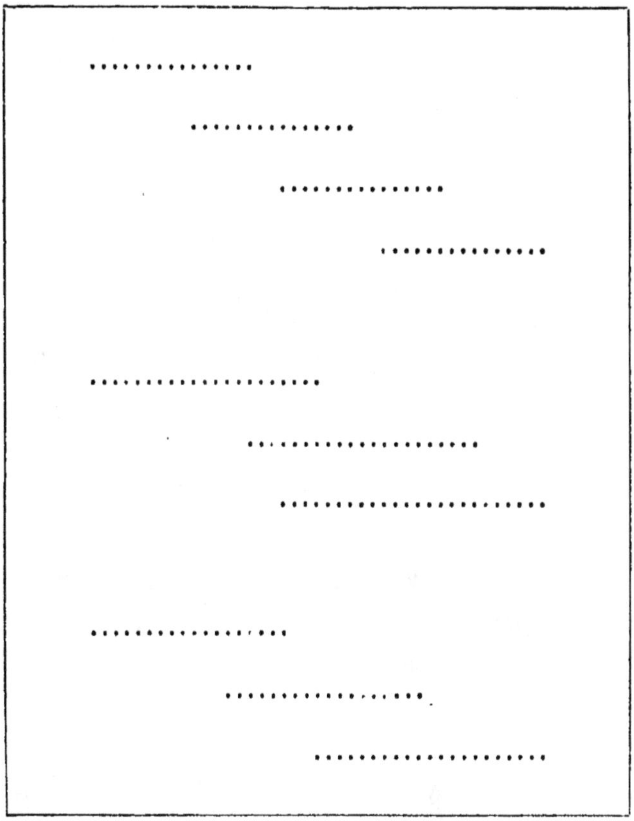

DIAGRAM III.

Diagram III is still better, for it is clearer : it allows of additions and alterations, and of Sub-Headings also. If little paper is allowed in an Examination, then this Scheme may do fairly well. But, like I and II, it does not allow of easy re-arrangement.

A fourth Scheme would be like III, but would put each Heading on a separate piece of paper or on a Card (see p. 186). This would be better, for the reasons given on p. 192: e.g. alterations, additions, Sub-Headings, and re-arrangement, would all be easy.

CHAPTER XI. WHAT THE IDEAS AND HEADINGS OUGHT TO BE.

1. THE Ideas should be as *complete* as possible. That is to say, nothing of importance should be omitted.

2. The next Law, which will counteract this and keep it within due limits, is the Law of *Unity*, which means that one shall only select such Ideas as belong to the subject and to one's particular Aim in Writing or Speaking, and that one shall reject every other Idea.

3. *Truth and fairness* are to be considered. There must be *no Bias*. If a biassed Idea *is* mentioned, then the *Objections* to it should be mentioned also. In fact, fairness demands that both sides of the question should be given. But (someone will ask) in preparing an Essay or an Article, may we not simply state one view of the case? Of course there is much to be said for this, and especially that it gives the ordinary reader one clear notion, and does not puzzle him with a lot of exceptions at the outset. So far this is all right, but the exceptions and the Objections should also be mentioned, and it is a safe rule even *to exaggerate the case for the other side.*

4. Anyhow the Ideas should be as *logical* as possible. And they should show a knowledge of human nature.

5. The Ideas should also be *moral and healthy*. Essays do not usually err in respect of unhealthiness, in fact, not nearly so much as Novels do.

6. As to the definiteness of Ideas, that is also to be

considered. The Ideas should be quite clear to the Author himself: for the meaning of this, see p. 228.

7. The Ideas should also be *illustrated* by Parallels, Comparisons, and Contrasts. This applies not only to those Ideas which would naturally be somewhat hard to understand otherwise, but to those Ideas which one wishes to Emphasise.

8. The Ideas also should show a certain *Proportion.* This of course depends largely upon the way in which they are expressed (see p. 271); but it has a good deal to do with the Ideas themselves as Ideas, and with their Arrangement. What is important should stand out in the foreground, and what is unimportant should retire into the background.

9. The *Connexion* of Ideas with one another also depends partly on the Arrangement, and partly on the Expression: see p. 263.

10. As to whether the Ideas should be *Original* or not, there has been a great deal of discussion. There are some who say that Writers and Speakers should only write or say what they have discovered for themselves. Others say that they may write or say anything which anybody has discovered, so long as they themselves have understood and felt what the Ideas mean. They must make the Ideas their own, before they hand them on to others.

11. But, be that as it may, the Ideas should be *Interesting*, not so much to the Writer or Speaker himself, as *to the reader;* and one department of this Interest would be the *Suggestiveness.* Essays should not merely give information, but they should also suggest problems and encourage the reader to think out his problems for himself. .

What the Ideas should be: in Rhyme.

Ideas should be the Author's own, seen clear by his
  own eyes,
free from wrong Aims, Omissions, Bias, Fallacies, and
  Lies ;
With Unity, Proportion, Order, Interest, and Style.*

* For the continuation of the Rhyme, see p. 204.

CHAPTER XII. HOW TO COLLECT IDEAS IN THE FORM OF HEADINGS AND SUB-HEADINGS.

THE Collection of Ideas (in the form of Headings and Sub-Headings) must be a process by itself. While it is going on, no attention must be paid to anything else; the whole mind must be *concentrated* on the Collection of Ideas. Even the Sub-Headings (under each main Heading) must not be thought of, though they must be put down when they suggest themselves.

Above all it is necessary to be able to express the whole Idea *by as few words as possible :* a single word is often quite enough. Thus no time will be wasted, and the writing will keep pace with the thoughts. See p. 66 for some helps towards this, e.g. the Analysing of Books or of Letters.

Of course the amount of time which can be given to the Collecting of Ideas, and the way in which they can be Collected, depends a good deal upon the conditions, for instance upon whether you have a week in which to prepare the work, or only a few hours ; whether you can refer to reference-books, or whether you are thrown on your own resources ; whether you are able to use the Card-system (p. 186) or whether you have to rely on paper of an ordinary kind, or whether you are not even allowed paper.

As a rule I should suggest that the Collecting of Ideas (Headings and Sub-Headings) for an Essay should generally take about *a third* of the whole time which the Essay itself will demand. With the extra process of Selecting and Rejecting Ideas, and Under-lining them, and Arranging them, I should say that not less than half the time should be devoted to this part of the subject, before a single sentence is expressed: the beginning and ending Sentences or Paragraphs may be excepted.

It is wonderful how the power of quickly Collecting Ideas increases with practice. I can now Collect Ideas perhaps four times as fast as I used to be able to. And not only that, but I can also form far more complete Lists. The following will give some idea of the relative 'proportions' in Essay-writing. On one occasion the Headings which I had Collected consisted of 100 words. I arranged these and read through them and mastered them in about 5 minutes. I dictated them in just under 5 minutes. I wrote them down afterwards in just under 25 minutes, and the whole amount, when written down, came to about 500 words. On another occasion, when the whole amount which I wrote down came to about 1000 words, and the Headings again to about 100 words, the dictation (to a Shorthand Clerk) took me 7 minutes, and the writing-out (by myself afterwards, as an ex-periment) about 42 minutes. It must be remembered that, whereas my power of writing out an Essay has not grown so very much quicker, my power of Collect-ing and Arranging Headings has grown extraordinarily quicker.

Besides the *General Lists* (pp. 83, 92), other helps to-wards the Collection of Headings would of course be the reading of Books and Articles, the listening to and the

taking part in Debates and conversations on the subjects, and the collecting and working out of *Parallels,
Comparisons, and Contrasts.*

These latter are among the most valuable means for
Collecting Headings for ordinary purposes. A good
instance would be an Essay-question like the Bonds
of Union between England and her Colonies. Of this
the average reader knows little, or rather he has little
that he can say on the spur of the moment. Let him
first of all get the underlying principle, namely that
he wants to find out Bonds of Union, and then let him
work them out *wherever it is easiest to work them out.*
For instance, let him ask himself what are the Bonds
of Union in an ordinary family, or in any other group
of people (such as a Club): he will think of a great
number of Headings in this way. Then let him think
of Comparisons: for instance, the analogy of the bundle
of sticks. Then let him think of Contrasts, e.g. what
it is that prevents people from joining together, or (to
take *an extreme case*) what is it that makes them quarrel.

It is important to *leave intervals,* that is to say not
to write the Essay or make the Speech immediately
after the Headings have been Collected, but to let the
mind lie fallow for a while, so that new Ideas may come
to the surface. It is surprising what a number of fresh
thoughts suggest themselves at intervals when once we
have been through a topic.

But it is generally absolutely essential that, before
the Essayist reads a single word written by anyone else,
he should *try to work out the whole topic for himself,*
jotting down those Ideas which are already in his mind.
Afterwards, by all means let him add to those Ideas:
let him read as much as he can on the subject, and let

F

him look at these Ideas at intervals; but let him
seldom, if ever, go straight to any Book for information.
Even a few minutes spent in working out a topic (see
p. 353) will not be wasted.

When he now has his Headings more or less ready,
let him write them either on *Cards* (see p. 186) or in
a permanent *Note-book*. He may have to re-arrange
them at intervals, and, if so, the *Cards* will be better
than the Note-book.

*He should always have a number of good subjects to
think out, during odd moments.* The amount of time
which might be spent on good and interesting subjects
during each ordinary day probably amounts to at
least one hour.

It is very well worth while *to practise writing down
Ideas by single words.* It is a kind of shorthand in
Writing. One does not write down the whole sentence, but one writes down the main Ideas, of which
the general effect will be like that of the Table of
Contents at the beginning of a Book or Chapter.
Only there would be a difference, namely that the Ideas
will be written *under one another*, and not in a single
line. This would also be useful for Telegrams. And
a good way of practising it would be to take a *Newspaper*, and, without looking at the Headings, to try to
devise Headings of one's own for each Paragraph, and
afterwards to refer to the Headings actually given.
Or, again, Letters which you receive might be analysed,
the analysis being kept e.g. in an Indexed Note-book.
Such a Note-book might be of great use.

This power of expressing Ideas by single words is of
enormous value throughout life. As I said above, in
the Collecting of Ideas the thought is apt to outrun the

pen. But when the thought is jotted down as a single word, or as very few words, then *the pen can keep up.* Personally, I believe that the habit of making Lists of things of any kind (e.g. of requisites for a journey, or of presents) will improve and be improved by this Collection of Ideas for Essays.

It is needless to say that it is very important to read Books, and Articles, such as the Articles in the "North American Review" or the "Nineteenth Century", and to listen to Lectures and Speeches and conversations; only it must be borne in mind that the Ideas gathered up in this way should be *reproduced on paper afterwards.* If you only have the Headings to reproduce, you can write them down in next to no time. It is also excellent practice for the *memory.* Afterwards the Headings can be corrected and added to.

A few miscellaneous Hints may be suggested here.

In Collecting Ideas it is often as well to get what may be called Tables, of Causes etc. (see pp. 112–113). They will enable one to think of a good deal which otherwise one might forget.

Secondly it is a great help to do this Collection of Headings while the mind is still *fresh*, rather than after any hard work. Nothing is so fagging to most people as writing consecutively hour after hour. At the end of this time the brain is no longer at its best; so the work of Collecting Headings should be done while one feels in the fullest vigour. This includes not only the beginning of the Examination hours, for example, but also certain times in the day (e.g. *not* between 1.30 and 3.0 p.m.)

It must be remembered that, as one writes down the Headings, *the symbols and signs for them need only be clear to oneself;* thus one can use Abbreviations (see below); and, generally, any means which brings a clear Idea before one's mind will be sufficient. One is not doing Headings for the benefit of anyone else except oneself. It is the Essay or Speech which is going to be read or heard by others, and not its Headings. A List of General Abbreviations is appended to this Chapter.

Between the Headings there should be *spaces*, so that additions can be made, and so that the whole result can stand out more clearly. It is a great mistake to economise paper. And, in the Arrangement of Headings, the principle of *indentation* should be used: that is to say, the main Headings should stand underneath one another, and the Sub-Headings should be a little to the right, a little inland, again underneath one another. This would be illustrated by the Diagram on p. 59.

When the Headings, and then the Sub-Headings, have been Collected, each can be gone through and revised. And a Scheme can now be made, perhaps on a single large page. Occasionally it will be found that, while one is actually writing out the Essay, new Headings will occur, being suggested by something which one has not worked out fully before. These should be added to one's Scheme.

The Scheme should not tie the Writer or Speaker down: it is meant to help him and not to hamper him, so that omissions, additions, alterations, and even changes in the Arrangement, can be made as the Essay is being written out or as the Speech is being spoken. And of course the occasional practice of an Essay or Speech without a Scheme at all will be an excellent lesson in promptitude.

It may be interesting to the reader to know that the dictation of this Chapter to a Shorthand Clerk, from a set of simple Headings, took about 20 minutes. It will give some idea of how much of the Essay is praetically already done by the time that the Headings have been Collected, and Arranged, etc. Of the Arrangement of Headings I shall speak in a subsequent Chapter.

In conclusion, I would add that I believe that the habit of Collecting Ideas (as Headings and Sub-Headings) will develope a general habit of Collecting, and that, conversely, the habit of Collecting other things (e.g. things for a journey) will develope the special habit of Collecting Ideas.

A few General Abbreviations (useful for Schemes, and for the Card-System).

∵ because, for

∴ therefore, and so

= is equivalent to, corresponding to, etc.

> is greater than, is better than, conquers, etc.

< is smaller than, is inferior to, is conquered by, etc.

− without, apart from

+ in addition to, with the help of

)(is contrasted with, in opposition to, etc.

→ developes into, produces, (? causes), etc.

← is produced by, (? is caused by), etc.

∥ in proportion to

↑ see above

↓ see below.

CHAPTER XIII. SOME HEADINGS WHICH ARE OFTEN OMITTED.

THOSE who look over Essays, or who hear Speeches, and who are not utterly uncritical or unoriginal, and who do not concentrate their attention on the Expression and Style, cannot fail to notice the frequent Omission of many Ideas which seem to them to be important or even indispensable.

Examples will be given below (e.g. see p. 79), but here let me briefly note a few of the commonest Omissions.

We have a Composition on some Period, let us say 'The Age of Louis the XIVth': we analyse it into Headings, and we find that no mention is made e.g. of

the Authorities and Evidences, and Fallacies;

the Previous Age, which will give some of the *Causes and Hindrances* (p. 126);

the Subsequent Age, which will give some of *the Results and Reactions* (p. 125);

Changes within the Age itself, which will give the tendencies (p. 127);

certain *Departments*, such as the condition of the Poor, the condition of Women, Finance, and so on (p. 83): see also the Classes, on p. 110;

Comparisons and Contrasts with other Ages (pp. 279, 281, 291).

And so with other subjects.   We have a Composition on Cicero as an Individual, and here again we find no Authorities or Evidences, no 'Hindrances' (p. 97), no Comparisons and Contrasts (p. 104), and no account of his Family and Social Life, and so on.

Obviously there is need of something to suggest these Headings.

CHAPTER XIV. ADVANTAGES OF GENERAL LISTS OF HEADINGS.

The General Lists, which will be given below, will at first look like a system of cramming. They will seem as if they were giving information in a very compact form. But as a matter of fact they do not give information, but *ask questions*, namely "What do you know about the following topic?" It is as if an architect, before he began his house, were to have a complete list of rooms which might be wanted. If · he had such a list he could, without trouble, select those rooms which he wanted, and reject the rest, whereas otherwise he might possibly forget something of importance. This is the real advantage of a General List.

Or, again, a General List may be compared to a shop full of things. The customer goes in and asks for (let us say) ten things, and, if the shop has a complete stock, those ten things are easily selected, especially if the shop is neatly arranged. In the shop there may be thousands of things which are not used at all, but the great point is that those which *are* to be used can be selected at once and without waste of time or trouble. In travelling, in the same way, it is usually much better to take too many things than too few.

1. The advantages of having a General List of Headings for an Essay or Speech do not appear until one

has tried to write the Essay without such a List (see
p. 79). Supposing a class at a School had prepared a
lesson, and then the schoolmaster said "Write out what
you remember of the lesson", the result would be very
muddled and very incomplete. As a matter of fact,
the master asks questions. He picks the lesson to
pieces, and asks about its various parts. *The questions
which he asks are not themselves information, but a means
of eliciting information.*

2. The Lists will of course differ for different Essays
and Speeches, but it is surprising to find to how many
topics the two Lists on pp. 83 and 92 will apply. A
collection of such topics is given on p. 183, and it might
almost be said that these two General Lists are *sufficient
for the main Headings of most topics*, and that then a
List of Sub-Headings for these main Headings might
perhaps be mastered in addition.

When once the Lists have been thoroughly learnt
and practised, then they can easily be applied to almost
any given subject. It will not make much difference
whether the subject be Aristocracy, Democracy, or
Monarchy (in political Essays or Speeches). The Headings will be very much the same for all   It does not
matter very much whether the Person be Caesar or
Pericles or Napoleon or Nelson: the General Headings
for the Individual, and for the special departments,
such as War, will apply to all these equally.

3. And, if these Lists are mastered, there will be *no
Omission* of any important subject. One of the most
maddening features of an Examination, for the examined,
is that he seldom puts down all that he knows: he may
really *know* the subject, but at the particular moment
he cannot bring it to the surface of his mind. His

mind may be compared to a pond, and the information which he wants to get hold of may be compared to 20 fishes. The 20 fishes are in the pond all right, but the difficulty is to catch them, and in an Examination the chance of 'catching' is extraordinarily ·small. It is possible to catch 15 out of the 20, but how are the other 5 to be secured? In an Essay or Speech exactly the same difficulty will be found. Probably my Headings are really well known to the Essayist or Speaker, but *at the time* he cannot recall them, and so he omits them altogether. Now with a General List like mine he could not possibly omit any Heading on which he could really say something of importance.

4. And this is not all: not only are there fewer Omissions, but a great deal of *time is saved* which would otherwise have been spent in searching for Headings, as if one were trying to collect pigs in clover.

5. As we have seen on p. 44, Essays and Speeches often suffer from bad *Arrangement* of their Ideas. Now if the General List contains the Ideas in a fairly good order (as it should do), then the trouble in Arranging these Ideas may be nearly saved. Of course each Composition will demand a certain amount of re-arrangement; but still the same Arrangement may be suitable for a great number of Compositions, *up to a certain point.* In fact, the Writer or Speaker will start at a very great advantage. Already he has a number of pigeon-holes, with labels all arranged in a fairly good order. What he has to do now, in Collecting his Ideas, is to put into each pigeon-hole that which he knows about the particular topic. Afterwards he may have to re-arrange; but not nearly to

the same extent as if his Ideas had been Collected 'higgledy-piggledy'.

6. If you have the General List *it is wonderfully easy to reject that which is not wanted.* A man who goes into a shop like Whiteley's should not object and say "There are too many things here; I don't want them all". He should choose just what he *does* want. He may have to see a number of things which he does not want, but the time wasted in this way is quite small. Anyhow he is very unlikely to omit anything of importance.

7. Nowadays, also, there is an additional advantage. We are beginning to regard subjects from many more different points of view. If you read an 'up-to-date' Newspaper (like the "Daily Mail"), and compare it with the History of Greece by ancient or even modern Historians, you will at first be inclined to think that *there are many more interests in the world* and many more departments of life than there have ever been before. But this is only half the truth. As a matter of fact, many of the interests have been there all along, only Writers and Speakers have not noticed them. A great deal is included now which was once thought unimportant. The lower Classes, for instance, receive their share of attention, and health and sanitary arrangements are another topic which would not have been considered in ancient times. Hence the modern Essayist or Speaker has to include a great number of Headings which the ancient Essayist or Speaker would never have troubled about. The modern world sees that the things which are mentioned are really important. There is a great deal to be discussed besides War, Religion, Government, and the gossip of the Court.

It is not meant that all Headings which you discuss are of equal importance : but it is meant that, if you go on in a haphazard method and put down just what comes into your head, you are as likely as not to leave out some Heading which really may be twice as important as what you have put in. Every day it becomes more and more unscientific to omit ; and what may be unimportant now may in future years come to have its importance brought prominently forward.

To prove this, let anyone take "Whitaker's Almanack" and pick out from the last two years the events, let us say ten of them, which he thinks will be most important twenty years hence. Very likely only three of his events will be remembered then ; as to the other seven, posterity may pass over them as being trivial.

8. There is yet another reason for General Lists being valuable ; and that is that they encourage *Fairness*. On p. 150 foll. we shall see that *Fallacies* are mostly due to some kind of Omission. And what looks very like dishonesty and unfairness may in reality be ignorance or forgetfulness. Now the chance of such Omissions, and therefore the chance of such Fallacies, is minimised if the General Lists be used.

9. These Lists also *save a great deal of trouble in learning*,* as the following example will show. Supposing we have learnt once for all the advantages of the supreme rule of one man, for instance, of Augustus at Rome, and supposing we have made a General List of those advantages, and have learnt this List, then, when we come later on to deal with any other good ruler like Pericles at Athens, or Peter the Great in

---

* In this they might be compared with Mathematical *Formulas*, e.g. for Arithmetical Progression.

Russia, or the German Emperor to-day, we should have a certain amount of our Ideas already found for us: we should have a number of things which the partienlar ruler *might* have done, and we shall just have to ask ourselves, "Did he actually do so-and-so?" Of course the difficulty is to choose as our starting-point that instance which is as near as possible to a complete List. If we needed a complete list of virtues, we should have no difficulty in our choice of an instance.

As contrasted with this, I notice many Books (of recent date) which give Outlines of Essays. They give Headings for hundreds of separate Essays, but *no General Headings for a few Types of Essays.* You find a Skeleton-Essay on 'Democracy': well and good. But the Skeleton-Essay on 'Aristocracy' (or 'The House of Lords') is given as something quite distinct. There is no attempt to say—'The Headings A, B, C, D, E . . ., viz. Causes, Hindrances, Comparisons, etc., are common to *both* these Essays, and in fact to a whole *class* of Essays, including even (see p. 96) Essays on Individuals'.

But, to return to what we said before, the chief advantage of a General List is that it almost does away with the chance of Omission. There are many people who do not speak until they are spoken to, or even until they are asked a question, and then they suddenly seem to blossom out. I remember one case of a man, whom I had never heard discussing cricket: when I asked him questions, however, I found that he knew nearly all the general results and important details of the leading matches of the last few years. And there are many people who are just the same in Essay-writing or Speaking. They need 'drawing out,' and these Lists will help to draw them out.

CHAPTER XV. HEADINGS FOR AN ESSAY, ETC., ON A PERIOD: WITH A RHYME.

WHEN a Period is to be reviewed, when two Periods are to be compared, and in many other kinds of Essays (such as the Influences of Geography, the Sphere of Government, the Results of War, the Causes of Success), it is absolutely essential to have a more or less complete List of Headings.

I observe that many excellent Schemes or Skeletons of Essays have been published lately: but they are all for individual Essays (e.g. a Scheme for an Essay on 'The Age of Louis XIV.'). There is little or no attempt to give a General List of Headings applicable to *any and every* Period: cp. p. 78.

The value of such a List cannot be estimated except by contrast. Try to review the Age of Louis XIV., or any Age, *without* such a List, and see how many Headings you can get. Probably there will not be more than three-quarters of those which are given here. You will have omitted many; and these will not necessarily be the unimportant Headings. You will have omitted several which, when once you are reminded of them, you will at once agree to be very important indeed: to prove what I say, make the experiment.

*   *   *

Now probably (unless you remember the previous Chapter) you will not have mentioned the Evidences, a review of every Class, the Period Before, the Period After, and so on.

If, however, you had had the List in front of you, you would have omitted no Heading of any great importance. *All your knowledge on the subject would have been drawn out.*

In the following List (for the many uses of which see p. 133) notice the opposites or Contrasts [in square Brackets]. For the List as a Rhyme, see p. 83.

Headings for a Period, etc.

[Interest of the Subject : see p. 255.]
Evidences.

G

Most of the above Headings may (see p. 362 foll.) become little Essays in themselves, and have Sub-Headings of their own. Some of these Sub-Headings may in their turn become little Essays and have Sub-sub-Headings of their own.

I give the List here in the form of a **Rhyme**:
for the best way of learning such Rhymes, see p. 88.

Give Evidences, points of view, and Fallacies (alas !) ;
Geography, and Public Works; the folk, of every Class,
the Intercourse, the Individual, Unions (large or small),
State-Government, and Order, Justice, Rights ; and
    Virtues all ;
Religion, aims, thoughts, customs, powers, and Educa-
    tion's parts ;
Language and Letters, Wisdom ; then the Sciences, and
    Arts,
and Inventions; social life, home-life, and women,
    dress, and Health,
Occupations (commerce, industries, professions, trades);
    and Wealth ;
Finance ; then *Other Peoples* in some way connected tell
(subjects, allies, and colonies, and enemies as well)
by marriage, intercourse, and trade, and travel, and
    by War ;
View th' Army, Navy ; then the Ages After and Before,
Changes within the Age itself, and stage of Progress
    state ;
Chief People ; give Quotations ; lastly recapitulate.
Many Headings have their *Contrasts*, and *Comparisons :*
    thus Rome
had Wealth, but also poorer folk, and so have we at
    home.

For Rhymes giving some of the Sub-Headings of
these Main Headings, see p. 139, etc.

FOR the use and value of all General Lists, I refer to p. 73 foll. Here I wish to point out once more (see p. 79) the value of these Headings, which I call Period-Headings, and which are collected in a Rhyme on p. 83; that is to say, such Headings as Government, Religion, Education, Commerce, War.

1. To begin with, we may use them when we have to describe the *Period* of some great man, of some great event, or of a certain year or number of years.

2. Of course, if two Periods are to be *Compared* or *Contrasted*, the Headings will be equally to the point.

But they cover a far wider ground than this.

3. If we have to give the *Results* of some Influence, let us say of Geography, Religion, Slavery, Naval Power, War, Monarchy (Democracy, etc.), Commerce, Industries, Wealth, Colonisation, Inventions, Literature, etc., or the effects of certain Individuals, we shall need to have before us a wide field: we shall need to survey the whole of life, as it were, and to ask, 'Was such-and-such a sphere affected, e.g. the position of women, the morals of the People, and so on?' Here the Period-Headings will again be needed.

4. If, on the other hand, we have to give

(*a*) the *Causes and Helps* (and perhaps the Means), or

(*b*) the *Hindrances* and Obstacles to the Influences of Geography, Religion, etc., then again the Period-Headings must be utilised.

For example, what were the Causes of Rome's Success, Rome's Failure, etc., or what were the signs and *Characteristics* of that Failure? Here, unless we have a long List of such Headings before us, we may easily pass over some Cause or some Obstacle of great moment, e.g. Geography.

The Causes of Unity (the Bonds of Union) e.g. between England and America, or England and Australia, might also be included here.

5. What is the proper *Sphere* of Government? How far should Government 'interfere'? Here we need to know how far Government *has* interfered or *can* interfere: we need to review the various departments of life. In other words, we need the Period-Headings.

6. In Essays on *Persons* (see p. 96 foll.) we have to consider what *helped* or *hindered* the Persons in their development; and of course many things might have contributed. We have to review their surroundings, their 'Environment'. We need the Period-Headings in case we should omit any important influence, such as Geography.

And this applies equally when we have to consider the *Effects* which these Persons had upon their surroundings and upon later Periods.

7. *Proverbs* are often set for Essays, and so are *Quotations* of a general character, such as 'Where ignorance is bliss, 'tis folly to be wise', or 'No single man ever yet altered the character of a Nation for any length of time.' Here, once more, we need *Instances* from every possible source: we need not only to review past and present 'History', but also to review its various departments, such as Religion. Otherwise we may be leaving out just those very Instances

which we really know best and which would be most
telling.

8. Even now I have not exhausted the uses to which
the Period-Headings may be put.   They will be wanted
also when we have to consider the *Evidences* for various
statements.   For, as we shall see on p. 145, in many
subjects Geography, Religion, Language, etc., may all
be valuable Evidences, besides (see p. 149) affording
valuable *Suggestions.*

9. If we wish to be able to take *a fair*, that is to say
a comprehensive,view of many questions great or small,
we may well set these Period-Headings before us before
we venture to form our opinion and to tell it to others.
We may think that a certain Political Party is right
in a certain line of action until we have examined that
line of action in the light of, e.g. Geography, Morality,
Education,. Commerce, the Subsequent Periods, and so
on.   Until this light has been thrown on the subject
we may, for all we know, be seeing only one side of the
subject.

CHAPTER XVII. **HOW TO LEARN LISTS OF HEADINGS.**

A. How to Learn Headings.

FOR general advice as to How to Learn and " How to Remember ", I must refer to a book on the subject, published by Messrs. Warne & Co. I should suggest the following helps here.

1. First of all try to *work out the Headings for yourself,* using common sense, Comparisons, Contrasts, etc. Then *correct* and add after an interval, and refer to the General Lists in Chapters XV., etc. Observe where you have omitted anything, and make notes of these weak points, and pay extra attention to these omitted Headings.

2. Then *write out the full List* from memory, and afterwards look again at the List and make additions and corrections.

3. With the List in front of you, *apply it* to various subjects. For instance, apply the List of Headings for an Essay on a Person (p. 94), to yourself or to anyone else that you know. You will find that, when you have used the Plan or Scheme a good many times, you will be able to do an Essay on another person without a Plan in front of you at all. In fact, the more Instances you get for each Heading, and the more you make certain of a few Instances for each, to start with, the more indelibly the Headings themselves will become impressed upon your mind.

4. It is as well to try to *reproduce* the Lists of Headings at odd moments, for instance, in the train.

5. For one List (see p. 108) I have suggested the system of learning by Initials: this I have found most useful in my own work. That is to say, one arranges the Headings in such an order that their *Initials* form some word or words, only it is always necessary to get the Headings thoroughly understood and grasped *before* one attempts this 'Initializing'. See, further, "How to Remember".

6. For some people, *Rhymes* will be the best means, but they also (see below) should not be allowed until the Headings have been thoroughly understood and frequently practised: then and not till then will the Rhymes be valuable. For a few Rhymes, to which the Reader can easily add many others, see pp. 36, 62, 83, 92, etc. As to the ways of learning Rhymes, I shall now proceed to offer a few suggestions.

B. How to Learn Rhymes.

There is a rooted objection, in the minds of many, to the use of Rhymes as a means of fixing Ideas in the memory, and this too in spite of the fact that people are wont to remember the number of days in the various months, and many other things as well,* by means of Rhymes. The objectors say that Rhymes are never to be used as a help to the memory.

Of course this is going ever so much too far, but it has some reason ; *it is a very great mistake to learn Rhymes as most people learn them*, that is to say *by mere sounds*, and as the parrot or the Phonograph learns Rhymes. The parrot or the Phonograph repeats

---

* See "How to Remember" (published by Warne & Co.).

Rhymes absolutely correctly, but even the parrot seldom understands a word or an Idea. And this is how most boys and girls learn Poetry and other Rhymes at School. This way of learning is generally rather worse than useless. Not only does it take a long time for most people to learn Rhymes thus, but for most people the Rhymes even when learnt do not stay in the memory, and even if they do they are scarcely ready for use.

The real way of learning a Rhyme, if good is to be got out of it, and *if* the Rhyme is worth learning, is *to read the words slowly as if they were not a Rhyme at all*, that is to say, to read them *thinking only of the sense*, and making no attempt whatever to learn the words as words or as sounds. It is best to say the words out loud and yet to think of the sense, and not to pass by any sentence until it has been understood.

When the words do not convey a clear meaning, then you must stop and think what they *do* mean. You might think of some actual *instance* (see p. 160): for example you might apply the idea to some particular example, or else work out the Contrast, which (see p. 291) will often throw light on the meaning.

When you have read through the whole Rhyme very slowly, making sure that you understand the general sense of the whole of it, as well as the special sense and the connexion of the various parts, then put it aside for a time, and, after an interval, read it through again, not troubling to learn it but simply realising it. Do this over and over again at intervals, at first very slowly and with concentrated attention, and (for it cannot be repeated too often) with thorough understanding.

For the very important Résumée-method, see p. 354.

After this has been done perhaps ten times, perhaps fifteen, not only will the Ideas and the sense be fixed in your mind as a valuable possession, but (curious as it may seem) the sounds will have been fixed in your mind as well. Without having made the slightest effort to learn the sounds, you will have learnt them merely by saying them out loud. Somewhat similarly, by hearing a tune often, you come to know it and to be able to reproduce it, without ever having consciously intended to know it. You take it into your brain willy nilly.

Before beginning a fresh Rhyme, go over the old Rhyme once more, that is to say, *make sure of the ground which you have already mastered,* before you try to master fresh ground. The early Romans were very careful to make their conquests their very own, and to secure them thoroughly, before they proceeded to fresh struggles and fresh conquests.

CHAPTER XVIII. GENERAL HEADINGS FOR SPECIAL SUBJECTS (e.g. COLONISATION, OR WAR): WITH A RHYME.

MOST learners who are told to write an Essay on 'Monarchy', or 'Slavery', or 'Naval Power', etc., have no notion as to how they ought to treat the subject. It is so vague. The following Headings will form a List from which they may *select*.

Let the reader apply these Headings to a subject like 'Government', or 'Religion'. But let him first try to collect the Headings for an Essay on these two Subjects, *without* looking at the List. Then let him see the List applied, e.g. on p. 96.

    *   *   *   *   *

Here, as before, we have

[The *Interest* of the subject]

  Evidences

    Authorities

           their failings 140

    Different points of view (Bias)................. 141

    Other Evidences 145

  Fallacies 150

To these we now add :—

Instances, including Extreme Instances 160

Causes and helps

Hindrances

Description
    parts
        their connexions
    extent and sphere
        in time
        in place
    changes
    [different points of view, fallacies, etc.: see above]
    appearance [esp. as opposed to reality]
Aims and hopes
Effects
    immediate or ultimate
    good or bad
Parallels, and Comparisons
    Contrasts

This is a rough-and-ready List, merely for the Collection of Ideas. In the Essay itself of course the Instances and Examples would seldom come all in a lump at the beginning.

Sub-Headings, and Headings for many Essays, in Rhyme.

[View Evidences, Bias, and chief Fallacies expose.]

———

'Neath the Main Headings Instances, then Helps and Causes range,
and Hindrance; next Description (parts and ties, extent, and change,
the standards and the points of view, appearance, aims and hopes);
th' Effects; Quotations, Contrasts, and Comparisons, and Tropes.

CHAPTER XIX. HEADINGS FOR AN ESSAY, ETC., ON A PERSON.

THE above Headings can be applied to a Person also: but the Headings for an Essay on a Person (e.g. Pericles, Cato, Watt, etc.) should be tried before the next page is read.

Persons are mostly chosen for some notable feature or features: they are usually Generals, or Politicians, or Scientific men, or Philanthropists, etc. For Authors, see p. 129. But, though they may differ in their peculiar line of work, they must all be treated alike to a certain extent.

The Rhyme (p. 92) was :—

[View *Evidences*, Bias, and chief Fallacies expose.]

'Neath the Main Headings *Instances*, then Helps and
    Causes range,
and *Hindrance;* next *Description* (*parts* and ties, *extent*,
    and *change*,
the *standards* and the points of view, appearance, *aims*
    and hopes);
th' *Effects ; Quotations, Contrasts,* and *Comparisons,* and
    Tropes.

This will give us :—
Evidences
    Authorities

CHAPTER XX. SUB-HEADINGS.

IT might be as well that, at some time or other, each Main-Heading should be treated as a separate Essay. A good many have been roughly outlined in this Book (pp. 96 to 132): the reader should try them all for himself before he reads these pages.

In an Essay on a Period, etc. (see p. 83), many of these Main-Headings will have to be treated as separate Essays, that is to say under many Headings there will be SUB-HEADINGS, which, if you have time, you will likewise not only Collect, but also Select, Underline, and Arrange.

It is almost essential for you to work out these Sub-Headings (i.e. Headings under each Main-Heading) before you can judge which Main-Headings are more important and which are less important, and therefore before you can Underline and Arrange the Main-Headings themselves. It is as if you had a number of parcels, each of which you wished to put in the best and most convenient place for certain purposes. Before you could fix on the places of these parcels, you would have to examine their contents.

The most useful List of Sub-Headings (e.g. Instances, Causes, Effects) will be found on p. 92. This List must assuredly be mastered, and on p. 87 are given suggestions as to *how* it should be mastered.

CHAPTER XXI. SUB-HEADINGS FOR AN ESSAY, ETC., ON A PERSON.

SOME of the above Headings, for an Essay on a Person, may now be considered one by one and in more detail. The reader should first take the Headings, and should jot down Sub-Headings under each. My List is very scanty, and only suggests a few ideas out of hundreds; his List should be much fuller than mine.

Instances: the Events of the Person's life.

These should be divided into Epochs, as far as possible. Certain crises and turning-points will probably be conspicuous.

Helps and Causes :—

(i) *Heredity* must be made to include not only the father and mother, but also the ancestors further back. It is here that our Evidence for judging people is so very meagre: we know so little about any person's stock-in-trade in early life, that we should be very careful in passing sentence. And yet we are wont to decide in a moment.

(ii) *Environment* is the second cause of a Person being as he is, the first being Heredity, and the third being that mysterious something which we may call Individuality (see 'Description').

Environment must include the places where the Person lives, the Age or Period (see p. 79 foll.), and, especially, the *Groups* among which he 'lives and moves and has his being': these may be his Family-group, his School-group, his Friend- and Acquaintance-Group, his Business-Group, and so on.

Hindrances will include these same two (or rather three) influences. They must by no means be neglected, for frequently a man's Individuality opposes or is opposed by his parents, or his conditions of life, or both. The life of Jesus is an excellent study in 'Hindrances' of the second kind.*

Description and Individuality.

This is undoubtedly not only the most important part of the Essay on a Person, but also the most difficult part. For we can scarcely describe at all without criticising, and, as we have just seen, Criticism is apt to ignore a great many 'extenuating circumstances' or the reverse, a great many disadvantages overcome or a great many advantages unused or misused.

Man may be considered from at least three different points of view: in any one sphere he is liable to be regarded as 'a success' or as 'a failure', without necessarily being the same in the other two. He may be regarded as a 'physical' success, e.g. as a fine football-player, while intellectually and morally he may be a grievous failure. Or he may be regarded as a brilliant genius, an 'intellectual' success, while he is physically unhealthy and morally unhealthy — we see too many instances of this in the Literary men of to-day. Or he may be regarded as "an unhealthy smug" and "a stupid ass", and yet be a stupendous 'moral' success.

The three spheres or parts may therefore be considered separately, to some extent, though the connexion between them should be pointed out wherever it is possible.

* See also "Earnest Men" (published by Nelson and Co.).

H

As to the *body*, we may consider such Headings as
' physique ', beauty, etc.

health (see p. 120)

rapidity, and promptitude (a somewhat different
quality),

endurance

strength

skill, and versatility (also a somewhat different
quality).

And we must consider the different ways in which
the body can be used.   Philip of Macedon is well worth
a study in this respect, and so is Caesar.

The Intellect can also be employed in many ways
and in many directions, e.g. in Government, Law,
Literature, Science, Commerce, War, etc.   See the
Various Headings on p. 83.

It is important to notice some of the same Headings
as above, e.g.

an eye for beauty and harmony, etc.

healthiness [as opposed to a morbid genius],

rapidity,

promptitude and readiness,

endurance (and memory),

strength, and energy,

skill,

versatility [here we must ask whether the Person
was good at one thing or at many: Alcibiades,
Caesar, and Gladstone, were versatile],

proportion [as opposed to giving undue importance to some things],

sound reasoning and inference, and " openmindedness ",

fairness [which is also a moral quality, being a love
of truth].

Enjoyment is hard to class: one has to say what the Person liked and disliked, and how happy or unhappy he was. He may enjoy bodily or mental activity, for example, or virtue especially.

The Moral qualities or **Virtues** cannot be severed from the Intellectual qualities. Thus the love of truth and the fearless search for truth are Moral as well as Intellectual. 'Openmindedness' seems to me to be almost as much a Virtue as Purity.

Again, true 'physical' Health seems to me to be as great a Virtue as Charity. I do not of course mean mere 'Muscle', but real Health which enables a man to work hard and well. It is seldom mentioned in the list of Virtues, however.

It is not always remembered that the Virtues can be and should be seen in every department of life. Demosthenes and Burke and Dymond insisted that a Nation has a Code of Virtue (kindness, forgiveness, honesty, etc.) as strict as that of an Individual. There are many who deny this, e.g. for Politics and 'Business'. Their reasons are often 'of the earth, earthy': they are even muddy.

Courage, steadfastness and *perseverance*, determination and energy [opp. to cowardice, to rashness, to weak-mindedness, to obstinacy, and to slackness].

Truth, truthfulness and *Fairness*, readiness to learn [opp. to lying and deceit, unfairness, implicit obedience to Custom, and Bias].

It is needless to say that the life of Jesus will give the best collection of Virtues. The Vices opposed to the Virtues often throw light on the nature of the Virtues, and some will be given in square brackets below.

Each Virtue (see p. 207) is a mean between two extremes (as Aristotle so justly said): thus Courage is a Virtue, but at one extreme is Foolhardy Rashness, at the other Selfish Cowardice.

A List of some Virtues.

Kindness, forgiveness, charitableness, kind correction [opp. to unkindness, malice, vengeance, and also mild acquiescence in evil, and over-clemency].

Self-sacrifice [opp. to selfishness].

Sympathy [opp. to want of sympathy, and narrowness].

Cheerfulness and hope [opp. to gloomy despair, and also to excessive hopefulness].

Optimism [opp. to pessimism].

Purity and *Healthiness* [opp. to impurity and morbidness, etc.].

Temperance and *Self-control* [opp. to obedience to the 'lower self'].

Meekness [opp. to pugnacity, and also to mere selfish cowardice].

Extent and Sphere. Here we may consider the 'sphere of activity', of body, intellect, morality, and enjoyment.

Changes. Any of the 'parts' of a Person may change during his lifetime, e.g. his Intellect or his Morals. A man must not be considered as always a consistent actor, though, if we knew all the Causes and Conditions, we might be able to explain the Changes. The **Tendency** of a Person's life is a far more important question than his actual condition or *action* at any given time.

Standards of Judgment.

Often a very great mistake is made here : often a Person is judged by one Standard only. For instance, Cato may be judged

(i) simply as a Roman of those days, i.e. he may be compared and contrasted with other Romans of those days ; or

(ii) he may be judged by the standard of the present Age, or of the writer's Age. One writer wondered how Cato could have regarded slaves as mere chattels. It was the regular way of regarding slaves *then*.

Or, again,

(iii) the *Ideal* may be taken as the Standard. Of course Cato, like most of the ancients (except Epaminondas and a few others), fell lamentably short.

Other critics, again, change their Standard without a word of warning. Now they are considering Cato as an old Roman, and now they are judging him as if he had been a Nineteenth Century Englishman ; this is even more misleading than to keep to one single Standard.

But, it may be asked, how *are* we to judge people ? I suggest the following compromise, and it seems to combine the three Standards, and to be the fairest possible test for every individual case.

"A certain Person, A, had such-and-such parents and ancestors, and lived in such-and-such an Age, and under such-and-such Conditions (p. 96). For such a man, under such conditions, there was a certain BEST POSSIBLE. How near did A come to this 'Best Possible'? What were his Tendencies, his Effects, and his Aims?"

The Appearance must (as far as possible) be distinguished from the Reality. Things are not always what they seem.

The *Aims and Motives and Hopes* must also be considered as well as the *Effects: failure* in defending the right is better than many so-called 'successes'.

Aims and Motives.

Of the Aims of Writers, we have spoken above (p. 48). Here we need only consider the Aims and Motives that lead most people to do what they do.

As we saw on p. 48, we are very apt to forget two points when we are asking "What were the Motives for this action?" We are apt to forget that the Motives may have been (*a*) mixed, and that (*b*) they may have changed even while the action was going on. Alexander the Great, for instance, did not invade the East and conquer the Persians simply for the sake of vengeance or glory: he had other aims, such as to get money, to unite the Greeks, etc. Having known Isocrates' views, he could scarcely have failed to have these Motives as well as the others. But, when he had finally conquered Darius' forces, and even before then, as he had to secure his rear by garrisons and colonies and roads etc., he may have wished to form a new Nation, a mixture of Greeks and Macedonians and Asiatics.

The following List deserves a careful study. It proceeds from the lower to the highest Motives, though the highest Motives may come into play without the lower Motives ceasing: the higher may be added to the lower. Sometimes, however, the lower Motives practically give way to the higher.

It is interesting to notice that precisely the same action may often be the result either of a purely selfish aim, or of a purely noble aim, or of a mixture of the two, or first of one and then of the other. A man, for example, may abstain from Alcohol simply in order to save his own health or even his life; then he may continue to abstain not only for this reason but also in order that he may do better work; then he may wish to set a good example to others as well, and to help them to do better work. Finally, this latter Motive may predominate.

Chief Motives :—

1. Slavish obedience to Custom and Authority.

2. Desire to escape or avoid
    starvation,
    pain,
    poverty,
    discomfort,
    disgrace and unpopularity, and obscurity,
    vice,
    etc.

3. Desire to get or keep
    food,
    pleasure,
    wealth,
    comfort, and luxury,
    fame, and popularity,
    virtue,
    etc.

So far, 2 and 3 mean only to escape or avoid, to get or to keep, certain things *in one's own case.*

4 and 5 will be to help *others* to do the same.

As to these 'others', they may be

    (i) few,
    (ii) many (see the 'Groups', on p. 112),
    (iii) the majority,
    (iv) all mankind,
    (v) posterity also.

Notice that the evils or blessings may affect

    (*a*) the body,
    (*b*) the intellect,
    (*c*) the morals and character,
    (*d*) the happiness ;

and that they may be sought not only for their own sake but for the sake of what they may bring with them or after them.

It is most essential to study Motives if we wish to appeal to others and to influence them.   Jesus' teaching shows that he 'knew what was in man'.

A good Exercise would be to study the 'actions' of others, as well as of oneself, and to classify the Motives under these Headings, making special allowance for the possibility of Mixed Motives.

The immediate **Effects** are *never* the full Effects (see p. 125).   Often the full Effects can scarcely be summed up for years or generations afterwards, even in so far as we can trace them for ourselves.   And of course we can only trace a part of them.

Parallels, Comparisons, and Contrasts may serve to emphasise and make clear the prominent points (see Philip and Napoleon, p. 281), to give interest to the subject, and also to 'show off' information which you have acquired.

· Here, if anywhere, the advice "not to search for Comparisons, but only to use them if they come naturally into your mind" is singularly out of place. In fact, a careful search is a most excellent exercise and may produce very valuable results. The chances are that a Comparison will not occur at all 'of its own accord'. See further p. 281 foll.

If the Person happened to be a **General**, then it would be necessary to know, among other things, the chief characteristics of good Generals : later on (p. 129) we shall treat of Authors, and the chief characteristics of good Authors. If space permitted, we should touch on the chief characteristics of great Scientific men, Statesmen, etc. But here we must be content to say a few words about Generals.

1. A good General keeps *Discipline* in his forces, and welds the forces together so that they act in harmony. Personal example (such as a simple active life) may do much.

2. He must have a sound *knowledge* of Geography, of mankind in general, and in particular of his own troops and officers, and the enemy's troops and officers. He must know the weak and strong points of both sides, the resources, etc.

3. He must be *original*, and yet must seek for advice, and take it, if necessary.

4. His plans must be *far-reaching* and not plans for the immediate future : and, if necessary, he must be able to conceal them. He must see to the safety of himself and his troops, especially in case of defeat.

5. *Versatility* is a fine quality in a General : to be able now to act with lightning rapidity, like Alexander,

and now to wait with snail-like patience, like Philip or Fabius, to be able to adapt oneself suddenly to new and unexpected conditions—this is essential.

6. Not less essential is careful *preparation* and provision of food, arms and ammunition, communications, connexions between the various forces, all in case of either victory or defeat.

7. Only the *most* consummate genius and instinct can take the place of a wide *personal experience*, as well as a wide theoretical *study*, of offensive and defensive war.

8. The merits or faults must not be judged by the immediate effects. A present victory may bring in its train a later defeat, and a present defeat and loss of life may be the only way of securing ultimate victory or even safety.

It is needless to give a list of great Generals: from Epaminondas, Philip, and Alexander, Flamininus, Fabius, and Hannibal, to Nelson, Napoleon, Wellington, and Kitchener and others to-day, the list is full of useful illustrations.

CHAPTER XXII. SUB-HEADINGS FOR THE PERIOD-HEADINGS.

FOR the *Authorities, Evidences, Points of View, Fallacies, and other Evidences*, see pp. 139, 145, 150.

Geography (including Geology) is a Heading very frequently neglected. If we wished to estimate its influences, e.g. on Roman History, or on English History, we should need some systematic plan of Sub-Headings. The reader might try to jot down these Headings for himself before looking at the List below.

    *   *   *   *   *   *

List of the 'Divisions' or Parts of Geography and Geology. These should be applied to a country like England, if they are to be properly understood.

'Neighbours', in the widest sense, i.e. Peoples who are near enough to affect the history of the People itself. Surrounding influences can also be classed here (e.g. the Gulf Stream). The position in the World or Continent etc. should be noted.

Boundaries, e.g. Sea, Mountains, Rivers, etc.

Shape, and 'Direction'.

Size, esp. as compared with other Countries.

Surface and Scenery.

The Surface may be flat or rough or hilly, dry or 'watery'; the level (above the sea) is also important.

In looking over the Country from a balloon, we should also be struck by the presence or absence of towns and buildings.

The means of Communication, e.g. rivers, would also strike one. And see 'Public Works', below.

Products, in the widest sense, may include Vegetable, Animal, and Mineral Products. These deserve careful study, since much of the history of a Country depends on its Products.

Under 'Vegetable' Products, the grains and fruits are to be remembered, and also the *Wood* (for ships, etc.).

Of Animals we need not give a List.

Minerals will include Stone (a product of enormous importance for buildings, etc.) as well as Coal, and the Metals.

The Air and Climate, etc.

The Air may be dry or damp, clear or foggy, hot or warm or cool or cold.

Here, especially, and also with regard to the Surface and Scenery, it is necessary to notice whether there is

Monotony or Variety in different parts of the Country, or at different seasons of the year.

The *Absence* of certain features is also suggestive. Very often we have to contrast our Country with another before we can realise what has been the result of our Country *not* having had certain features (e.g. excessive cold).

The above Headings are well worth remembering. Their initials are N.B., S.S.S., PAVA.

Public Works.

In England to-day the Public Works, e.g. the roads and buildings, must be reckoned as part of our 'Geography'. Though the work of man, they have yet become as much a part of our land as the trees are, and (alas!) even more so. We are apt to look upon our Geography as fields and trees and rivers: but, for many millions of us, the Geography is the city with its streets and lights and buildings. The Public Works cannot be treated simply as Geography, however.

The following List will apply chiefly to early ages. As time goes on, the Public Works (such as Libraries, and School-buildings) become more and more numerous.

Among those which are connected with *Water,* are the following :—

  canals, reservoirs (aqueducts, etc.) ;
  baths ;
  bridges ;
  harbours ;
  drainage ;
  ships.

For *War* and Defence, besides
  ships of war, etc., we have
  fortifications, such as towers and walls ;
  armour, and weapons.

For *Communication,* etc., besides
  canals, etc. (see above), we have
  streets and roads ;
  railways ;
  postal arrangements ;
  lights.

For *Health, etc.,* we have, besides
  drainage, baths, etc. (see above),
  parks and open spaces ;
  Gymnasiums, etc.,
  granaries.

For *Education, etc.,* we have
  Schools ;
  Libraries ;
  Public Statues ;
  Museums, Art-Exhibitions, etc. ;
  Concert-Halls, Lecture-Rooms.

Miscellaneous works would be
  Monuments ;
  Churches ;
  Buildings for Meetings, e.g. Town-halls, Houses of Parliament ;
  Prisons ;
  Mines.

The People of Every Class.

Under 'Fallacies' (p. 150) we see how apt Writers and others are to judge of the whole by some one or more of its parts (especially if these parts be very prominent), and to *omit* the other parts: in other words, to ignore the Law of Averages. We know how the Egyptians, for example, were classed as 'highly civilised people', because the Few, the members of the upper Classes, were highly civilised. If we take the average, and include the lower Classes, the labourers and slaves, we shall probably change our opinion. Those who laud to the skies the Civilisation of 'Greece' are apt to forget that many parts of Greece (e.g. Acarnania and Epirus) were quite uncivilised, and that even in Athens the women and slaves would bring down the average very considerably. And they *must be included.* And so it is with our own country: those who are puffed up with national pride, e.g. at our huge Navy and Commerce, should read Wallace's "Wonderful Century", and remember that London has slums.

The Classes most commonly neglected are Children, Women, Servants and Slaves, and Resident Foreigners.

A complete List of the various Classes will not be attempted here: but it should be tried by the reader. Some of the 'Occupations' will be found on p. 120.

The following points generally call for some consideration: they should be applied to England and to other Countries, for practice.

(i) The *Sources* of the population, e.g. immigration;

(ii) The *numbers*, esp. in proportion to the size of the country. Emigration, etc., may come in here.

(iii) The *distribution*, in towns, suburbs, villages, open country, on the sea, and *abroad*.

(iv) The relative *size and importance* of the Classes: the importance may appear in Politics, in Society, in War, etc. It may also change (see p. 127 below).

(v) The *subdivisions* of the various Classes, the Employments, and the *Cross-divisions*, are to be noticed; and also

(vi) The relations of the different Classes, whether it be friendly help and co-operation, or opposition.

Communication, not only between Classes, but also between Individuals, and between them and other Peoples, is to be noticed.

Communication may of course be by river or canal or lake or sea, by path or street or road or mountain pass, by railway, and so on. Needless to say, free Communication may do much to unite the People and to open their minds.

Unions, and the Individual.

As civilisation advances, a very marked feature is that (see p. 135)

(i) on the one hand many Unions grow larger and larger;

(ii) on the other hand the Individual is more and more recognised as an Individual, a Unit, with rights and privileges and choice of his own, instead of merely as a *member*, e.g., of a Family: see p. 116.

One of the meanings of the words 'Freedom' and 'Liberty' (words so often misused) is that the Individual has a conscience of his own, which he ought to obey rather than such commands as go against his conscience.

Among Unions may be mentioned the following *groups:* of course the same person may belong to several groups.

Family, Clan, and Relations;
Village, and Tribe;
City-state, Town, and Locality generally;
Nation;
'Occupation'-Groups, e.g. Groups according to
> business or profession [politics, war, etc.];
> pleasure or exercise [a powerful group in England];
> social life [wealth, culture and education, etc.];
Religion.

We shall have to ask how far the Individual is independent, and how far he depends on one or more of these and other Groups and its Customs, etc. In other words, what claims has each Group upon the Individual?

A splendid Essay-Question is: **"What are the Bonds of Union within any particular Group, or between any two or more Groups?"** For example, "What are the Bonds of Union between England and America [or Australia] to-day?"

Here we should start with the Family as the basis, because (see p. 65) it is better known to us. The reader should work it out first by himself.

*   *   *   *   *   *

We only need to mention here a very few out of many Bonds—

(i) connexion by blood and marriage; and by traditions;

(ii) similarity of
    appearance,
    dress,
    manners,
    speech and sayings,

(iii) locality and its associations, including the 'home';

(iv) Government (by the father, or mother);

(v) similarity of interests;

(vi) ? hostility to, or jealousy of, some other Family;

(vii) the habit for a Family to be closely united together; it is partly an instinct also;

(viii) intercourse;

(ix) religion.

There are many other Bonds of Union, which the reader should work out carefully in odd moments, and then apply, e.g. to the Bonds of Union between England and America.

State-Government.

This by itself will form a vast Essay, and even one kind of Government alone (e.g. Aristocracy) is a large topic. Only a few Sub-Headings, therefore, can be suggested here, in addition to those on p. 92 foll. (e.g. Helps and Causes, Hindrances, Aims, Effects).

1. First of all, as opposed to State-Government, we may have Party-Government or Government by a single person, Local-Government (e.g. in Counties or Districts), Tribal or Family-Government, Individual Independence (such as Herbert Spencer advocates), and Anarchy.

On the other hand, we can have above the State-

I

Government, League-Government, or International-Government (like that of the United States). Some day there may be a World-Government.

2. An excellent Essay-Question would be '*What is the Sphere of State-Government, and what ought it to be?*' The Period-Headings (see p. 83) should here be gone through one by one, e.g. Communication, Unions, Order, Justice, Rights, Morality, War, etc.

It is well worth considering how far the State-Government ought or ought not to 'interfere' in certain departments: Herbert Spencer seems to be in favour of the smallest amount of interference by any Government. But much depends on the character of the Government (ours is partly a Government by the elected Rich), on the State of Civilisation, etc. There seems little doubt that, *if* the Government is intelligent, it can 'interfere', better than any other power, in matters like Health, Education, War, etc. But Commerce, Religion, and other spheres, are far more doubtful.

So far, then, we have :—1. Contrasts to State-Government; 2. Sphere of State-Governments.

We might then consider

3. Who govern?
4. How are they (*a*) chosen,
               (*b*) supported,
               (*c*) checked?
5. How long do they govern?
6. By what means?
7. How well, or badly?
8. The *Appearance* is often to be distinguished from the *Reality* (see p. 155). Thus our own Government is often classed as a limited Monarchy, though the Queen's

power is chiefly Social; Rome at one time was governed practically by the Senate, but *theoretically* by the Popular Assemblies.

Of the above Headings, No. 4 (*a*) and (*b*), *the Basis of the Government*, deserves a special Essay to itself. The Period-Headings (p. 83) will suggest many of the Bases of any Government, e.g. of the Roman Senate when it was *in its prime:* for instance,

Unity;
Excellence (intellectual and moral);
Religion;
Character (of the Romans);
Custom;
Wealth;
War;
etc.

Order, and Justice.

Similar Headings would apply here. For we might

1. contrast disorder and injustice;
    and then consider
2. the sphere of Justice, i.e. the offences with which it deals, and the penalties which it inflicts.
3. Who judge, and who decide the penalties?
4. How are they (*a*) chosen,
    (*b*) supported,
    (*c*) checked?
5. For how long do they hold power?
6. What are the processes?
7. Are the decisions fair or unfair?
8. Is Justice expensive or cheap?
9. Is it the same for all? and so on.

Rights of Individuals, as well as of ' Groups.'

We may consider how the Rights are enforced, e.g. by the Government and Law and the Executive, or by Custom.

Among the Rights of Individuals may be :—
> safety of person and property ;
> healthy conditions for body and mind ;
> education ;
> freedom of
>> movement (locomotion) ;
>> speech ;
>> action ('the freedom to do right', 'the liberty of conscience') ;
>> intercourse ;
>> redress ;
>> etc.

A good many of these will be opposed to an arbitrary and 'interfering' State-Government.

For *Virtues*, see p. 99, above.

Religion.

As opposed to real Religion we have not only Superstition and mere Ceremonies, but also Scepticism, etc.

We may consider here :—
> the God or gods ;
> the priests, and how far they form a separate class or caste ;
> the places of worship ;
> the ceremonies, festivals, etc. :
> the expenditure of money and time.

The beliefs must be often distinguished from
    (*a*) the beliefs or spirit of alien Religions;
    (*b*) Scepticism, free thought, and Philosophy;
    (*c*) Science;
    (*d*) *the actual life and ' works ' of the people.*

This last is the most important distinction of all. No Religion, perhaps, has ever shown such a contrast between its real spirit, and the actual lives of most of those who profess to hold it, as Christianity.

Of course here, as under most of these Headings, the *Effects* are to be estimated, e.g. the Effects on Government, on Virtue, and on the Intellect. The actual Effects of the Religion should be worked out as a separate Essay, the Headings on p. 83 being taken one by one.

For the *Aims and Motives*, see p. 102, above.

For the *Thoughts and Ideas*, see p. 98, which will also give some ideas about—

the *Powers and Capacities*. For the Physical or Bodily powers, see p. 98.

Education.

In its widest sense Education would not be a knowledge of hosts of isolated and useless facts, all more or less "the same size", but would be opposed to the state of the person whose mind, body, and character are undeveloped. People are usually said to have had an Education even if they have never learnt how to use their limbs rightly, how to keep healthy, how to earn a livelihood, how to make use of what they have learnt and what they can observe for themselves, how to draw inferences, how to speak moderately well, and—among numbers of other signs of an all-round Education—how to be happy and to do good to others.

The best *Means* of Education deserve a careful study, not only for the purposes of Essay-Writing and Speaking, but for the purposes of daily life. Among them are the following :—

Health and Exercise. I put these first, for they should begin with the earliest years and be kept up till nearly the end of life. Some Exercises are better than others. I consider games like Football to be the best.

Reading (books, papers, etc.).

Learning (at Schools, Lectures, etc.): among the subjects should be
>Physiology and Health,
>Natural History,
>Music and Art,
>etc.

Intercourse, of the People with one another, and with those of other Nations (by travel, etc.).

Free speech and free writing.

These are only a few Headings out of many. Some day I hope to write more fully on the subject.

Language.

Besides its value as Evidence (see p. 146), the Sources of its Vocabulary are to be noted, and the extent of its Dialects, and the general characteristics (merits and faults) of the Spoken and Literary Languages.

Among other questions, one may ask—

How far are foreign Languages known and spoken?

How far does the Literary differ from the Spoken, and this from the 'Vulgar' Dialect?

Literature.

For a list of some of the departments of Poetical and Prose Writings see p. 131 ; and for Criticisms, see p. 132. Literature might include

Philosophy, and, to some extent, the *Sciences*, which tend to become better known among the Common People.

For the '*Arts*', such as Music, Painting, Sculpture, and Architecture, see under the 'Occupations' (p. 120).

Inventions are worth notice. The effects of the Steam-Engine, of Machinery (e.g. for Printing), of Electricity, of Photography, etc., are of course well worth a separate Essay.

Social Life, and Home Life.

Ancient Histories used to say little on this topic. Wars and Battles, Kings and Governments, Religion, etc., these were the main themes.

Now, however, we tend more and more to look into the state of Social Life and Home Life. A book like Escott's "England" shows how important these topics are.

Among the Headings might be :—

Intercourse ;

Amusements :—

games, athletics, and 'sport',

exercise in general,

entertainments (theatres, dinners, etc.),

festivals and holidays ;

temperance and moderation, or the reverse ;
customs and habits ;
daily life ;
position of women, and of various classes (p. 110).
marriage, and divorce.

Under *Home Life*, we might also note
the relations of father, mother, children,
servants, and relatives ;
education of children, and of servants.

Here also we might note
the position of women:—e.g.
their occupations indoors and out-of-doors ;
their aims ;
their education.

Dress is a matter of no small importance, as we shall realise some day. Whether a certain fashion is natural and healthy, or unnatural and unhealthy, is a subject deserving careful attention.

Health.

Here, as elsewhere, the *average* Health of the population is to be observed. We must not take a few athletes as typical of the whole Nation.

Among the tests* will be :—
the appearance ;
the work done by the body and the intellect ;
the standard of morality ;
the flourishing (or the reverse) of doctors, drugs,
stimulants, etc., and of diseases.

Occupations. See also the Classes (p. 110).

The *place* of the Occupation is worth observing, whether it be in town or country, on the sea-coast, or on river or at sea.

* See "Muscle, Brain, and Diet" (published by Messrs. Sonnenschein).

The amount of idleness is also to be observed; whether it be 'sheer' idleness, or be due to want of employment or to ill-health, etc. The ignorant would like to class here the professional athletes and many amateurs also. But the openminded and intelligent public will realise that games and exercises are one of the most important 'Occupations' of the British people: without them we should soon become 'a nation of shopkeepers', or, rather, something far worse.

Among 'Occupations' may be mentioned these :—

Country life;

Professions, etc. :—

    Politics and Government-work,

    Law,

    Religion,

    Education,

    Literature,

    Science,

    Arts,

    War,

        Army and Navy,

    Health,

        Doctors and Inspectors,

    Engineering.

Commerce, and Trades :—

    Financing—

        Banking, Money-lending, etc.

    Commercial life (of merchants)—

        Clerkships, etc.

    Shop-keeping (wholesale or retail),

    Agencies.

Industries :—
    agricultural and 'pastoral',
    food, etc.,
    building, etc.,
    manufactories,
    dress,
    carrying and conveying.

Servants, and Slaves.

Wealth and Finance (cp. above).

The Wealth of the State,
    of groups (e.g. Companies),
    of classes (e.g. the 'Aristocracy'),
    of individuals,
may be noted.

The Wealth of the State may be considered with reference to
    its sources (esp. Taxation), and amount ;
    the ways of collecting the Wealth ;
    the ways of spending it.

The Wealth of individuals also has
    its sources and its character,
      e.g. land and its 'products' (p. 107),
        coinage,
        paper money,
        'credit',
        etc. ;
    the amount of it, and its distribution ;
    the ways in which it is spent.

Under *Finance* we may call attention to
    charity ;
    banks ;
    the relation of work, payment, selling, and buying.

Other Peoples, connected in some way.

The actual Connexions may be very various, and often hard to define; e.g. see the Bonds of Union (p. 112).

The list of these Other Peoples might include :—

1. *Subjects*, who form the Empire proper: what is their relation to the home-country, and what is the nature of the rule? And see Headings on p. 83.

2. *Allies*, for a time, or as members of a more or less permanent League, or as 'United States'. And see Headings on p. 83.

3. *Colonies.* Here, also, what is the relation to the home-country? How far off are the Colonies? And see *id.*

4. People connected by
   blood,
   marriage,
   intercourse and travel
   trade and commerce. Here the question of Protection will come in.
   See also Headings on p. 83.

5. *Rulers.* An Essay on India would have to include an account of England, the ruler of India. And see *id.*

6. *Enemies.* See below, and under 'War'.

With all these Peoples, *something* might be said under many Headings, such as
   Geography,
      communication,
   all the classes,
   Government;
   and see the Headings on p. 83.

The effects of the home-people on the Other Peoples, and vice versa, must be estimated.

War: see the General Headings on p. 92.

In contrast to War, we have Peace, Arbitration, Compromise by fines etc.

A few Headings (from p. 92):—

> the causes and aims, and the side with which the greater part of the blame seems to lie;
>
> the expenses of money, life, property, prestige, etc.;
>
> the characteristics—e.g.
>> ways of fighting,
>> length of war.

The Army.

Many questions might be asked here: e.g. with reference to

> compulsory service,
> standing army,
> subdivision of work (specialisation).

As to *the Troops*, from what classes are they chiefly drawn,

> citizens (include volunteers here);
> mercenaries;
> allies?

The proportions should be given.

The divisions, large and small, e.g.

> heavy-armed ⎫
> light-armed ⎬ infantry and cavalry,
> artillery and siege-train,
> commissariat,
> transport-service,
> garrison-duty,
> etc.

The tactics.

The arms, etc.

The privileges of troops and officers,
    their position,
        rewards.

For the General, see p. 105.

The *Navy* might have somewhat similar Headings.

The relative size and importance of Army and Navy should be considered.

Of course both War, and the Army and the Navy, cannot be considered apart from the Geography of the Country (p. 107).

The Subsequent Period should have Headings like those of the Period itself (p. 92).

This Period is important because it gives many *results* of the Period itself: in the earlier Period were the germs or eggs which were only developed or hatched later on. See 'Fallacies' (p. 150).

We are wont to judge the policy of a Politician or a Party by its immediate effects. This *may* be quite unfair. It is possible that the real and vital effects will not come into being till 20 or 50 or even 100 years later. Thus Pericles' policy must not be judged by his own Period alone: we must look *beyond:* when we do, we may consider it bad. 'By their fruits ye shall know them.'

An Individual also must be judged not only by what he *is*, but by what he is becoming (his *tendency*), and also, to some extent, by what his children are : see p. 100.

It is this principle (of taking into account the following period) that gives Ancient History its unique value. We are not yet in a position to teach the History of to-day. We shall not be, for at least another fifty years.

The Previous Period is no less valuable. It should also have much the Same Headings as on p. 83.

While the Subsequent Period gives some of the results (of course it does not consist entirely of results), the Previous Period gives some of *the causes* and *helps*, and—a vital consideration—some of the *hindrances* as well.

In other words, the Period itself did not suddenly start into being, self-made, as it were: it was what it was, *to a great extent* because of, or in spite of, the Previous Period. There lay the germs which developed within the Period itself.

Thus each Period is not simply a unit, but is also a link—the link between the Previous Period and the Subsequent Period, and *to some extent* the result of the former and the cause of the latter.

And yet each Period *is* a unit too. The people do inherit a certain state and certain conditions: but it rests with these people to make or to mar. Only let us remember that the Previous Period *does* impose certain limitations, and the Subsequent Period *does* give us evidence as well.

We saw that the Individual also *is* what he *is* partly because of his *heredity*, i.e. the 'Previous Period', so to speak. We saw that his effects might continue after his death, or indeed might not appear or flourish at all till after his death, in the 'Subsequent Period'. Nevertheless, he *is* a unit, an Individual. His heredity and his conditions or environment give him his stock-in-trade and his sphere of action. It rests with him to make or to mar: and the real and full result of his life may not come till a decade or a whole century shall have passed.

Changes *within the Period itself.*

As with the Individual, so with the Period, it is necessary to discover the Changes and tendencies in any direction, e.g. Changes of population (immigration and emigration, growth of the town-population, etc.). Many of the above Headings should be taken. The Previous Period and the Subsequent Period will perhaps be the best guide as to the tendency, even if these exaggerate it.

The Stage of Progress.

As we must not judge a man apart from the Period in which he lived (his environment), so we must not judge a People apart from its environment. We must not expect in an Ancient Nation the standard of virtue which we may demand to-day.

For different signs of Progress, see p. 135 foll. Here just a few features of modern times may be mentioned.

1. Geography (see p. 107) is better known and better used.

2. States are larger.

3. More classes are included or considered, esp. women, children, and foreigners.

4. The individual (p. 111) is also recognised as a unit, not merely as a part of the machinery of the family or City-State, etc. He gets more share in Government, justice, comfort, education, and so on (p. 116).

5. *Specialisation* is more and more marked. In Government, for instance, instead of a single person or set of persons managing War, Justice, Religion, Finance, etc., we have sets of persons who take up

one of these things as a speciality, and, later on, only a part (perhaps only a tiny part) of one of them, e.g. one department of Criminal Law.   And so it is with Commerce, Industries, Education, etc.

6. Fresh Inventions are constantly made, and also made known to the public.   Knowledge generally becomes more accurate and more widely diffused.

Many other features should be considered.   But here it is enough to say that, when we judge a People, we must take into account not only the Geography of the People, and other advantages and disadvantages, but also the general state of civilisation at the time.

It is this that makes the Athenians so wonderful.

Leading Men and Women may be

α. typical of the People, in most respects; or

β. an exaggeration of some of their features, perhaps also anticipating some of the features of a later Period;

γ. contrasts to the People, in most respects, or 'protests' against them, as Socrates was, and as Jesus was.

For *Quotations*, see p. 163.

For *Contrasts*, see p. 291.

For *Parallels and Comparisons*, pp. 279, 281.

CHAPTER XXIII. HEADINGS FOR AN ESSAY, ETC., ON AN AUTHOR, AND FOR LITERARY CRITICISM.

AT first the Author should be treated (briefly) *as a Person:* see p. 93. We should consider the evidences, the events of his life, the helps and causes and hindrances (heredity and environment), the description, including changes, the aims, the effects, etc.

Then we should consider him as *an Author,* and here the Headings will be somewhat similar (see p. 92).

We shall have (e.g. in the case of Vergil or Livy):—

Evidences, etc.

Instances, viz. his works, which can be classified in various ways, e.g. by their subjects.

Helps and Causes, and

Hindrances.

Here we should have not only the heredity, and the Period, the groups of family, friends, etc. (p. 112), and the training, but also

(*a*) previous Literature,

(*b*) Literature of the Period itself.

Description and Individuality of the Work.

In estimating the work, we must remember to separate [see p. 213 foll.]

I. *the Ideas,* from

II. *the Expression* of the Ideas, and the Style.

> For the Ideas may be disgustingly unhealthy even though the Style be most exquisite.

Under I., the Ideas, will come the Ideas themselves, which should be interesting, show knowledge of the subject, of human nature, etc., be fair and true (e.g.

showing sympathy with those who hold opposite views),
healthy, well-selected, well-proportioned, well-arranged,
etc.   See p. 60 foll.

Under II., the Expression of Ideas, will come such
Headings as

> Clearness,
>
> Brevity,
>
> Variety,
>
> Rhythm,
>
> etc.   See p. 202 foll.

III. It must be remembered that the different *parts*
of an Author's work must often be judged quite
separately; e.g. Cicero's Letters, his Public Speeches,
his Philosophical Writings, and his Poetry.

IV. The *Aims* and objects of the Author are of
importance : we have to consider not only

(i) what his Aims were, and how good or bad they
were, but also

(ii) how far he succeeded, according to these Aims.

Critics often forget that an Author may succeed in
what he aims at doing, even though he may be aiming
very low.

V. *Changes* are common.   An Author's early writings
may be better than his later writings, or vice versa.

The *Effects* (good or bad) may be traced

(i) upon people, and their lives,

(ii) upon Literature ; and these Effects may appear

(iii) immediately, or

(iv) not till after a long interval.

Here, as everywhere, the most important points must
be made clear and emphasised by

Comparisons, and

Contrasts,

If we compare and contrast Burke with Demosthenes, or vice versa, we shall throw light on, and emphasise, every point in which they agree and every point in which they differ.

Quotations may be used (see p. 163).

A few Classes of Writings may be noticed :—

A. *Poetry.*
    Heroic or Epic Poems.
    Hymns, and Sacred Poetry.
    Songs, and Personal Poetry.
    Dramatic.
    Comic.
    Epigrammatic.

B. *Prose.*
    History and Narrative.
        Biography.
        Special Periods.
    Geography.
    Essays and Articles.
    Oratory.
    Philosophy, and Religion.
    Learned Work.
        Sciences.
    'Art' and Illustration.
    Education, and Training.
    Translation.
    Humour.
    Drama (Tragedy and Comedy).
    Fiction.
    'Journalism'.
    Criticism.
    etc., etc.

Both lists might easily be extended.

Note.

In Literary Criticism it is absolutely vital to separate the estimate of the Ideas from the estimate of the Expression or Style; and not only this, but also to separate the different ways of regarding the Ideas and the Style.

For instance, an Author may have very unwholesome Ideas, but the Ideas may yet be true to nature, and may be 'well-proportioned' (p. 268), and well-arranged. Or, again, his Ideas may be wholesome, but untrue. Or they may be wholesome and true, but ill-adapted to the 'audience'.

It is our part to consider which merits and which faults the Author combines. The number of 'combinations' is enormous.

And so with the Expression. It may be clear, forcible, rhythmical, etc., without the Ideas being at all worthy of praise either for their healthiness, or for their truth, or for their fitness for the Author's purpose. Again, the Expression may be quite clear, but wanting in brevity, and in Rhythm.

Here, again, we shall have to consider which merits and which faults the Author combines.

As to Expression, the passage from the New Testament (p. 211) should always be borne in mind. It will recall most of the merits of Style.

It must be repeated that the Author's advantages and disadvantages, his aims, and his 'changes' (p. 100), must always be kept in view.

CHAPTER XXIV. TOPICS FOR COMPOSITION, WITH HEADINGS FOR AN ESSAY ON PROGRESS.

Some Types of Subjects (cp. p. 9).

I. *For the ' Period'-Headings (see p. 83).*

(*a*) The Elizabethan Age.

(*b*) The Results of English Conquests.

(*c*) The Causes of England's Success.

(*d*) The Bonds of Union between England and her Colonies.

(*e*) The Proper Sphere of Government Control.

(*f*) Progress (see p. 135).

(*g*) 'Failure is the only sure Foundation of Success'.

II. *For the ' General Essay'-Headings (p. 92). Many of these involve the Period-Headings also.*

(*a*) Absolute Monarchy [or, Aristocracy, or, Democracy].

(*b*) Slavery [or, Liberty].

(*c*) War.

(*d*) Naval Power.

(*e*) Colonisation.

(*f*) Games and Athletics.

(*g*) English Public Schools.

(*h*) Printing.

(*i*) Decision.

(*j*) Education.

(*k*) Amusements.
(*l*) Travelling.
(*m*) Books and Reading.
(*n*) Newspapers.
(*o*) Music.
(*p*) Poverty.
(*q*) Fire.

Hundreds might be added.   See 'Pros and Cons' (Sonnenschein and Co.).

III. *For the Headings for a Person* (*p.* 93).

(*a*) Philip of Macedon [or Caesar, or Napoleon].
(*b*) Cicero [or Gladstone].
(*c*) Watt [or Stephenson].
(*d*) Lord Shaftesbury.

IV. *For the Headings for an Author* (*p.* 129 *foll.*).

(*a*) Thucydides [or, Carlyle].
(*b*) Livy [or, Macaulay].
(*c*) Vergil [or, Milton].
(*d*) Browning.
(*e*) Matthew Arnold.

Progress.

To illustrate the use of the 'Period'-Headings (see p. 83), an Essay on 'Progress' (or 'Evolution') might be sketched. The Ideas here are not yet complete, nor are they yet 'Selected', Underlined, or Arranged.

Evidences (esp. instances and examples)
    Authorities
    points of view
    Fallacies, e.g.
        judging by upper classes only
            by comfort only
            by Churches only
            by 'Freedom' only

Geography and Geology
    more understood and used
    e.g. wood, water, metals, coal

Public Works
    e.g. walls, drainage

Population—every Class—
    increasing
    more Classes included (p. 110)
        esp. women and slaves

Communication
    increasing (steamers and railways, postage
        and telegraphs)
    opening of minds to new ideas

Unions
    larger, but
    more care for Individual (p. 116)

State-Government
> less control over individual
> sphere changed
> local freedom
> division of labour and specialisation

Justice, and Rights
> Justice separated from Government
> more Rights for individual

Virtues
> higher (Ideal) standard (p. 99), for
>> *a.* individuals
>> *β.* States, and other unions or groups.

Religion
> tolerance
> philosophy

Aims and Thoughts
> originality allowed and encouraged

Capacities
> specialised (p. 127)

Education
> much of it useless
> extended to more classes (e.g. women)
> cheaper

Language
> expresses more things in more ways
> a few Languages are widely spread

Philosophy, Sciences, and Arts
> more numerous Sciences
> each subdivided (specialisation)
> used for man's benefit
> more accurate methods of research

Inventions

Social Life, and Home-life
> birth less important, wealth often more so
> father's power less supreme
> individual freer

Health
> bodily perhaps worse
> professed care
> unnatural conditions (city-life, etc.)

Occupations
> more numerous
> specialisation and co-operation
> town-life and industries
> > Commerce
> > Free Trade
> > Professions
> > more (e.g. teaching) recognised as re-
> > spectable

Wealth
> money and paper-money
> investments
> huge fortunes (uneven distribution)
> credit
> > Finance
> > taxation fairer
> > Political Economy studied

Other Peoples connected
> Subjects
> > huge Empires
> > more consideration for subjects--
> > > less oppressed
> Colonies
> > more independent
> > further afield

Allies
    balance of power
Visitors
    more numerous
    better treated
    they are educated by the visits, and them-
      selves serve as educators
Traders
    international rights
    Free Trade
Enemies and War
    more arbitration, but
    huge Armies, of soldier-specialists,
      Navies
    expense
    deadly weapons, etc.
Leading Men and Women
Changes and tendencies
    towards a huge World-State
    gradual

To illustrate the use of the 'General Essay'-Headings (see p. 92), we might notice, e.g.
Causes and Helps
    God's guiding hand
    man's work
Hindrances
    do.
    backward movements
      Progress not a straight upward line,
        but a series of curves
Objections
    some say there is no 'Progress' and improve-
      ment, but only change, or Evolution.

CHAPTER XXV. AUTHORITIES, AND THEIR FAULTS AND FAILINGS: WITH A RHYME.

WITH regard to the quoting of Authorities, see p. 163, and for the right way of reading Books and listening to Lectures, see pp. 352, 358. It is pointed out there how the information must not only be absorbed but must also be thoroughly understood, digested, and thought over, and also (if possible) applied.

Here I shall speak of Authorities only in so far as they are Authorities for the Ideas in the Essay. Every Essay should mention the Authorities on which its statements are based, that is to say, if there *are* any such Authorities; there is too great a tendency to trust implicitly to the statements made by well-known people, and it is important that every statement should be given only for what it is worth. There should be a distinction between ' This is so,' and ' Sir —— says that this is so '.

It is necessary for every Writer and Speaker to know exactly where his Authorities are deficient and to state these deficiencies clearly. It is especially necessary when the subject is about former times, or when it includes former times, as in a Historical Sketch, or in parallels from Ancient History.

Faults and Failings of Authorities.

Supposing we had to do an Essay on 'Rome in the time of the Early Republic,' our Authority would in the main be Livy, just as for English History our Authorities might be Macaulay, etc.: we should have to consider how far such Authorities were adequate or inadequate.

1. On p. 150 we shall see how many errors are due to the *omission* of something, and, with regard to our Authorities, we notice that many of them are lost either wholly or in part. The Historians from whom Livy drew his narrative are mostly lost, and a great deal of Livy himself is lost also.

2. And this is not all: for the writers *omit* a great number of important topics. We know how, till quite recently, English Histories were full of Wars and battles, lists of Kings, and Court-intrigues, changes in Government, and so on. They omitted things which now we consider scarcely if at all less important than these, and which, as the years go on, may gradually come to be considered as even more important, for instance, health, the state of the poorer classes, the daily life of average people, the Colonies, and so on. Hence the Authorities are as a rule singularly inadequate when we come to deal with any of the large problems of Ancient Times or even of what may be called the earlier Modern Times.

3. Once again, the Authorities are apt to fall into terrible Fallacies (see p. 150), e.g. fixing their attention

on a part, and excluding the other parts which may be equally important, and drawing their conclusions from the one part only, as (see p. 151) Max O'Rell is wont to do.

4. Nearly all writers are *biassed* in favour of their own times and their own country, and against other times and other countries; few writers have erred more in this respect than English Historians. The writing of History in an impartial spirit has scarcely begun in our country. Writers are also biassed and prejudiced in favour of their own party or group, for instance, their political party, their friends, and their family: which means that they are biassed against the opposing political party, against their personal enemies, and so on.

5. The *Method* of many Authorities, too, is very unsatisfactory.

The Summary of Events in " Whitaker's Almanack " gives the events of the year according to the days of the year: we pass on from the name of the Lord Mayor to a war in the East, from the death of a member of the Royal Family, and the birthday of another member, to the opening of some charitable institution; then there may come another allusion to the War, and so on. The whole account would be described in technical language as wanting in continuity and connexion, as wanting in *proportion* and perspective, and as wanting in unity.

6. This want of proportion is noticeable. While the writer who lives long after the events must err because his evidence is meagre or unfair, the writer who lives at the time of, or soon after, the events, is almost bound

to err because he cannot yet see things in their real bearing : for the results (see p. 125) are not yet visible.

7. The *Aim and object* of Authorities often makes them quite unfitted for use as Evidences. Many of them wish to gain something by their writings, to please people, to instruct them, or to blame or to justify. With these aims in view, they do not mind omitting, adding, or altering.

8. Nor must we lose sight of their *forgetfulness*, their laziness in not examining Evidences, and also

9. *the faults and omissions of the Authorities and Evidences which they have to use;* and we shall see that thousands and thousands of the statements, which are made and repeated with absolute confidence in Books and Essays and Speeches, are insufferably unreliable.

10. Only then is the writer wont to feel any doubt, when the Authorities for a given point are found to disagree ; when there is only one Authority, then the writer accepts that Authority ; he assumes that, because it is not contradicted, therefore it must be right. But, when we come to think over the matter, the statements made by only a single Authority are apt to be quite unreliable, as we can tell by the mere fact that, when several Authorities are found side by side, they nearly always differ; this should lead us to suppose that, where we only have *one* Authority giving *one* account of the matter, if we had other Authorities surviving as well we should probably have other accounts of the matter. But this vital principle is little known to the public. It is frequently ignored even by the most critical Historians and Essayists and Speakers, with the curious result that, *where the Evidences are most*

meagre, the statements are made with the most absolute confidence, and, where the Evidences are most complete, scarcely any certain statements can be made at all.

As a matter of fact, the strongest Evidence for truth is not that which one Authority says but *that about which many Authorities agree*, though they may differ on other matters.

These are only a few words out of many which the subject of Authorities demand, but it is enough to show that an Essay or Speech must not merely repeat statements as absolutely certain, but must give the Authorities for them and examine how far these Authorities are reliable or the reverse.

We shall now show that the same will apply with regard to the Evidences for any statement, apart from the written Authorities.

Even what we discard may have its value: we may not only (see p. 149) draw inferences from what is *omitted* by the writer, but we may also draw inferences from what we ourselves decide to discard. We may say that so-and-so is a mere exaggeration, a piece of colouring, a myth : but the mere fact that it was accepted by so many people, and accepted perhaps without any suspicion, may give us valuable information as to the minds of these people, their characters and habits of thought.

But even where we may seem to have abundance of Authority, and abundance of Evidence, it may often be best to be both candid and cautious, and to say, ' This we should *almost certainly* reject (or accept); this very probably; that probably; that possibly; and that, again, probably not'. Accuracy often says ' Be content with various degrees of *probability* '.

As an *Exercise* in finding out the chief faults of Authorities, it might be as well to make a list of, and classify, and find the causes of, the faults of the following:—Fairy Stories, Legends and Myths, accounts by common people or children, the writers in the time of Louis XIV., 'How Bill Adams won the Battle of Waterloo'. There are plenty of other fields for practice e.g. in everyday conversation.

A Rhyme, giving some Failings of the Authorities.

> Authorities are often lost, they sometimes
>   add, or change,
> exaggerate, accumulate, omit, or rearrange,
> from interest, or desire to please, teach,
>   blame, or justify,
> or from forgetfulness or sloth, or from
>   some Fallacy.
> They often lack proportion, continuity,
>   broad grasp,
> and show us such a Bias as should make
>   the critic gasp.

CHAPTER XXVI. OTHER EVIDENCES.

By Evidences I here mean something besides the actual Authorities for any given statement, for which see p. 139 foll.

Supposing that all English History Books, up to to-day, had been burnt, how could we restore English History?

Putting aside the Inscriptions and Documents and Letters and other Literary sources, what would there be to tell us about the past? In coaching at Cambridge I have often been surprised at the ignorance of pupils as to what Evidences there are for any given statement apart from the actual written Authorities themselves.

1. First of all comes *Geography*, which may be made to include Geology. A great deal of our past History can be learnt from a map of our country. When we see the coal-fields and the mines in the North and West, when we see the network of rivers and canals, the neighbourhood of France and of the North-Western coast-line of Europe, when we see how easy it is to get from England all over the world by various routes, when we see how England, though far Northwards, still has the Gulf Stream to keep it warm, we cannot fail to be able to restore a good deal of our past.

But, if we wanted to look for remains and traces of the past, whether these remains be changed or whether they be, as it were, fossilised, where shall we be inclined to look?

2. *Religion* will be one of the best places. Just as one looks for fossils in a cliff, so one looks for old-fashioned things in Religion. Where else do we find the language of 1611 in daily use, and a great deal as well that belongs to periods far earlier than that?

3. *Law*, again, preserves (to the woe of the poor) many traces of old things, such as customs which have disappeared elsewhere.

4. *Buildings* also carry us back a long way—some of them, like Stonehenge, to the very early times of our country.

5. *Language and Philology* are most valuable as Evidences. Our English names of towns in -don, -ham, -chester, -caster, etc., tell us a little history all by themselves. They tell us that we are a mixed people, or rather that we owe our civilisation to many peoples. Our very Language itself points in the same direction. See "How to Learn Philology" (Sonnenschein and Co.).

6. And if we were to make *Inferences* from these and many other Evidences, as to what our past History had been, I think that all its most important features could easily be reconstructed. We might not recover many names and dates and details, and the inferences would have to be corrected, but anyhow the exercise of making them would be admirable for the mind.

7. In one respect, indeed, Evidences apart from written Histories would correct almost every written History that we have. If we carefully examined the shape of the skulls of English people to-day, we should be able, in fact we should be bound, to correct the statement so common in History books, that we belong almost entirely to the Teutonic stock. Language of

course is no safe guide here. The skulls show us to be not only Teutonic, but also to a large extent Celtic.

The great advantage of studying Evidences, besides the exercise it gives for the mental faculties, especially that of drawing inferences, is that it compels us to examine customs, and the sayings of high authorities, both of which are apt to be false and far from good and true. *We are apt to be fettered by custom and by what well-known people are pleased to tell us.* We are apt to take for granted that this must be best, without examining the question for ourselves. For us, as reasoning beings, it is a serious duty to examine the Evidences for any given statement; without such an examination we are incurring a heavy responsibility. Some day everybody will be required to justify himself for whatever he has done, and, if he does not get into the habit of examining Evidences, he will be forced to fall back upon that very silly reason 'I did it because a great number of other people were doing it as well'.

Take, for instance, the doctor. Why does he recommend such-and-such a drug? Because some high Authority recommends it, and because it is usual to recommend it. What are the Evidences for its value? Surely that is a far more important question.

There is an extra advantage besides, and that is that the Evidences often form an interesting Beginning for an Essay, or for a Book, or for a Speech. They are seldom given in such Compositions: in fact, of the Essays which I have examined, scarcely one out of a hundred gives its Evidences And yet these are undoubtedly of very great interest and importance.

Besides the above branches of Evidences there are many others.

8. On pages 279, 281, 291, we shall see that *Parallels and Comparisons and Contrasts* are a kind of Evidence. At any rate they suggest things which *might* be true, and occasionally they go a great deal further than that. If we find that similarity of appearance is a bond which holds a family together, we may conclude that similarity of appearance is a bond which *may* hold a Nation together to some extent, and even two Nations, e.g. ourselves and the Americans or Australians.

9. The branches of Evidence most commonly omitted are the *Previous Conditions and the Subsequent Conditions.* Nothing can be fairly judged without a consideration of these two points. There never was a truer saying than '*By their fruits ye shall know them*'. And yet people *will not* judge things by their results. They *will* take the opinion of others for granted and repeat it like parrots and not like rational and civilised animals. Before we dare to criticise another person, for instance, we should always carefully examine what may be called his Previous Conditions and, as far as we can, his Subsequent Conditions. The Previous Conditions will include his heredity (his parents and ancestors), and his environment, that is to say, the circumstances and conditions under which he has lived: without these, we cannot form a true estimate of the person himself. Nor can we really see *in what direction he is tending* (which is vitally important), unless we see the results. This it is that *makes a judgment on something which is going on in our own times almost impossible.* For we cannot know it by its fruits: its fruits may not appear for twenty years or more. In

an estimate of past heroes or 'villains', the previous conditions and their effects upon the person must always be taken into account as Evidences.

The subject of Evidences would form a good subject for a long book or series of books, and it is impossible to treat of it adequately in a single Chapter. Here I have only suggested one or two thoughts out of some hundreds. The reader would do well to work it out as a special Essay-subject all by itself. But just two more points must be noted.

10. *Extreme cases* and simple cases are of the very highest value. Buckle, when he wished to find the influences of Geography on man and on History, started with such countries as Egypt: here he had an extreme case and a simple case. It was an exaggeration of certain principles, but it showed these principles clearly and simply. This was far better than starting on a 'complicated' country like France.

11. *Omissions* are not without their value. 'If this had been so, the writer would certainly have mentioned it' may often be a sound line of argument. This is especially the case, e.g., where a writer omits to blame someone whom he elsewhere loses no opportunity of blaming. But, like so many other branches of Evidence, this is valuable rather as suggesting or confirming some point, than as actually proving it.

CHAPTER XXVII. FALLACIES: WITH A RHYME.

THE reader will naturally ask why I devote a special Chapter to Fallacies. There are several reasons.

1. Fallacies are to be carefully avoided everywhere, and they cannot properly be avoided unless their nature and their causes are first seen. One must learn to detect Fallacies in others as well as in oneself.

2. The detection of Fallacies and the study of Fallacies is very good exercise, not only for the *reasoning* faculty, but also for what we may call honesty and *open-mindedness*, and even for Progress itself. The opposite of a Fallacy may often be considered as Bias, and Bias is very frequently in favour of custom. It assumes that what is customary is best, and it opposes any and every change.

3. For *Literary* purposes there is no better *Beginning* to an Essay than the exposing of a Fallacy. The instance from the New Testament (p. 211) shows this, and Guizot in his " History of Civilization " shows it also. That book has a model Beginning.

One of the reasons for this is that everybody likes to hear others criticised or to criticise others for himself. It *interests* the reader to expose a Fallacy, and it prepares the ground very well for what you consider to be the true view of the subject. Before you say what a thing *is*, you often make your task and your reader's task easier if you say what it is *not*. In fact very often one can go little further in a subject than to expose the Fallacies. One may not like to venture on many positive opinions.

I have collected here one or two Fallacies from a book which had a large sale at one time, namely "John Bull and his Island", by Max O'Rell. The reader should take the words and find out where the Fallacies lie, and should then classify the Fallacies for himself. He might compare his results with mine and accept whichever he thinks the more reasonable.

The references are to the pages of the reply by "John Bull to Max O'Rell" (Wyman and Sons).

1. "John Bull has muscular arms, long, broad, flat, and very heavy feet, and an iron jaw that holds fast whatever it seizes upon." (17)

2. "A head-master knows personally every pupil." (78)

3. "In England an intelligent boy costs his parents nothing to educate." (78)

4. "Football is a wild game, fit for savages." (78)

5. "Summer and winter, the Englishwoman takes a cold bath every morning." (22)

6. "The aristocracy, the upper and middle lower classes all go to church or chapel; the lower classes go to the tavern and get drunk." (39)

7. "The French workman is an artist in his way; the work of the English artisan is purely manual, and he only turns out substantial things." (93)

1, 2, 3, and 4 are Fallacies because they seize on one part or set of instances, and ignore or omit other parts. They generalise without consulting the Law of Averages (p. 157). 4 especially is a Fallacy due to judging by appearances (p. 155). It obviously is not by a man who has played the game hundreds of times with gentlemen.

5 (like some of the above) seems to be due chiefly to bad Evidence: though it is like 1, 2, 3, and 4 also. The part here is a very exceptional part.

6. Here also a very exceptional part is chosen, and the Evidence (esp. as to the Public Houses) is partly to blame.

7. Shows National Bias, though it contains a germ of truth. It also generalises by one part, and ignores and omits the other parts.

For the purpose of criticism, he need not here trouble as to whether the Fallacies were intentional or unintentional. He may even assume that they were unintentional and due to ignorance or carelessness: that is the more charitable view. It does not matter much, for our present purpose, whether the writer was himself deceived or whether he intended to deceive others.

Putting aside actual mistakes, we may mention a few Fallacies which are exceptionally common, leaving the reader for the most part to think of his own instances.

He will find that *most Fallacies are Fallacies of Omission.* The mistake is generally that something of importance is *omitted.*

Let us take, to start with, a Proverb, "Take care of the pence and the pounds will take care of themselves." Everyone knows that there are hundreds of cases where this does not apply at all, where the person takes care of the pence and the pounds do *not* take care of themselves (except in the sense of keeping clear of the 'economiser'). The Fallacy here is that something is omitted; and the omission would be—'Take care of the pence, *if* it is economy to do so'. In the same way, it is not always really true that 'A penny saved is a penny gained'. Something may be omitted. I have known cases where a penny saved has been five shillings lost. The omission may be similar to the above: some other point of view has been unknown or else ignored.

Supposing, now, we take that very common Fallacy, the Fallacy of trusting to *Authority,* perhaps to a very high Authority: why should it be wrong to assume that 'a thing must really be so, because A has said that it is so.' Well, here one omits the fact that the

Authority may have made a mistake and that other Authorities who are equally reliable may hold different opinions, and that anyhow everybody has a right to his own opinion and is not forced to admit the thing merely because A says that it is the case.

Let us take the most terrible Fallacy of all the Fallacies, that what is *customary* is therefore *best*. How often we hear people say " It is wrong to do that ", or " It is right to do that ", and then give as their only reason, for its being wrong, that *most* people don't do it, and, for its being right, that most people *do* do it. The fact is that something is omitted here, and the chief Omission is the future. The person who says that what is customary is best omits to consider that the future, say in another thousand years, may be an improvement. Custom may alter. Now if the custom, in a thousand years' time will be better than the custom now, as we hope it will be, then the custom now may not be best : it may be even execrable. It also omits the consideration of the past. People have *always* said that custom is the best, and yet in the past we have seen many changes. Each state of things was considered best until something new had been tried. This was nearly always *at first* considered as bad, yet it made its way and is now received into the sanctuary of custom.

Very like this is the Fallacy due to *Bias*. A person will not look at a thing from any point of view but one. Read many English Histories and see how the English are always in the right, however wrong they may be. Then read a French History and see how the French are always in the right ! What has been omitted here ? Surely the point of view of the other side. The truth undoubtedly lies as a rule somewhere between the two extremes. Bias to a certain extent is inevitable, but it is a great thing to get into the habit of detecting it and of seeing that other people regard things from quite different points of view. Read the speech of Demosthenes and the speech of Aeschines on the Crown: each seems to be speaking the truth, and yet the orators are perpetually contradicting one another. Perhaps a third orator might have described the same incidents from a third point of view. All three would have been liable to fall into Fallacies.

The Fallacy of fixing the attention on one part, and of ignoring the other parts, is one of the commonest that we have to be on our guard against. We shall see below that, when writers tell us that the Athenians were highly civilised, they omit a great deal—they omit, in fact, two parts of the State which were not prominent, but extraordinarily large, so much so that they were far larger than the mass of Athenian citizens themselves. The reader will guess that these two parts of the State, which frequently were scarcely at all educated, were the women and the slaves. To fix the attention on one part and to ignore the parts which are less prominent is one of the grossest Fallacies of all. It might surprise the reader if one called into question the statement that England is a prosperous country: he would immediately say 'Look at the amount of money that Englishmen possess, look at her position, and her merchants, and look at her possessions abroad!' These however are only parts. I have a perfect right to call attention to other parts. In fact I insist on doing so, and I might just as well judge her by the wretched millions in the cities. After all, they form a very great part of England. So, before we decide, we must consider not one part only, but every part.

One part on which the attention is very commonly fixed and concentrated is the *appearance*. It is a great Fallacy to judge that a man is strong and healthy because he looks strong and healthy. For instance, a man may have a big chest and may appear, for this reason, to be very powerful. But when one finds that this chest is in a bad state, and cannot contract or expand much, one sees that the appearance was in this case deceptive.

Fallacies about *causes* are also common. To fix the attention on one cause and to ignore the others is again a Fallacy of Omission. We read in Histories how one great event was due to a glass of water, another to a petty quarrel about a woman, and so on. Now all these were causes, it is true, but they were not the full causes, they were only a part of them. It is especially common to give the *immediate* cause. For instance, how often one hears that " The open window gave me a chill "—it may have been an open window that was the immediate cause, but it does not in the least follow that it was the full cause. There may have been many factors without which the open window would have produced no such result.

And similarly with regard to *motives*. Now little account is taken of the number of motives which may induce a person to do a thing, and the changes which may take place in these motives as the person is in the course of doing the thing (see p. 108). The writer is generally content to fix on one motive and to give it as practically the only one.

And, as people make mistakes about causes, so they make almost equally serious mistakes about *hindrances:* they even omit them altogether. They condemn a man, for instance, because he is a drunkard; they omit the fact that his temperance was terribly hindered and handicapped by heredity, and by unwholesome surroundings and temptations. If they did not omit this, they would scarcely condemn as unsparingly as they do.

Once again, with regard to *results:* a man, let us say, is guilty of excesses in eating and in drinking, and he keeps this up for five years. He says, 'They are not affecting my health'. The Fallacy here is that he omits the future. Look at him in another twenty years' time, and then you may see where the Fallacy lies. He has been fixing his attention on only a part of the time during which the result would appear. Here again people are apt to judge too much by the immediate results.

Another Fallacy would be where people make a wrong *inference.* I once read that "Reasoning cannot be taught". The reader might do well to see where the Fallacy lies here, and he will do so best, I think, if he turns this into the personal form (see p. 233), asking himself "Who does what?" At first the answer is not obvious, but after a time it appears to be as follows. The person who made the above statement, that "Reasoning cannot be taught", should have said "I myself and others have not been able to teach reasoning; therefore we conclude that reasoning cannot be taught at all". The Fallacy was that this person omitted the possibility that someone in the future, someone who should be even wiser than himself, would have the power of teaching reasoning. Because he and others had failed, it did not follow that everyone else in the whole future would be certain to fail also.

When once we come to details, Fallacies are legion. The Fallacy, for instance, that it is a mistake to explain things to people, and that they should be left to find out everything for themselves, is not uncommon. Here, what has been omitted is that many people are not trained to find out things for themselves, and it does not occur to them to do so ; and unless they *have* been trained in this, or even actually told to do it, they will not do it for themselves. Of all the Fallacies which are worth working out, possibly the one I mentioned, namely, that Athenians were highly educated, would be the most instructive, for it is an offence against what may be called the Law of Averages. The speaker fixes his attention on the people who lived in some parts of Athens, the better classes, and who lived there at one period, as opposed to the early Athenians who were not very highly educated, and the later Athenians who were perhaps, if the expression may be pardoned, too highly educated to be really educated. They ignored those who were in other parts of Athens and Attica, and who lived at other times. They did not take an average before they made their statements. And the same applies to the statement that England is a prosperous nation. Let the reader now, in conclusion, examine the statement that England owes this prosperity entirely to beef and beer, for it is a good type of a Fallacy.

I have only given a very few examples and general principles here, and space forbids me to add anything ; but the reader will find it worth while to make a special study of Fallacies and their detection. He might take one of the Daily Papers (I will not give a list), and run through it, mentioning and classifying the various Fallacies which it contains. It would be a good morning's work.

The following Rhyme may be of use, as including many kinds of Fallacies.

It's Fallacy to judge by one sole standard, (and neglect
time, place, conditions, causes, aims, the tendency, the
effect).

It's Fallacy to treat the outward semblance as the soul,
number and size as proofs of great importance, part as
whole,

Authority as truth, and custom as the best of all;
things done as things done purposely, one cause (however small)

or a circumstance or hindrance as the one and only
source;

some one man's act as a Nation's act (and the converse
too, of course);

the immediate as the full effect; one meaning of a word
as another; or to base remarks on premisses absurd:

false Deduction, false Induction (like the pyramid re-
versed),

have many different aspects, and I know not which is
worst.

Bias may be for self alone, or family, or friends,
or for a group in politics or for religious ends
or other ends, or else for State or Nation as a whole:
and 'Bias—*for*' will also be *against* the other pole.

CHAPTER XXVIII. DEFINITIONS.

MANY Writers and Speakers rush straight away into their subject without any Definition at all, and hence there are apt to be obscurities and misunderstandings. If we examine a discussion in a Paper or Review, we generally find that one cause of the quarrelling is that neither Writer has defined his subject, or else that the one Writer uses a certain word or words in one sense while the other Writer uses them in another sense. For Political arguments Sir George Cornewall Lewis' work has done much to remove misapprehensions. I remember hearing one discussion on Religion : both parties were in a furious temper, and, though I did not see the reason at the time, it occurred to me afterwards that by Religion one of them meant superstition and meaningless ceremonies, whereas the other meant a following of conscience and an attempt to lead the highest possible life. On thinking over their arguments I found that neither party really disagreed with the other on any important point.

Supposing the subject is 'Democracy', it is essential to define 'Democracy'. Is it to mean what *we* call Democracy, that is to say, is it to mean a Government by those rich men who are chosen by the whole population of householders?

Again, when it is 'Freedom' that we are considering, is it Freedom from legal justice, or Freedom from what?

1. It is often necessary, in defining terms, to take

the Period-Headings and apply them ; e.g. they would help a good deal towards a Definition of Freedom, by showing in what spheres the Freedom is to be found.

2. If we look at a statement like this : "The art of Essay-Writing cannot be taught", we must define what is meant by this.   Does it mean the power of writing Essays perfectly or the power of writing them better than we wrote them previously?   Now a great help towards a Definition and indeed, as we shall see, towards Clearness in general, is the use of a *personal and Concrete* form, in answer to the questions (p. 233), "*Who does What*, etc?"   The New Testament is conspicuous for this personal expression, whereas many treatises on Ethics and Religion are one mass of abstract terms.

3. *Instances* also help the Definition considerably. If we are asked for an Essay on Tyrants (see p. 54), we must think of Instances of Tyrants : e.g. Phalaris was a General before he became a Tyrant, and as a Tyrant he was said to be cruel; Pisistratus was popular among the poor, while he himself was rich.   The Instances must be collected from every place and every time, and *Parallels* must be included.   Thus, besides Greek Tyrants, one might mention the Czar of Russia, or Napoleon.

4. *Comparisons* (see p. 281) may help a good deal, and *Contrasts* also.   For example, we cannot well define 'Freedom' until we know what it is to be contrasted with, whether it is to be slavery or something else.

5. Buckle, in his "History of Civilisation in England", arrives at some Definitions by taking *Exaggerated and Extreme cases*, see p. 149.   By this means he saw some one aspect by itself and saw this very clearly.

6. Besides this, *Questions* (cf. above) are of very great value; and Definitions should be tried experimentally. Guizot, in defining Civilisation, asked a number of Questions, and tried various answers: Was it this . . ., or that . . ., or that . . .?

7. This might also be called the process of *Excluding*. One excludes whatever is not really essential to the idea. For instance, Phalaris was said to have burnt people in a brazen bull, but the brazen bull was not essential here; the essential point was e.g. the cruelty. To arrive at a Definition, one should find out first of all what is common to all the Instances, then what is common to many of them, and then what is common only to a few, and lastly what is incidental or exceptional. By this means one can make up *a general kind of Formula.** For instance, Tyrants were absolute rulers: in Greece Tyrants generally ruled only for a short time, they spent a great deal of money, they put down the oppression of the Nobles and raised up the oppressed Commons, and united the whole State together. The Tyrant also was outside the Laws of the State and unprotected by them. He usually had to rely on military force.

8. Last of all, it is only fair to give *the views of others.* We have to decide, it is true, on some single Definition, but, on the other hand, we must mention the fact that others may not accept this Definition when they use the same word: they may use it in quite a different sense.

And, having made our Definition, we must be very careful to keep to it throughout: not to use a word now in one sense and now in another. This is the commonest trick of dishonest Speakers and Writers and the one to be most conscientiously avoided.

* We often have to be content (see p. 222) with certain features *which the given Idea must contain.*

M

CHAPTER XXIX. PARALLELS, COMPARISONS, AND CONTRASTS.

(See CHAPTERS LI.–LIII.)

I HAVE treated Parallels, Comparisons, and Contrasts, under the heading of the Expression of Ideas, as I have considered their chief functions to be (see p. 281 foll.) to make Ideas clear, interesting, and suggestive, and —if necessary—to emphasise Ideas.

Nevertheless, Comparisons and Contrasts are (or should be) by no means confined to these functions: still less are they, as some seem to think, mere 'Rhetorical Tricks'. They are also valuable in the Collection of the Ideas themselves: in fact (see pp. 286, 293) they are almost certain to bring to light Ideas which might otherwise have escaped notice altogether.

In a word, I do not think that the Ideas *can* be adequately Collected without the aid of Comparisons and Contrasts: I consider them an integral part of the *Scheme* of an Essay or Speech, before we have yet come to the Expression of Ideas. A Scheme with bare Ideas, unillustrated and uncontrasted, I should regard as an incomplete Scheme.

But, for the sake of convenience, I have treated the two aspects of Comparisons and Contrasts (viz. as affecting the Collection, etc., of Ideas, and as affecting the Expression of Ideas) in single Chapters, in the Third Part of this Book.

SOME Books, such as Sir John Lubbock's "Pleasures of Life", simply teem with Quotations: and, as the book is apparently written for the People as well as for the cultured Few, this may be quite sound. For the People love and respect Quotations from Authorities, somewhat as they love personalities about great or famous men and women, however trivial these personalities may appear. And the People respect Texts, even Texts which are pulled out from their context like pieces of Mosaic pulled out from their pattern.

But this must be said on the other side. Quotations often are a pandering to the taste of the People, or forcing upon them of words which may be very rhythmical and high-sounding, but which are often ill-understood or even misinterpreted.

The whole question of the use of Quotations is one well worth a special treatise: only a few of its many sides can be touched on here.

First of all, as to the Quotation of actual words.

Quotations of Poetry should of course be given word for word, but opinions differ as to Prose Quotations. There are many who say that they also should be given word for word.

A very great deal must depend on how far the Ideas are well and clearly expressed in the Quotation. It would seldom be a good thing to quote Herbert

Spencer word for word, for, among other things, his English is seldom clear to an average reader.

Besides this, it is hard to remember Quotations word for word, and there have been many who have learned such Quotations and who now think of the words rather than the sense : they repeat them as a parrot might, and not with understanding. This may be (see p. 87) chiefly the fault of the way of learning the Quotation.

Nevertheless, there must be many Prose Quotations which must be quoted absolutely as they are in the original.

Those who are against such Quoting say that you ought rather to get hold of the underlying Idea and express it in your own way : the Idea then will not be your own original Idea, but will be the next best thing to it. At any rate you will be sure to have made it your own before you offer it to the reader ; whereas, if you quote the exact words, there is little guarantee that you have understood the sense, or that the reader or hearer will understand it.

This applies in particular to *foreign Quotations.* These should nearly always be translated, unless they be for learned Readers only. The number of such Quotations which average people can understand is very very small, and a translation which gives the sense is generally much better than the original words. In our ordinary Classical teaching at Public Schools and at Cambridge, I have found by experience that almost the whole of the attention is given to *the words* and Language, and that the learners go away from School or from Cambridge with the very vaguest notion as to the Ideas themselves. I believe that the Classics would teach them far more if, throughout Schools and the Universities, they were studied in good English Translations *at any rate to begin with;* but this is by the way.

A few poetical Quotations are extremely good for both Books and Essays and Speeches: many from Shakespeare, and some from Cowper and Tennyson, for example, may be used again and again and again. It is worth while to buy a good book of Selections from the Poets, and to learn once for all (see p. 88) a few of these which seem most likely to be of use in Essay-Writing or Speaking. A friend of mine had one Quotation from Tennyson, and he (of course exaggeratingly) said he would defy anybody to give him the Essay-subject into which he could not introduce that Quotation.

NEITHER in the Collection of Headings, nor in this department, the Selection and Rejection of Headings, should there be any thought as to how these Headings are to be Arranged, or how they are to be Expressed. *The attention must be concentrated* on the question, 'Which Headings, if any, are to be rejected?'

A great deal will depend upon the readers or hearers whom one is addressing, the chief principle being *Appropriateness*. It is not enough that a Heading should have something to do with the subject, but it must be appropriate to the particular readers or hearers, and to the particular object and aim which one has in view.

Another principle is *Economy*. It is a pity to waste time and attention on certain Headings and Sub-Headings, when that attention had better be given to comparatively few but vital points. This is particularly the case (see p. 19) with Speeches.

This does not mean that every detail should be rejected, but (see p. 216) it means that you should reject only those details which do not throw light on, or emphasise, the main point.

One or two further considerations are worth noticing. First of all, whether you think a Heading is worth putting in or not must be a matter of personal opinion and taste; and this is one of the occasions where *Originality* comes in : you will have to judge for yourself, though of course you may do well to ask for advice.

Secondly, it may be right to adopt certain Headings of which the importance is not quite obvious to *you :* every year people are finding out that something, which used to be neglected, was really worth taking into account; the *interest* of the thing is at length discovered. Hence there are some points which may have to be inserted in Essays of certain types, even if you cannot *yet* say that these points are important or even interesting. You can easily add a note to the effect that they *may* prove important and interesting some day.

Headings may be rejected, then, partly because they are inappropriate to the reader, considering the object which one has in view. This of course will include the rejection of Headings which have nothing to do with the actual subject.

Headings may also be rejected because, if they were to be put in, they would make the Essay or Speech too long ; they might be interesting but they would tend to distract the attention.

Other Headings may be rejected because they are untrue or unfair, although *to mention an unfair argument, if you also say why it is unfair,* is often the very best way of dealing with it—far better than omitting it altogether.

Other Headings can be omitted or should be omitted, either because they are unhealthy, using the word in a wide sense, or else because they are unkind or apt to hurt people's feelings. On the other hand there is in

England a great deal too much *prudery* about mentioning subjects which are some of the most important
in life, and there is a great deal of misguided 'charity'
which shrinks from mentioning things for fear of
offending someone or other, and probably for fear of
some personal loss. The motive may seem excellent,
but the effect may be exactly like that of never correcting the faults of children.

As helps towards rejecting Headings, the Aim and
the readers should constantly be kept in view; and
there is something to be said for the plan of *writing
the end of the Essay before one does anything else*, if by
this means the goal will be kept in view throughout.

Two or three Exercises may be suggested as practice
here.

1. First of all, take your own Composition, or any
other, and, after you have got the Scheme or Analysis
of it, *cut out* whatever you consider to be inappropriate,
etc. Of course it is very hard to cut out some Idea
which you wish to air, for instance some interesting
suggestion. And there is scarcely any learned man
who has not spoilt many of his Books or Articles or
Speeches, or some of them, by masses and masses
of information which may be interesting in itself but
is not appropriate, either to the aim or object in view,
or to the readers. To take an instance, Commentaries
on the Classics or on Ancient History should be studied
from this point of view: they contain folios of such
learning as is singularly out of place just where it *is*,
e.g. in School-books, however accurate it may be, and
however interesting, for other purposes.

2. Another Exercise is to '*mark*' *the Ideas* according
to their importance, for instance, to give the most

important Ideas ten marks and the least important one mark or none at all. See further the following Chapter.

3. But a still better Exercise perhaps is to take great Orators and Writers, and to make an Analysis or Scheme of their Ideas, and then to see how much they have rejected. You will find plenty of facts and plenty of arguments which *might* have been inserted, e.g. in a speech of Demosthenes. But now you can ask yourself whether the omitted things were omitted because they were not appropriate to the readers or audience, or to the Aim of the Author or Speaker, or whether they were not put in because they never occurred to the Author at all. This will lead you to think over the reasons for Selecting and Rejecting Ideas.

In my own opinion the Rejecting of Ideas is the hardest part of Essay-Writing: it needs tremendous *self-control and self-sacrifice,* and it cannot but have a powerful effect on the character. To be able to say to oneself, 'Such-and-such a Heading will interest the readers, but I must reject it because it has nothing to do with my present Aim', and actually to reject it, not only needs very great self-control at the moment, but must be most excellent self-discipline for the whole of life.

CHAPTER XXXII. HOW TO PROPORTION AND UNDERLINE THE HEADINGS.

WHEN the Ideas have been Collected and Selected, then the Writer or Speaker must concentrate his attention on Underlining those Ideas which are most important, or rather those which seem to *him* to be most important; for here personal opinion and taste must again come into play.

The Collection of Ideas, and the Selection and Rejection of Ideas, are already off his hands: he need not trouble about these any longer. And he must not yet trouble about the Arrangement of Ideas, or about their Expression : these will come later on. Nor need he trouble about how he is actually to Emphasise the Ideas; that will be left to the Arrangement of Ideas, and (see p. 268) to various other means, such as Repetition, Comparisons, Contrasts, etc.

Here he only has to decide which Ideas he considers to be rather important, or appropriate, or interesting and suggestive, and under these he should put a single line ; more important, etc., Ideas should have a double line under them ; and the most important, etc., Ideas should have three lines.

But the other extreme, the least important, etc., Ideas, could either be cut out or else have no particular sign to mark them. The Sub-Headings, that is to say, the Ideas under the Main Headings, can be marked (see p. 59) by being *Indented.*

It will be necessary for you to Collect the Sub-Headings before you Underline: for, until you know the Sub-Headings of any given Main Heading, you cannot safely say whether that Main Heading is very important, etc., or not.

CHAPTER XXXIII. HOW TO ARRANGE THE HEADINGS AND SUB-HEADINGS.

WHEN once you have begun to express Ideas in language, it is far too late to think of Arranging them: that is to say unless you have a special genius for this. The ordinary Essayist or Speaker who begins to write down or speak his Ideas at once, is (as we have seen on p. 45) trying to do a threefold or fourfold task, each part of which is extremely difficult in itself. He is, or ought to be, Collecting his Ideas, Selecting, and Proportioning them, Arranging them, and Expressing them.

Of all these different tasks, probably the Arranging will be the hardest for him, partly because it is the least practised. After all, one has a good deal of practice in Collecting Ideas, and a good deal of practice in Expressing them: but in Arranging them one has little or none. In the whole of my education, I do not remember to have had a single lesson in the art. Obviously, however, this Arranging of Ideas should have been studied as a separate process all by itself.

As a starting-point, I shall take a quotation from a celebrated authority on Essay-writing. I give it as a type of bad Arrangement, and, singularly enough, it comes out of a book on "the art of writing English". It will be seen, for instance, that the Arrangement of the Ideas is very faulty for at least two reasons: first, that the order is altogether wrong, and secondly that what might have been expressed, and should have been expressed, under 13 headings has been expressed under 28. A third fault would be that very important Ideas, such as No. 28, are put on exactly the same level as petty and trivial pieces of advice, which are scarcely worth mentioning at all. In Arrangement or classification, and in Proportion, the list is altogether to be censured.

As an Exercise in Arrangement, let the reader himself take these pages, and let him criticise the Arrangement, and then re-arrange the Ideas in a logical order.

Let him devote some time to this, because the Ideas themselves will be of great value in Essay-writing.

"GENERAL RULES.

"1. Vary the length of the sentence. Vary also the form.

"'Diversify the sentence-type,' says Dr. EARLE. 'The one rule is to be infinitely various'.—R. L. STEVENSON.

"2. Never use foreign words or phrases, unless you are compelled to do so.

"3. Never begin a sentence—or a clause—with 'also'.

"4. Let the relative stand as near the antecedent as possible.

"5. Qualifying phrases and modifying adverbs should be placed as close as possible to the words they are to qualify or to modify.

"6. Let your sentences be always clear to yourself, and ascertain whether they are also clear to others.

"7. A participle, being an adjective in function, must always have some noun or pronoun to which it is attached.

"8. Avoid such phrases as 'Of all others,' 'than any other'. 'Other two' for 'two more' is a Scotticism.

"9. Let there be one subject in a sentence.

"If more than one be required, let its relation to the main subject be quite clear. Or: 'Do not change your nominative.'

"10. Avoid tautology.

"11. Avoid pleonastic expressions—like 'return back' or 're-turn back again'.

"12. Avoid exaggeration—even in the height (or the depth) of emotion.

"13. Avoid such clumsy connectives as 'therein', 'thereby', 'whereto', 'whereupon', 'wherefore', etc.   All of these are more or less antiquated.

"14. Use as many connectives as you can.   Such easy connec-tives as 'again', 'once more', 'on the other hand', 'besides', give lightness to the composition.

"15. Shun clichés.

"16. Do not begin your paper with 'The above title,' 'The subject of this paper.'

"17. Be careful about the position of the word 'only'.

"18. Avoid repetition, unless it is really necessary or distinctly telling.

"19. Avoid archaic, quaint, or Biblical phrases.

"Such phrases are not admissible in ordinary prose.

"20. Be clear.

"'Care should be taken, not that the reader may understand if he will, but that he must understand, whether he will or not.'—QUINTILIAN.

"21. Be simple.

"22. Avoid the use of unnecessary adjectives.

"23. Do not search for similes or metaphors.   If the subjec naturally suggests them, they will come of themselves ; if they dot not, they are better away.

"24. Emphasis may be gained by an inversion of the natural order of words.   If you employ inversion, recollect that the most striking position in a sentence is the beginning ; and the next most emphatic, the end.

"25. Be careful to avoid DISLOCATION.

"26. Draw up a short skeleton of what you are going to write about.

"27. Read your essay aloud after it is written—either to your-self, or to a friend, or to both.

"28. Cut out those words you can do without, provided the sense and rhythm are not injured by the process."

*   *   *   *   *

The following errors may be mentioned, as a few out of many :—

(i) No. 26 says "Draw up a short skeleton of what you are going to write about". This is quite in the wrong place : it should come first ;

(ii) No. 16 says "Do not begin your paper with 'The above title', 'The subject of this paper'. This should not be as late as 16 ;

(iii) Nos. 4, 5, 17, and 25 might all come together; and so might

(iv) Nos. 10, 11, 22, 28 ;

(v) Nos. 13 and 19 ;

(vi) Nos. 6 and 20. To put these two Sections apart is a piece of carelessness : no one who had carefully prepared his Scheme by the Card-System (p. 186) could possibly have fallen into this error.

Let him now see whether his results are like mine : of course I do not put mine forward as final. But it will be seen that I suggest 13 Headings instead of 28.

I put in brackets some comments to advice which I do not consider to be quite sound; and of course the Hints are very incomplete, and some are trivial (e.g. 16) ; the second remark in 8 is pedantic.

I. [*Collection of Ideas and Arrangement*] :—

(26) "Draw up a short skeleton of what you are going to write about." [See p. 186.]

II. [*Beginning*] :—

(16) "Do not begin your paper with 'The above title', 'The subject of this paper'." [See p. 258.]

III. [*Fairness*] :—

(12) "Avoid exaggeration—even in the height (or the depth) of emotion." [See p. 301.]

IV. [*Variety*] :—

(1) "Vary the length of the sentence. Vary also the form. . . ."

V. [*Subject of the Sentence, etc.*] :—

(9) "Let there be one subject in a sentence. . . ."

(7) "A participle, being an adjective in function, must always have some noun or pronoun to which it is attached."

VI. [*Clearness, etc.*] :—

(20) "Be clear. . . ."

(6) "Let your sentences be always clear to yourself, and ascertain whether they are also clear to others." [See p. 227.]

(21) "Be simple.   That is, be yourself!" [But see pp. 45, 236.]

VII. [*Connectives, etc.*].

(14) "Use as many connectives as you can. . . ."

(3) "Never begin a sentence—or a clause—with *also*."

(13) "Avoid such clumsy connectives as *therein, thereby, whereto, whereupon, wherefore,* etc. All of these are more or less anti-quated."

VIII. [*Connexion and Order*] —:

(25) "Be careful to avoid DISLOCATION."

(4) "Let the relative stand as near the antecedent as possible."

(5) "Qualifying phrases and modifying adverbs should be placed as close as possible to the words they are to qualify or modify."

IX. [*Choice of words*—cp. VII. (13)] —

(19) "Avoid archaic, quaint, or Biblical phrases. . . ."

(2) "Never use foreign words or phrases, unless you are com-pelled to do so."

(15) "Shun clichés."

X. [*Brevity and Economy, etc.*] :—

(22) "Avoid the use of unnecessary adjectives."

(28) "Cut out those words you can do without, provided the sense and the rhythm are not injured by the process."

(11) "Avoid pleonastic expressions—like 'return back' . . ."

(10) "Avoid tautology." [But see p. 254.]

(18) "Avoid repetition, unless it is necessary or distinctly telling."

(8) "Avoid such phrases as 'Of all others', 'than any other'. . . ."

XI. [*Emphasis*] :—

(24) "Emphasis may be gained by an inversion of the 'natural' order of words. . . ." [And see p. 268.]

XII. [*Metaphors*] :—

(23) "Do not search for similes or metaphors. If the subject naturally suggests them, they will come of themselves : if they do not, they are better away." [But see p. 162.]

XIII. [*Revision*] :—

(27) "Read your essay aloud, after it is written—either to yourself, or to a friend, or to both."

For another instance of bad Arrangement, see Bain's "Rhetoric and Composition" (vol. i., p. xvi), where he has one great Heading for

"CLEARNESS

opposed to obscurity . . ."
followed by another great Heading for

"SIMPLICITY

opposed to . . . difficulty in being understood."

For every subject, for every set of Ideas, there is *one best possible order*, for each set of readers or hearers, for each class of Composition, and for each aim and object of the Writer or Speaker.

A great authority on Style, namely Flaubert, used to spend whole days in finding the exact words by which to express his Ideas. One cannot consider it altogether a waste of time if one considers how much it must have improved his power of perseverance and accuracy, and his conscientiousness. But the art of Arranging Ideas would be equally worthy of such thorough treatment. The Ideas which one has Collected should be Arranged once, and, after an interval, should if necessary be re-arranged.

N

To spend hours and hours or days and days over this process cannot be time wasted, because *the power of Arranging must affect every single department of life.* It can hardly be too often repeated that a power like this, when rightly acquired in any *one* department of life, can then be applied to any other department. The power of Arranging Ideas for an Essay will even help the power of arranging, let us say, things in a room or books on a shelf or things in a box or bag; that is to say, *provided that the art has been practised in the right way.* In other words, it will produce a general power and facility for Arrangement.

Only a few principles can be mentioned here. Very much, of course, as we have already said, must depend on the readers or hearers, on whether they are stupid or educated, whether they are general readers or specialists; much also must depend on the aim or aims of the author; much also on the subject itself, for instance, whether it is in the nature of scientific proof or in the nature of a light and easy conversation or talk.

For example, a difficulty often arises as to whether one shall put the Instances before the Principle, or vice versa. One has Instances to illustrate a Principle, and a Principle which may be illustrated by Instances. Which shall come first? A safe scheme for average purposes I have found to be the following, and I see it has been (unconsciously) applied by a large number of well-known Essayists and Speakers.

1 and 2. The *Evidences* for a statement or principle should be given. Or, as an alternative for No. 1, *Fallacies* and wrong ideas on the subject may be refuted. Or either of these might be 1, and the other would then be 2.

3. A single *Instance*—let it be as clear and as interesting as possible, to the readers—may now be given. The Instance might be introduced by some *Comparison*, if it were not sufficiently clear and interesting in itself (see p. 281).

4. From this Instance should be drawn the *Principle* which it illustrates and embodies:

5. This Principle may be still further illustrated by *other Instances*, or

6. *by Contrasts*, which would perhaps do more to illustrate and to emphasise it than anything else possibly could (see p. 291).

7. If there are *other Principles*, they may be introduced in the same way, viz. at first by a single Instance.

8. A *Summary* at the end may gather together and *tabulate* all the Principles, which may now need to be re-arranged in the best possible order.

9. Exceptions to the Principles, and Objections to them, with answers, may come at the end, or they may precede No. 8.

Of course this is only a general order, and is liable to many changes.

Some *tests* of good order, in many types of more serious Essays or Speeches, would be as follows:—

1. When you have read the Essay, and have remembered the first Heading, then the other Headings ought to follow easily, as if all of them had been linked together: just as, if you were given *one* link in a chain, you ought to be able to pull the whole chain towards you by means of that link.

But this is a test not only of Arrangement but also of *Connexion*. There are very few Essays which will

stand this test.   Most of them contain several transitions of a very jerky kind.   The reader has to jump
from one point to another, and does not slide unconsciously over the joint.

2. Anyhow, certain *clear Ideas* should be left behind
in your mind as to the 'Pros and Cons' of the case,
and *there should not be too many Ideas left behind*, but
rather several very important points in the foreground,
and much in the middle distance, and still more in the
background.

3. Throughout, the Essay should have been *interesting* (and, if possible, suggestive).   Of course the
Interest cannot be entirely dependent on the Arrangement alone.   But it is surprising how, with a given
number of Ideas, expressed in similar words, one
Arrangement will make them interesting and another
Arrangement will make them dull.

Among the difficulties of Arrangement is the difficulty
of harmonising these two principles, namely *Interest
and Connexion*.   Both of them must be considered, as
well as the other principle of *Proportion*.

The Ideas should be arranged according to their
importance, and in such a way that one may naturally
lead to another, and that the Interest may be sustained
throughout.

It will be noticed here that I have said nothing about
the omission of unnecessary Ideas.   This belongs, not
to Arrangement, but to another department of Essay-
writing and Speaking, namely to Selection and Rejection.   The Essayist or Speaker should have Selected
and Rejected his Ideas before he thinks of Arranging
them.

The following *general principles* may apply to a good many Compositions.

1. When you have Collected the Main Headings, and under them the Sub-Headings, and under these again the Sub-Sub-Headings, then take the Main Headings first and Arrange *them*. This is best done by the Card-System (see p. 186). *Group together those which are akin, under one great Heading or general* notion. This should be the first aim, namely to collect together such Headings as come into the same class, beneath the same roof, as it were.

On p. 92 we have seen that a 'group' might be formed of Ideas which are all Causes or Hindrances of something, or which are Effects of something, or which are Objections to your Ideas, and so on.

2. You may possibly have two or three such classes (see p. 185); but outside these classes there may still be certain isolated Main *Headings which do not seem to fall into any one class.* How are these to be Arranged? Often one is driven to Arrange them in a certain order merely because *some casual item* under one Heading will lead on to the next Heading, that is to say, there may be no *real* vital connexion between the two but a mere word about one will serve as a transition to the other, just as it so often does in conversation: e.g. 'Talking of so-and-so and William Arthur, reminds me that Arthur Jones is ill'.

3. The order adopted by *Demosthenes* was very different from this. As one reads one of his Speeches *there seems to be no Arrangement whatever*, and yet he must have Arranged his subjects as carefully as possible; and the same will apply to the section (which I have given on p. 212) from the "Sermon on the Mount".

There is apparent disorder and want of Arrangement, whereas there is really an extremely scientific Arrangement, which has succeeded in appearing casual. It has concealed its art.

What is the principle of this? It is in the main to lead up to a single Idea from different points (see p. 215). To start with something which, apparently, is merely interesting and has no connexion with the topic, and then gradually to lead on to the Idea which one wishes to emphasise; and so the point comes for the first time. Then a new topic is started, interesting again, but apparently unconnected with the first; but gradually this leads up to the same point as before. When this has been done four times, let us say, then that point has been *emphasised*. This method is particularly adapted for appealing to average people, for instance, to a large popular audience. The advantage of it is that the Interest can be kept up throughout. The curiosity can be excited, for the people will be saying to themselves, 'Why on earth is he talking about this, which is surely quite off the point?'

And not only is there Interest, but there is also Variety. In the reading of that passage on the Sermon on the Mount, it does not occur to the casual reader that Jesus, *throughout, was speaking of only one thing.* He seemed to be speaking of many things: of the preacher, of sheep and wolves, of fig-trees and thistles, of the Day of Judgment, of the house built on rock or on sand; and yet all these parts have one Aim. They are all on the same subject, but they approach it from different points of view. For teaching purposes, this method is almost as indispensable—as it is unusual.

When an Essay or Speech adopts a more 'methodical' Arrangement, it should work on the following lines.

The *Beginning*, or rather the Beginnings, should be *Interesting*.

The '*Middle*,' or mass, should be more *solid* and should contain the most important part of the work; but, within the Essay or Speech, Proportion must be observed, so that Ideas which the writer thinks important may stand out as important, and trivial ideas may be thrown into the background.

The Ending, except in lighter literature, should be not so much Interesting as Impressive.

This rule, which applies to an Essay or Speech, applies equally to a Book, as we all know (see p. 258), and to a Paragraph, and to some extent even to a Sentence. But, in these two latter spheres, the principle of Connexion (p. 263) is also to be considered.

What is the best *practice for Arrangement*?

1. To give oneself an object in view, one ought to 'Arrange' for some special purpose, whether it be for Teaching or for Lecturing or for an Article; this will make the work more interesting.

2. And notice that the first Arrangement should not be accepted as final. Second thoughts are sometimes the best. An interval (see p. 330) may be a wonderful aid.

3. What is called *Précis-writing, or Summarising,** is a great help to Arrangement. That is to say, one hears or one reads some subject (e.g. a series of Letters or Articles), and then one reproduces it. Only this itself is hardly practice in Arrangement. The Arrangement must come afterwards. Supposing a Master read

* For the suggestion as to Summarising Parliamentary and other Speeches, see p. 387.

out to his class an interesting Article on some subject, his class could write down on Cards the Ideas which they remembered, and the full List of Ideas or Headings could be given by the Master ; so far, again, there would be no practice in Arrangement. But if the packets of Cards which each boy had were *shuffled* and then were *re-arranged* by each boy, and if then the Arrangement were *criticised* by different boys or by the whole class, and if free criticism were allowed, then we should have an excellent piece of practice in Arranging, as well as in Collecting and remembering Ideas.

4. It should be always borne in mind that many different Arrangements may be fairly good for the same set of Ideas, e.g. according to the different objects and aims of the Writer or Speaker.

5. Finally, Indenting is of importance. When one Main Heading has under it certain Sub-Headings, these Sub-Headings should always go just a little 'inland', not directly beneath the Main Heading, but just a little more *to the right*. The advantage of this is obvious. It makes the Main Headings easier to revise by themselves, and the Sub-Headings by themselves, and it helps to show what is more important and what is less important. The 'Sub-Sub-Headings' should be still further indented.

The power of Arranging Ideas is seldom born with a man. It nearly always has to be 'made'. But it is wonderful how practice will improve it. One might compare what practice will do in the way of packing bags. A skilful packer will get into a bag half as much again as an unskilful packer. There are some who are born with the art of packing bags, but most people have to (or ought to) learn it for themselves.

Another comparison suggests itself here, and that is that, after a railway journey, a bag which has seemed quite full at the start is shown to have sorted its contents somewhat differently, and, of its own accord, as it were, to have arranged them more scientifically and more economically. The brain does very much the same with its Ideas. Leave your Ideas alone in your brain for a week, and you will probably find that in the meanwhile they have arranged themselves quite satisfactorily, and have bred other Ideas as well.

In spite of the great value of Arrangement and of practice in Arrangement, however, it is a part of Composition that is very little studied : its importance is seldom insisted on, nor is bad Arrangement easily detected. This may be partly because, as we actually Write or Speak (or read or listen), we are apt to concentrate our attention rather on, e.g., the Vocabulary, the Rhythm, the order of Words, the Syntax, and the Ideas themselves. Another reason would be that its Principles are little known or studied or applied as a special art. A third reason would be that Analysing and Précis-writing are a 'habit' little practised and cultivated in our ordinary Education : and, without such Analysing, the Arrangement of Ideas or Headings is incredibly difficult.

As an Exercise in Arrangement, let the reader try to Arrange the Causes of Rome's Success (see pp. 10, 83, 263): e.g. The Senate, Alliances, Family Life, Geography, Roads, Etruscan Kings, Colonies, Character, Slaves, Individual Leaders, Mixture of Peoples in Rome, Extension of Rights to Aliens, Organisation (in Religion, etc.), Treachery, Unity, Isolation of Others, Weakness of Enemies, Slaves, Gradual Conquest, and so on. One Arrangement will be suggested in " How to Remember." For another Exercise, see p. 277.

CHAPTER XXXIV. THE CARD-SYSTEM.

THE Card-System applies, as we shall see, not simply to Ideas and Headings for Essays and Speeches, but also to Mems and Quotations; and for Index-writing it is inestimable.

There are certain *Objections* to the Card-System, and the first might be that it would be *expensive*. But, as a matter of fact, each Card might be used four times, or even six or eight times. Supposing, however, that each Card were only used three times, even then the rate for a thousand words of Writing or Speaking would be quite trifling, if each Card contained, let us say, ten words; for the Cards only cost half-a-crown a thousand, and *can* be had for two shillings.

At first, also, it might be thought that the Cards would be *inconvenient* to use, but the personal experience of thousands shows that, at any rate for business-purposes, exactly the reverse is true. The Cards are quite easy to carry about when one is travelling, if only one uses elastic bands or Cabinets or Card-holders; and any kind of inconvenience will very soon disappear after a little practice.

And the same will apply to the objection that the System is *unusual*. Seldom have there been any new suggestions which have not been condemned as 'unusual', and, if one tried to introduce the System in Examinations, where it certainly ought to be introduced, one would be met by this objection—'We are not in the *habit* of allowing Cards'. But this is no fair condemnation. In Examinations, paper can be torn up into small oblong pieces, which will serve as Cards.

The System may now be explained briefly. It has often been misunderstood. For instance, one lady entirely missed the point, and wrote down twenty Ideas on a single card. In such a case the Card-System had no great advantage over the ordinary Memorandum-system, or even over the Note-book.

1. The principle is to buy Cards at half-a-crown a thousand, or even less, and on them to write *Headings, and not Sentences, copying only one Heading on one Card, and of course writing only on one side of the Card at a time.* The Cards can be turned afterwards.

2. If there are any Sub-Headings, these can come either on separate Cards following the main Heading, or (but this is not so good) on the same Card, but indented (see p. 59). To keep the Sub-Headings on separate Cards is far the best way.

3. These Cards (if used only once) should be *labelled and catalogued* very carefully.

4. A great help towards Arrangement and Clearness is to have Cards of *different sizes and shapes*, and of different colours, or with different marks on them: see below. There should also be a Card-Tray, or a box with compartments in it, such as shown in the following illustration. Of course the Tray might have an open top.

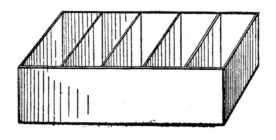

5. Above all, there must be *no false economy*, for the Cards are extraordinarily cheap—so cheap that there can scarcely be one of my readers whose time would not be far more precious to him than the few pence which he might save by such economising.

6. It is also important to have thin elastic bands with which to tie up the packets.

7. In using the Cards, and in filling in the Headings, one should employ *Abbreviations* freely : a few of them have been suggested on p. 70.

Some special Marks may be added here.

Special Marks on Cards :—

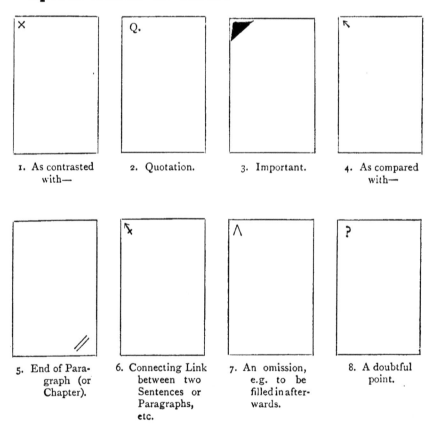

| 1. As contrasted with— | 2. Quotation. | 3. Important. | 4. As compared with— |
| 5. End of Paragraph (or Chapter). | 6. Connecting Link between two Sentences or Paragraphs, etc. | 7. An omission, e.g. to be filled in afterwards. | 8. A doubtful point. |

These are only a few Samples : they could easily be altered or added to. *The Abbreviations and Marks need be clear only to the Writer himself.* They save ever so much time.

8. After the Headings and Sub-Headings have been written, they can then be *Arranged,* and

9. finally can be *embodied in a Scheme,* if there is time. Before they are ready for the Scheme, however,

10. they should be *put aside for a long interval,* so that, e.g., additions can be made to them. When they have been finished they may be spread out on a table or on several tables. If you can get a table with pegs, or something to mark the divisions between the packets, it will be so much the better. To mark Main Headings you might have coloured Cards, for instance, blue Cards, or else larger Cards.

11. *You should always carry a few Cards about in your pocket,* in case you should think of anything useful, for instance, during a walk. It will be very easy to distribute these Cards afterwards in their proper packets. You should keep a special place for these *miscellaneous* Headings, and these you should sort at intervals.

12. So far we have considered only just the Main Headings and the Sub-Headings. But it would be possible, and it would be advisable, if the work has to be carefully done, to apply the Card-System to '*Connexions*', i.e. to write on Cards the connecting link between each Idea and the Idea that follows ; and it may be as well to apply the System even to Paragraphs, that is to say, before you write a Paragraph to write on Cards the Headings for the different sections of it.

It may be mentioned, by the way, that to treat the written Paragraphs on a similar System is also a great saving of time, that is to say, when you are copying out the Essay itself, to write each Paragraph on a separate piece of paper. If you do this, you will have far less re-writing when you come to copy out the Essay finally. But this applies rather to Writing for the Press.

13. *At first it is a mistake to think of anything else except the mere jotting down of Ideas.* The Ideas should be jotted down, each on its own Card, and the Sub-Headings should be jotted down on their own Cards, a little way 'inland'. Afterwards there will be time enough to subdivide the topics, and to re-arrange them ; but at the beginning you must concentrate your attention on the Collection of Ideas, and must not think at all about the Arrangement.

This is the great advantage of the Card-System over the ordinary Scheme (on a single sheet of paper), for with the latter one has to be thinking of two things at the same time, namely, of the Arrangement of the Ideas as well as the Collection of the Ideas.

14. When it does come to the Arranging, *the Cards should be arranged something like a hand at Whist.* And you will find it very easy to alter, to add, or to take away, for you can always *substitute a new Card or remove an old one.*

15. The old Cards can be used in many ways. You can turn them upside-down, and treat the other end similarly, then you can turn them over and the backs of them will give you two more spaces to be used. Some might even use the four sides also! After the Cards are entirely covered, they can be used for scrap-books for Hospitals.

16. The System can be applied to other purposes

besides Essay-writing, such as, for instance, *the Arrange-ment of people at a dinner-party;* but here I am only speaking of their use for literary purposes. The ad-vantages of this System I shall treat of in the next Chapter, but I may say here, by way of anticipation, that they enable one to concentrate one's attention on the Collection of Ideas as apart from their Arrange-ment and Expression; that they are easier and quicker to use, if alterations have to be made; that they can be worked with extraordinary rapidity, especially if they are combined with Dictation (see p. 69), and if they have been practised for some time. As to rapidity, it is possible to dictate from Cards an Article of three thousand words, that is to say, such a one as might appear in the "Nineteenth Century", in half an hour. The preparation by the Card-System might take twenty minutes, if one knew the subject well; the arrangement ten minutes; and the dictation thirty minutes.

I arrived at the Card-System by degrees, and was glad to find that Prof. Wendell also recommended Cards. I have elaborated the System considerably in the last few months, and now I generally use the Cards of the Library Bureau (Bloomsbury Street, London), or those by Messrs. Evans and Hallewell, 5, Ave Maria Lane, London, E.C. The latter are the cheaper.

CHAPTER XXXV. ADVANTAGES OF THE CARD-SYSTEM.

ON the advantages of the Card-System I have already said a few words. These advantages can now be considered somewhat in detail.

I have already spoken of their use for purposes of Connecting, e.g. of giving Causes and Effects, and for keeping the right Proportion of importance (see p. 189). Other points now remain to be considered.

1. As I have said, they are very *cheap*, for they can be obtained at less than half-a-crown a thousand ; and each Card can be used at least four times.

2. They are very *portable*, especially if they have holes in them, and if boxes are made in which they may be kept: see p. 187.

3. They are useful *for other purposes*, besides Essay-writing and Speaking. For instance, for Addresses, for Bills, and for Memoranda.

4. They encourage a *business-like brevity*.

5. They ensure wonderful *rapidity*. A whole book of thirty thousand words I have prepared (though of course only roughly) in two hours, by the Card-System. Such a pace would have been impossible otherwise. This does not include any of the Dictation ; it merely includes the Collection and Selection of Ideas, and their Arrangement. The System is a wonderful *saving of time*, partly because so few Headings have to be

re-written. Each Idea has only to be written once. Another reason why it saves time is that here you can *imply* things instead of having to express them in full, for your Card-System and its Headings need only to be clear to yourself (see p. 67), whereas a complete Essay or Speech must be in Sentences and must be clear to your readers or hearers as well. In the Cards you can use all kinds of Abbreviations (p. 70): these, again, need only be clear to yourself.

6. As to the effect upon the writing-out, *very few pages have to be re-written.* Instead of perhaps twenty or thirty pages in a Book, you will have to re-write not more than two or three, and these will generally be in the Preface, where re-writing is almost inevitable.

7. Another good effect upon the writing-out will be that *the number of words will be very small.* It is worth while to make the following experiment. Take an Essay-Subject and work it out in the common way, namely, by writing the Essay straight down, just as you think of the Ideas. Let us say that you give two hours to doing this. Now take this Essay, and count the number of words which it contains : let us say that it contains fifteen hundred. Next take the Essay and analyse it, writing down each Heading and each Sub-Heading on a separate Card. Take these Cards and re-arrange them, and, if necessary, alter, and add new Headings or Sub-Headings. Last of all, do the Essay over again from the Cards, and count the number of words. The Essay will probably be far better than it was before, better in Completeness, better in Clearness, and better in Arrangement ; yet I doubt if it would come to more than five hundred words, at any rate, if you are an average Essay-writer. It is quite obvious

o

that the gain both for the Writer or Speaker, *and* for the reader or listener, may be very considerable.

8. It has been seen above that part of the System is *to leave an interval* after the Cards have once been written. During this interval, let us say of a week, if you can spare it, changes will be sure to occur to you. You will want to *add* some things, to *alter* others, and possibly to *omit* others. Now, *supposing you had already written your Essay out*, it would be very inconvenient to make these alterations; to put in a fresh paragraph here, or to alter half an old paragraph there, is tiresome work for the Writer, and produces an unpleasant result for the reader. With the Card-System this disadvantage is minimised.

9. But the great merit is, as I have already stated,.that the Card-System enables you *to focus your attention on one task at a time, and especially on the Collection of Ideas.*

At first it may not seem obvious that this *is* a gain. But, considering the matter scientifically, you must see that your work will be better if you have not to bother about the *order* in which your Ideas have to come, but can freely write them down on Cards, by a process which is considerably quicker than Shorthand, and be quite sure that the Arrangement of these Cards afterwards will be easy as a separate task. Later on, you can concentrate your attention no longer on what your Ideas are to be, but on how they are to be Arranged. And again, you can concentrate your attention, by means of the Card-System, on what Comparisons or Contrasts you are to use, what Fallacies you are to expose, and so on. Not only will you have Collected the greatest possible number of Ideas, and have Arranged them in the best way you can; but each individual section of your Essay will be better and better Arranged by this System than by any other. Finally, when your Cards have been prepared, you can concentrate your whole attention on how to Express the Ideas.

10. The Card-System will therefore be *good practice for Writing generally*, and I very often use it for important *Letters:* not merely because it improves the Letter, but also because it actually saves time. But it is not only for Writing that it is valuable: it is valuable for Speaking also. Anyone, who has practised the Card-System for some time, can prepare a Speech in a very few minutes: and this gift is simply inestimable.

11. The power of *Summarising* and of Précis-writing which the Card-System gives is extraordinary: whereas to Analyse a piece of English (see p. 233) used to take me perhaps half an hour, it now takes me something like five minutes. It is interesting to notice, in a Telegraph Office, how long a time people take in composing their telegrams, and how the final result is often not nearly as good as it might have been. It is obscure, and perhaps a whole penny has been wasted! The Card-System, which jots down Headings clearly, but briefly, is very good practice for this.

12. Under 8 we have already seen how, as one is actually writing on or Arranging the Cards, there is a very good chance of new Ideas suggesting themselves *en passant;* and, when these new Ideas have suggested themselves, it is, as I have said, very easy to add them. It is easy to add new Cards to the pack, either at the time or later on. It is easy to take out Cards that you do not want, and to alter the Headings on those Cards which you already have. Again, when the Cards are

Arranged, the Card-System enables one to revise the Arrangement very quickly, and to alter it if necessary. And it is wonderful how it *improves the power of order and Arrangement.* The process of solving the problem 'Here are ten Ideas, eight of which have Sub-Headings: how ought I to arrange these Headings and Sub-Headings?' this process by itself is a valuable mental exercise.

13. Once again, when these Cards have been written and Arranged, they are *easy to refer to at a moment's notice. They become a possession for ever, and not a 'stereotyped' possession either :* for you can always alter, add, or change, which is a great consideration. If you keep your Essays *as* Essays, it may take you a quarter of an hour to find some Idea in them if you wish to refer to it ; whereas, by the Card-System, the Idea can be found in a minute, simply because it *is* an Idea or Heading, and is not dressed (or hidden) in a Sentence or Paragraph.

14. The Card-System would be useful for every kind of Book and Essay and Speech, and for most kinds of Letters. It is even a good thing to use it before an important *conversation.* Within the Book itself, it will apply to the Sections, Chapters, and Paragraphs. *Each part of the Composition will benefit by it, but most of all the Expression and Style.* This sounds at first a contradiction, because one would say that this was just the part of Composition which the Card-System did *not* concern ; but it is for this very reason that the Card-System helps Expression. It does everything else for you *except* the Expression, so that, when you come to this, it is the only thing left to be done, and you can devote every atom of your energy to it. I cannot but

think that one of the reasons why ordinary Writings and Speeches are so obscure is that the Writer or Speaker has had to be Collecting his Ideas and Arranging them and thinking out which are the most important, at the same time that he is trying to Express them (or rather that he ought to be trying to express them) in a way intelligible and interesting to the reader. How on earth can an ordinary person succeed in doing these many things at once? Obviously he is setting himself a Herculean task. By the Card-System, he would split up this task into parts, and would win a victory by conquering the enemy in detachments.

Three words may be said by way of Summary.

Firstly, do not economise Cards or paper.

Secondly, make your Headings very brief; they need only be clear to yourself; and put each on a separate Card.

Thirdly, do not be surprised if the System is a little awkward to handle at first. There never yet was any great result achieved in History without a slow and steady and even unsuccessful beginning. With time, however, the System will become easy and quick. You must not expect to reap the fruit till you have sown the seeds and watered the ground.

PART III.

PART III. **HOW TO EXPRESS IDEAS: STYLE.**

CHAPTER XXXVI. EXPRESSION OF IDEAS, AND STYLE: GENERAL NOTES.

THE Expression of the Ideas (Headings and Sub-Headings) cannot be finely distinguished from the Collection and Arrangement of Ideas. Thus we cannot say that the working out of Comparisons and Contrasts, for important Ideas, belongs entirely to the Collection of Sub-Headings or to the Expression of Headings. This is a place where the two Parts of Essay-writing meet; and this is not the only place.

My division of the Art of Composition into two main Parts is therefore convenient rather than accurate: the two Parts overlap and have neutral grounds.

In order that the attention may be concentrated on the Expression of Ideas, the Collection, etc., must already have been finished. Even the Comparisons (p. 281), and the Contrasts (p. 291), should have been worked out carefully. Perhaps the Card-System (p. 186) has been used, or a Scheme (p. 59), or else the Card-System first, and the Scheme afterwards.

The Ideas, then, we suppose to have already been Collected, Selected (and Rejected), Underlined, and Arranged. They now have to be Expressed; and they should first be glanced through very quickly.

In Expressing Ideas it is far harder to separate the processes in a similar way, and to attend to them one at a time. The next best thing is to *criticise* the

Expression afterwards, first with regard to Clearness, then with regard to Appropriateness, then Brevity, etc. leaving Rhythm till the end.

It may be said that *there is, for each Idea, a best possible Expression*, according to

> the subject;
> the class of Writing or Speech (e.g. Book, Essay, light Article, etc.—see p. 16);
> the readers or hearers;
> the Aims of the Writer or Speaker (p. 48).

Occasionally (e.g. in Shakespeare) we come across Expressions which we feel to be the best possible for all purposes and conditions. But these are rare. As a rule there will be a *different* 'best possible', for different conditions.

Flaubert, partly to distract his thoughts from his grievous ailments, used to spend hours and hours in searching for the best possible, especially the best possible word. And there is also, of course, the best possible Sentence, order of words, Rhythm, and so on.

A Rhyme (continued from p. 62), **suggesting some Characteristics of Expression and Style.**

Style varies with the subject, causing anger, tear, or smile,

excitement, scorn, calm reason, action, sympathy, or fear,

(to the aim and audience fitted); holds the attention, and is clear.

Music and Balance, Contrasts, 'Tropes', and Rhetoric should be seen.

Then Punctuation, Grammar, Language, where 'Good Use' is queen.

CHAPTER XXXVII. DIFFICULTIES AND FAULTS IN EXPRESSING IDEAS.

WHEN an Essay is being corrected at School, the Faults are usually marked (e.g. underlined) without any distinction: they are marked simply as Faults. But, if the Writer is to improve, he should find out exactly *where the Fault lies, and how it might have been avoided.*

We have already spoken of Faults which are Faults with regard to the Ideas. You may have made some mistake in Collecting Ideas, in Selecting them, in Proportioning them, or in Arranging them, quite apart from the way in which you have Expressed them, although even here the Expression cannot be altogether kept out of sight.

But in the following pages I shall only speak of the Faults which people are apt to make in Expressing Ideas, apart from the Collection, etc., of the Ideas themselves. In other words, in this Chapter will be found the mistakes which people might make when they have already prepared their Scheme of the Essay or Speech, and now come to turn it into language.

The Faults which I shall point out will be *only generally Faults, and not universally so.* For instance, there may be the Fault of what is called *Prolixity*, that is to say, where too many words have been put in; but an apparently unnecessary number of words is not always a mistake. Brevity is a virtue in Style, but not when the Ideas are too compressed. There can be excessive Brevity. In the same way, there may be the

Fault of a want of easy Rhythm, but easy Rhythm is not always a gain. There are occasions when the Rhythm can be too easy, when the attention can be fixed on the beautiful sound, as it often is in the reading of the Bible, so that the sense and the Ideas do not receive nearly enough attention. It would be interesting to analyse the effect of Bible-reading, so as to find out to what extent the beauty of the language *prevents* or *distracts* people from paying attention to the sense, in the same way that a beautiful tune might prevent people from paying attention to the words of a song or hymn.

The following Faults, then, will be only generally Faults : and, at the outset, it is interesting to notice that *Aristotle's definition* of a Fault holds good almost throughout. He said that virtue was *a mean between two extremes,* e.g. that the right degree of Courage was somewhere between arrant cowardice at one extreme and foolhardy rashness and thoughtlessness at the other ; that Economy was somewhere between mere niggardly stinginess and lavish spendthrift carelessness. Throughout life, and throughout almost every subject, it is surprising how true this definition is.

Take, for instance, Grammar or Syntax (see p. 320). There are certain rules of Grammar which it is a mistake to violate. One obvious extreme would therefore be to ignore the rules of Grammar altogether. On the other hand, one can go too far in the direction of what one thinks to be good Grammar, and one may be fairly condemned as a pedant and an unpractical stickler for what may be called over-correctness. The objection to certain common constructions, which sound quite right to nine hundred and ninety-nine people out of a thousand, is generally due to an ignorance of the principles of language. People insist to-day on a rule which held good perhaps fifty years ago. They forget that language has changed and is still changing. A good instance would be those who insist on people saying '*in* the circumstances', and not '*under* the circumstances'. This is surely pedantry, and the defence of '*under* the circumstances' would be first of all that it had come to be used by a number of good writers, without its offending the ear of a number of able critics, and secondly that its origin was quite easy and natural. '*Under the conditions*' has always been a proper construction,* and, *on the analogy of this*,† people have come to say '*under* the circumstances' also. Those who condemn this construction have not studied the principles according to which language has developed. I have seen a whole book written on this principle, namely, that whatever was a rule fifty years ago, must still be a rule to-day.

Obscurity and want of Clearness is a great Fault. The words may be too technical for ordinary readers or hearers, or the wrong words may have been chosen (see p. 325); or the words may be in the wrong order (p. 317). As to the other extreme, it is a question whether a sentence *can* be too clear, whether the Idea *can* be too simply expressed ; and, if we once admit that Carlyle's writings produced a greater effect and a better effect than they would have done if they had been perfectly clear, then we must admit that *for certain purposes* absolute Clearness is a Fault.

A good illustration of Aristotle's rule is that of the

---

* Cp. Latin.
† See ' How to Learn Philology' (Sonnenschein and Co.).

right *Length.* Excessive Brevity, whether of Paragraphs or Sentences or Words, is generally a Fault, and may be called Baldness.   Excessive Length, on the other hand, is a still greater Fault.   To have too long Paragraphs, too long Sentences, too long Words, is worse than to have these too short.

To take another instance.   There can be too much uniformity and *Monotony.*   If an Essay or Speech goes on in a similar Rhythm, with the Sentences and Paragraphs of the same or similar structure and length throughout, it will be guilty of the Fault of Monotony. If, on the other hand, the Writer or Speaker is perpetually changing his Rhythm, and the length of his Sentences and Paragraphs, unnecessarily, then he will be going to the other extreme of needless Variety. Here, as elsewhere, the 'mean' must needs depend on a number of conditions, such as the subject, the Writer or Speaker, the Aim, and the audience.   To change words unnecessarily is a great mistake.   On the other hand, Tautology is to be avoided.   In the two sentences which I have just written, the reader would do well to decide for himself whether I ought to have changed the words as I did, or not.   In the sentence from Froebel, on p. 325, the change is certainly unnecessary.

Want of connexion, either between one Paragraph and another, or between one Sentence and another, or between the various Words in a Sentence, is to be avoided.   Can there be at the other extreme too close a connexion within an Essay?   It is quite possible that occasionally a break and a fresh departure are necessary, in order to relieve the attention; and a popular audience (see p. 212) often needs an (apparent) absence of connexions.

As to *Comparisons and Contrasts*, the commonest Fault is to use too few. Sometimes there are none at all, and sometimes those of the wrong kind are chosen. On the other hand, it would be a mistake to have too many Comparisons and Contrasts, especially where the sense would be clear without them, and where the Idea is not to be emphasised.

Repetition, in the same way, is not to be avoided altogether and is not bad altogether, especially where Clearness or Emphasis are helped by it, but otherwise mere Repetition for the sake of filling up, i.e. Repetition which does not help Clearness or proper Emphasis, is an equally bad fault.

As to *Emphasis*, again, it is a mistake to have no Emphasis at all, that is to say, to present all one's Ideas as if they were equally (un)important. A learned pedant was once described as having a brain full of millions of pieces of information which were all of the same size. Such a man had no *Proportion*. On the other hand, Emphasis may be grossly misused in the sense of being over-used. There is no better illustration of this than certain American Papers, which have devoted so much attention to Emphasis, and so many devices (such as thick type and notes of exclamation and underlining) in calling attention to what did not deserve attention at all, that, when they come to an Idea which really deserves attention and Emphasis, they have little or no means left by which to call special attention to it.

The devices which are called Rhetorical Devices, such as the Question, the Epigram, etc. (see p. 299), are by no means to be avoided, but they must not be used to excess, especially when the subject (e.g. quiet

P

description) is unsuited for them. Balance again is a noticeable feature of Rhetoric, but Thucydides is fond· of using it to excess.

Another Fault is the use of a harsh *Rhythm*, or of an inappropriate Rhythm : for (see p. 305) the two things are not the same.

Bad *Punctuation*, or insufficient Punctuation, is another fault. It is doubtful if excessive Punctuation may not be a fault also. I am (probably rightly) accused of excessive Punctuation.

Such are a few of the commonest Faults in Style or Expression. Others might be worked out by a consideration of the Merits of Style (see p. 204), and by a working out of the Faults by contrast with these Merits.

CHAPTER XXXVIII. HOW TO FIND CHARACTERISTICS OF EXPRESSION AND STYLE: MATT. 7. 15–27, AS AN ILLUSTRATION.

MANY Writers have earned a great reputation for Style, and some have undoubtedly deserved it. And yet, when we come to ask what Style consists in, no Writer seems to be able to tell us. Put a piece of bad Style before a critic, and he will say that it is bad; he may even say *where* it is bad. Again, put a piece of good Style before him, and he will say that it is good. But ask him exactly *why* it is good, and he will probably be at a loss. The attempts of so many who have a good Style themselves, to tell others the secret of it would be lamentable if they were not so ridiculous. I once read a long-winded Article in flowing English entitled "Style"; after a great deal of inflated wordiness, the Writer eventually decided that Style was something which could not be described.

Up to the present moment I have never come across any Writer who gives clear instruction as to how to find out the characteristics of anyone's style, and this Chapter must therefore be a somewhat crude attempt, seeing that it is, as far as I know, the first attempt in this direction.

Let the Reader take a passage from the "Sermon on the Mount", and let him try to find out for himself what are the characteristics of its Expression and

Style; let him write them down as separate Headings, one under the other.

15 Beware of false prophets, which come to you in sheep's
16 clothing, but inwardly are ravening wolves. By their fruits
   ye shall know them. Do men gather grapes of thorns, or figs
17 of thistles? Even so every good tree bringeth forth good
18 fruit; but the corrupt tree bringeth forth evil fruit. A good
   tree cannot bring forth evil fruit, neither can a corrupt tree
19 bring forth good fruit. Every tree that bringeth not forth
20 good fruit is hewn down, and cast into the fire. Therefore by
21 their fruits ye shall know them. Not every one that saith unto
   me, Lord, Lord, shall enter into the kingdom of heaven; but
   he that doeth the will of my Father which is in heaven.
22 Many will say to me in that day, Lord, Lord, did we not
   prophesy by thy name, and by thy name cast out devils,
23 and by thy name do many mighty works? And then will I
   profess unto them, I never knew you: depart from me, ye
24 that work iniquity. Every one therefore which heareth these
   words of mine, and doeth them, shall be likened unto a wise
25 man, which built his house upon the rock: and the rain
   descended, and the floods came, and the winds blew, and beat
   upon that house; and it fell not: for it was founded upon
26 the rock. And every one that heareth these words of mine,
   and doeth them not, shall be likened unto a foolish man, which
27 built his house upon the sand: and the rain descended, and
   the floods came, and the winds blew, and smote upon that
   house; and it fell: and great was the fall thereof.

*   *   *   *   *   *

The reader will doubtless find the task very hard. He probably will not have any scientific method of procedure, and, when I tell him that the first thing to do is to take away the Ideas, and to leave them out of the question altogether, he will probably be very much surprised. Nevertheless it is so: if he wishes to criticise Style *as* Style, he must not consider the Ideas themselves for a moment: *they* may (to a great extent) be criticised apart.

Let us then see what are the Ideas of this passage, or what is *the* Idea of it, and then we shall be able to concentrate our attention on finding out how the Idea or Ideas are Expressed. We shall therefore have to analyse the piece, and write the abstract of it, before we begin to examine into the Style.

The gist of this piece is the answer to the question, 'Who are the really good?' This, in the language of the Authorised and Revised Versions, would be, 'Who belong to the Kingdom of Heaven?', which conveys quite a different meaning to most ordinary people. This then will be the Idea of the piece, and the answer to the question is, that the really good are those who are good in their inmost nature, at their foundations, as it were, so that everything that they do, and everything that they produce, is bound to be good also.

The reader, having now found the Idea, can come to see better how it has been Expressed. He can now try once again to find the Characteristic of Style, asking himself what is it that makes the Expression of this Idea so excellent in this passage. For in this passage a large number of the excellencies of Style are combined, that is to say in the original Greek.

In case the reader should omit to notice that the language is simple, I offer a Version in simple English, from " The Teaching of Jesus To-day " (Grant Richards).

Be on your guard against all the pretended representatives of God, who come to you looking like sheep, when all the time they are really hungry wolves : it is by what they produce that you must class them ; for instance, you don't get bunches of grapes off thorn-bushes, or figs off thistles, do you? It is the very nature of good trees to produce good fruit, and of rotten trees to produce bad fruit : it is as impossible for a good tree to produce bad fruit, as it is for a rotten tree to produce good fruit ; you know this is so, for the trees which do not produce good fruit you cut down to be burnt. Yes, it is by what they produce that you must class them.

It is not every one who goes on calling me 'Master' that will enter into God's unseen world : they only will enter in who do what pleases my unseen Father. When the day comes, many will say to me : 'Master, Master, surely we called ourselves "Christians"? Surely we preached as "Christians", surely as "Christians" we were kind to those that were ill, surely as "Christians" we did many wonderful things?' Then I shall speak straight out to them and tell them : 'You have had no kind of connection with me : away from me, you who are sinful in what you *do.*' Any one, then, who listens to what I say and also does what I say, may be compared to a sensible man who had built his house on rock : afterwards, when the rain came down and the rivers were flooded and the winds blew and beat against that house, it did not fall, for its foundation was rock : but any one who listens to what I say, and does not also do what I say, may be compared to a foolish man who had built his house on sand : afterwards, when the rain came down and the rivers were flooded and the winds blew and beat against that house, it fell : and its fall was terrible.

*

Let us notice, by way of preface, that the speaker knew his subject thoroughly, and of course had had practical experience in it. It was a part of his very self.

He also spoke in *simple and graphic* language : it is very seldom abstract (see p. 231). Throughout, it is *personal*, and generally speaks of persons as doing or saying something ; notice especially verse 21.

Not only did he know his subject and speak in simple language (which I have tried to represent on p. 213), but he also knew human nature and the *motives* which influence it, and the nature and the motives of his hearers in particular.

His Ideas were of course all that Ideas should be; but it is not of these that we shall speak here. Here we shall speak only of the Expression and Style.

(1) But observe how the one Idea is *emphasised*, because it is so important.

(2) The next thing which strikes us is the Clearness and Simplicity (see above).

(3) Then there is the *Interesting Beginning*. The word "Beware" would itself arouse attention, and the "Sermon on the Mount" starts with the words "Blessed are the poor", which (see p. 258) must have forced people to listen. The *Ending* is *Impressive*.

. (4) In the first verse (15) we also find a *Contrast, or Exclusion*. Instead of saying directly who the really good *are*, he says who they *are not*: they are not those who pretend to be God's representatives. 'Contrast' is also seen in verse 17, where the good tree and the corrupt tree are opposed to one another. Cp. verse 21, and again verse 24 foll., where the house on rock is contrasted with the house on sand.

(5) In these last verses (from 24 to 27) the *Balance and Parallelism* is perfect. Each clause about the house on sand corresponds to a clause about the house on rock.

(6) *Comparisons and Metaphors* abound, and they are those which *the particular hearers* would understand. In fact they were chiefly taken from their daily life or from the surrounding scenery. The sheep and the wolves, the fruit-trees, the grapes and the thorns, the figs and the thistles, the cutting down of trees, the building of the house upon rock or upon sand, the rain, the flood, and the wind—all these were familiar to those who were present. The principle was to start with that

which was *familiar* to them, and in the light of this to explain that which was less familiar to them.

(7) The Comparisons involve a good deal of *Detail*, but notice how the details all help to make a picture. The Writer or Speaker should never avoid detail and concrete instances, so long as they throw light on the important aspects of the subject in hand.

(8) In verse 16 and verse 22, we have the use of the *Question* rather than the Statement: see p. 296.

(9) In verse 17 and verse 18 we have *Repetition*, and so again in verse 20. Either the Idea is repeated in different words, or the very words are repeated.

(10) In verse 19 and in verse 23, and again in verse 27, there is an appeal to a *Motive*, and that Motive is fear. It is one of those features of the speaking of Jesus which are rather apt to be ignored, but undoubtedly Jesus *did* appeal to fear among other Motives. The general principle, however, is that he constantly appealed to some human Motive or other.

(11) In the whole Section we have the principle of *Variety* well illustrated. There is only *one main Idea*, but it is repeated again and again, and *approached from different points of view*.

(12) These are only some of the features of Style. Of the *Rhythm*, the Grammar, and Punctuation, and so on, we cannot speak here because the Greek original is unfamiliar to most readers; but the Authorised Version has a splendid Rhythm and swing throughout the New Testament.

The *advantage* of taking this New Testament instance is not only that it illustrates so many of the excellencies of Expression and Style, but also that it is *familiar to the readers;* in fact most of them know the Authorised or Revised Version of it by heart. Besides this, the Ideas are perfect, and indeed are Ideas which everyone *ought* to know, and Ideas which —very few people take the slightest notice of in daily life. How many persons judge things by what they produce, rather than by the popular opinion and judgment about these things? About one person in a thousand.

And another reason why this passage is so good, as a lesson in Style, is that, however steadily people refuse to carry out in action the Ideas which appear here, yet at any rate they profess the greatest respect for them.

Besides being a passage which illustrates very many points, and which is familiar, and which is worth study-ing for the sake of its Ideas alone, and which is respected by the majority of mankind, there is this further advantage that near this passage, that is to say, in the " Sermon on the Mount " before we come to this Ending, there are many more passages which can be treated in the same way.

Last of all, the Verses here are a good instance because they were spoken to *a popular audience.* Supposing, for the moment, that the " Sermon on the Mount" was spoken all at once, then it most decidedly was the greatest sermon that has ever been preached, though not by any means the longest. Almost from beginning to end it was probably understood even by the most stupid people in the crowd. I do not think that this applies to the Authorised (or even to the Revised) Version, which is not good as a mere rendering of the *sense* of the Greek. How could a 1611 Version be expected to be so? But the original Greek was most extraordinarily simple and easy to 'see through'.

At the same time the Sermon, and especially this Ending, had in it a great deal that would give the more intelligent and educated people food for reflection. It is a piece of Composition which must appeal to absolutely every class of readers and hearers.

CHAPTER XXXIX. ORIGINALITY.

FOR the purposes of this Chapter, I shall treat a thing as no less Original because it has already been found out by someone else : in other words I shall include under the word 'Original' whatever the Writer has worked out for himself, whatever he has made his very own, even if others have thought of it first. I am compelled to include here Originality in Ideas as well as in the Expression of Ideas : the two departments (cp. p. 202) cannot be separated.

In a still wider sense, I might almost include anything which a person understands so thoroughly that he can describe it clearly to anyone else, and give good Comparisons and Contrasts ; about which he can answer questions satisfactorily, and of which he has a definite picture in his mind's eye. This is not Originality, but is very near akin to it.

The first requisite is that a person should *see a thing clearly ;* he must not merely be able to say so many words, but he must have a clear view of the Idea. And this will often mean that he must have thought over the Idea, looking at it from every point of view ; but this does not yet make Originality.

Nor has a person quite become Original when he has made his own inferences, nor even when he has criticised the Idea and formed his judgment of it. There is something needed besides, and Originality seems especially to be *the combining of things in a new way ;* for example, finding a link between two things which before had seemed to be unconnected.

Originality in the process of Essay-Writing or Speaking will come in again and again, if the Essay or Speech be prepared according to my method. In the Collecting of Ideas, in the Selecting of them, in the Underlining, in the Arranging, and in the working out and choosing of Comparisons and Contrasts, Originality will constantly be needed. For instance, the Essay-Writer or Speaker will constantly have to appeal to his own judgment (see pp. 167, 170) and to say what he thinks best.

With regard to the Arranging of Ideas, the whole treatment of the subject may call for Originality. Let me take one example. If we are to consider what effects Geography has had upon English History, we have to choose between three methods of treatment: either we can take the divisions of Geography (see p. 107), and consider the effects of each, or we can consider the History, and see how far it was affected by Geography, or, thirdly, we can combine these two methods; and perhaps this would be the best way: we might begin by pointing out certain features of the Geography (such as the Coast Line, the many Rivers, the Variety of Climate and Scenery, the Gulf Stream, the Coal Mines, and the Metal Mines), and we might estimate the effects of all these features, and then we might consider the History, and see how far it has been due to these and other causes. By this means we should be able to repeat the most important Ideas, from different points of view. We should ensure Variety.

Originality is demanded in nearly every branch of Expression and Style. To find out the clearest way of Expressing something, to find out how to make the Expression interesting and (if necessary) emphatic, to decide how far there should be Variety, in fact to use your common sense everywhere—all this gives ample play for Originality. For you have to perpetually appeal to your own ingenuity and your own judgment, and yet at the same time to remember that you are submitting what you do to the judgment of others also.)

FEW words are commoner, in reference to an Author's Style, than these words Force and Vigour. How often we read, " His Style is Forcible and Vigorous ", or, on the other hand, " His Style is tame and lifeless ". And yet no one has adequately described what Force and Vigour are. A critic can tell you whether the quality is present in a given piece of Writing or in a given Speech, or whether it is absent. But exactly in what the quality consists he does not say :, still less does he give *practical* advice as to how the quality can be acquired. It is a most mysterious element in Style, and as yet we have not come *very* much nearer to a definition of it than we have to a definition of, let us say, life itself.

Nevertheless there are certain features without which Force and Vigour can hardly exist. We cannot say that they actually *are* Force and Vigour, but at any rate they are essential to it: they are a *sine quâ non.* See the footnote to p. 161.

First among these comes personal conviction and *earnestness:* the Author or Speaker must have a *motive,* and must be deeply convinced of the truth of what he is saying. This does not mean that he must speak the truth; for thousands of people have been deeply convinced of the truth of what is in reality absolutely false : it merely means a certain object in view, and a conviction as to the Ideas being right.

Now a man can scarcely be convinced about Ideas unless he has *a clear notion* of what these Ideas are! To take an extreme case, if a man did not understand the meaning of a piece of Hebrew, he could scarcely—apart from Translations, etc.—be *really* in earnest about the Ideas in that Hebrew ; and so (Force and Vigour can hardly be found except where the Author clearly understands the Ideas and (see p. 231) has a picture of them in his mind's eye. Yet some of the most Vigorous Authors have been very far from clear in the way they have Expressed their Ideas.) A few instances will be sufficient. Thucydides, Tacitus, Carlyle, and Browning would be four Authors, out of many, whose Force and Vigour are indisputable, but whose Expression is apt to be very obscure.

(As a rule, however, Vigour is found where the *words* are Clear, Simple, Dignified, and Striking.)

The Concrete *Instance* is often more 'vigorous' than the General Statement : even *details and small touches* (see p. 216) may help to give vigour.   Thus contrast—

> 'Sailors like their special luxuries'

with

> 'Jack loves his baccy and his grog'.

Again, how much more forcible than

> 'a short moment'

is the pictorial touch,

> 'the twinkling of an eye'.

One general feature besides this is that there should be *no waste of words :* Brevity is not always the same as Vigour, but the two generally go hand in hand. In fact, Vigorous Style may often omit words which seem almost to be necessary, so that, if one put in these words, the Vigour would be almost gone.

Suggestiveness is an instance of this. Professor Barrett Wendell, in his excellent Book on English Composition, hints that Force is suggestive : that it implies rather than expresses. You feel that there is something kept in reserve. The Expression is striking, and leaves the reader or hearer to work out something for himself. The following quotation seemed to me to be an instance of Suggestiveness : I do not know how far it will be considered Forcible.

" Just before going to bed, I do not like to eat lobster salad or to read about prisoners in Siberia."

Force and Vigour nearly always attract the attention somehow or other, and striking *Comparisons* (including Metaphors), which appeal to the readers or hearers, will often of themselves give Force. One cannot help feeling that a little child's remark about the effects of influenza, namely, that it made her legs 'giddy', was very Forcible : it must appeal to what every individual will understand and feel for himself.

And Vigour will differ according to the class of Composition, as well as according to the readers or hearers, and according to the Aims of the Writer or Speaker. Here, as elsewhere, there is a certain *Appropriateness.* There are certain Sentences which would be Vigorous wherever we found them ; thére are others which are only Vigorous *in certain Contexts ;* so that there are occasions when Humour may be Vigorous, and when nothing else would have so much Force as an appeal to the sense of the ridiculous. Even Bathos itself (see p. 260) may be the most Forcible form of Expression under certain conditions, e.g. for purposes of ridicule.

A Sentence or a piece of Writing cannot be properly Forcible if all the rest of the Sentences and Paragraphs are equally Forcible; that is to say, when Vigour and Force are not necessary (for instance, in a quiet description), there they should not be used; they should be reserved for passages *where they are really needed*, or else they will lose their effect, when we come to these passages. As we shall see in the case of Emphasis, which is closely related to Vigour, a (passage is much more emphatic if whatever surrounds it is unemphatic) (see p. 278). A light shows far more clearly when it is surrounded by darkness, and a person would never appear so truly Vigorous among those who were no less Vigorous than himself, as among those who were dying in a hospital or those who were dead on a battle-field; here as elsewhere there must be Contrast.

Another element is the *Rhythm*, which will of course depend largely upon *the length and the order of Words*. For the order of Words and the Rhythm, as helping to give Force and Vigour, the New Testament is far the best study. The reader should take some of the most Forcible Sentences, and change the Words, and the order of Words, and the Rhythm. If he does this, he will often find that the Force and Vigour almost completely disappear.

There is no space here to follow out this very important aspect of Vigour, but I hope to follow it out in subsequent years; at present I can only refer to the Chapters on the Sentence and on Rhythm.

Q

As I said above, Force and Vigour are closely related to Emphasis (for which see p. 268). A Sentence which is Forcible and Vigorous can scarcely fail to be Emphatic also. But the converse is not necessarily true, and this is why I have treated Emphasis separately. For Emphasis may be obtained by means of sheer Repetition, and Repetition may be quite as different from Force and Vigour as five tame taps with a hammer are different from a single energetic tap. Nevertheless, the ultimate effects may be very similar; the stone may be hollowed in much the same way by the frequent dropping of water and by the sudden blow of the steel.

It is almost needless to add that Force and Vigour are often felt merely because the *Emotions* are appealed to; and it would not be waste of time to work out a list of those Emotions which are (*a*) more or less common to all humanity (e.g. love, indignation and anger), (*b*) more or less common to certain Classes or Groups (e.g., in women, pity, and the love of personalities; in Englishmen, pluck and obstinacy). For some words will be Forcible for all mankind, others more especially so for a certain Group, for example for those of a certain Nation or for those of a certain age. The Emotion which is to be excited must be appropriate to the subject, to the Aim of the Writer or Speaker, and to the reader or hearer as well.

CHAPTER XLI. CLEARNESS, AND SIMPLICITY.

'*Clearness*' is hard to separate from '*Simplicity*', as Bain should have realised: see p. 177. But the following may be one difference. We saw (on p. 226) that we could scarcely have Force and Vigour without Emphasis, but that we *could* have Emphasis without Force and Vigour (e.g. by mere Repetition of the words). So, here, we can scarcely have true Simplicity without Clearness, but we can have Clearness without Simplicity. A clear Sentence may be very long and very florid and ornamental: Juvenal is often clear without being simple. Possibly the word *Precision* includes the two ideas.

The words which one writes should be something more than Clear: they should be actually *transparent*. There *are* occasions when one wishes to express a thing somewhat obscurely (as Carlyle did), but they are exceptional. As a rule the words should be so clear that not only do they have *only one meaning*, one single meaning, but that they also show this meaning immediately; the reader or hearer should never have to pause and ask himself 'What does this mean?' or 'Which Idea does this mean?' The reader of a certain orator's Speeches frequently has to ask himself one of these two questions, especially the second. Not unfrequently he asks himself yet a third question, 'Does this mean anything at all?' This is perhaps the severest criticism of a Writer or Speaker which a reader or hearer can ever offer.

The difficulty of being clear is prodigious. What a Writer writes, and what a Speaker speaks, may may be perfectly clear *to himself*, but it does not in the least follow that it will be clear or even intelligible to the audience. I do not doubt for a moment that the following passage was clear to Herbert Spencer when he wrote it, but I very much doubt if the ordinary reader would understand it, at any rate in less than three readings. It is from page 58 of his " Sociology ". N.B. Herbert Spencer's punctuation is seldom careful.

"The reader doubtless anticipates the analogy. What Bio-
"graphy is to Anthropology, History is to Sociology—History,
" I mean, as commonly conceived. The kind of relation which the
" sayings and doings that make up the ordinary account of a man's
"life, bear to an account of his bodily and mental evolution,
"structural and functional, is like the kind of relation borne
" by that narrative of a nation's actions and fortunes its historian
"gives us, to a description of its institutions, regulative and
"operative, and the ways in which their structures and functions
" gradually established themselves."

· The more learned a writer is, the more he has read and studied and *confined himself to*, his special subject, the less he is able to write on it with transparency) that is to say as a general rule. I find that a certain Scientist's earlier works were far clearer than his later works, which are so full of abstruse Technical Terms that the ordinary reader cannot grasp the sense at all.

Another Quotation will illustrate the obscurity of writing which is full of Technical Terms. These Technical Terms were quite clear to the writer: in fact, he probably could not have expressed his Ideas otherwise, at least without very great effort. But for the general reader the Ideas are shrouded in obscurity.

"In a similar way, in America, the shock of political thought "brought about in the interior of each of the thirteen colonies, "by the delegation of important prerogatives to a new-fashioned "central government, rendered the criticism of that Government, "of its functions, and of its rights and duties, as natural as, "in other times and circumstances, was the unquestioned sub-"mission to the claims of any Government believed to be duly "authorised.

"The origin of a disposition to reject the pretensions of "Government to occupy any field of action it chooses, without "accountability to any other standard than the apparent demands "of the moment, must be sought chiefly in the first of these "causes."

The chief reason why these writers fail to be clear is that they have seldom, if ever, practised (Clearness as a special Exercise.) One of the best Exercises is the turning of a piece of English into Latin or Greek Prose, where Clearness is insisted on : for *the Latin or Greek must have one transparent meaning, and only one.* Cases are well known of clergymen and public Speakers who, in order to ensure Clearness, have first written their thoughts in Latin, and then have translated them into English.

A second cause of Obscurity, in addition to the excessive 'learning' and technicality of the Writer or Speaker, would be that he has not his Ideas definitely before him in his mind's eye : he has not pictured to himself the 'action' of which he is writing. These *mental pictures* are indispensable.) How far they differ from the Abstract phrases with which Books and Reviews are crowded can be judged from the following two passages, put side by side.

"The quantitative value "of animated life, as a geo-"logical agency, seems to " be inversely as the volume "of the individual organism" (Marsh, "The Earth as Modified by Human Action", p. 78).

"It seems to be true that, the smaller the animals are in bulk, the more effect they have on the 'Geology' of a country, because of their greater numbers."

Another cause is *excessive Brevity ;* it is partly this which makes Tacitus so hard to understand. Another great error is the wrong *Order of the Words ;* instances are given on p. 325. The Arrangement of Words in Sentences is very little studied in Schools. Professor Meiklejohn gives excellent instances of mistakes of this kind. Two instances may be sufficient here : I found them in a Novel.

" He returned home with the ring which had caused him such trouble in his waistcoat pocket."

Had the order of words been changed, or had the Author said

"When he returned home, he had in his waistcoat pocket the ring which had caused him such trouble,"

his meaning would have been perfectly clear.

The second is " She announced her engagement to Mr. Brown."

It must be borne in mind that very often the Writer or Speaker himself will be unable to see that what he has written is anything else but perfect. Perhaps he himself knows what he means, but he cannot put himself in the position of anyone else who does not yet know this.)

Another common cause of obscurity is that *the wrong Word* has been chosen. This is too obvious to need illustration here.

As helps towards Clearness, the following suggestions may be found of use.

(First of all, *the reader or hearer has to be considered, rather than the Writer or Speaker.* The latter should say to himself, " I want the average reader or hearer, or one who is below the average, to see this Idea as clearly as *I* see it." Now, in order to attain this Clearness, the Writer or Speaker must himself see the Idea with unusual plainness and definiteness : he must have a very definite picture in his mind's eye. Strange as it may sound, the habit of drawing pictures will do much towards making the Expression of Ideas *unmistakable.* This is not merely an allusion to pictures of people, but also to Diagrams and Plans of every kind.)

But a still better means is to turn whole passages of abstract writers (like Herbert Spencer) into simple English, which should as a rule answer such questions as " *Who does what?* " Sometimes other questions must be answered, such as "When? Why? How? etc." In other words, as a rule, persons should be imagined as acting or speaking or thinking, etc. ; this is one of the secrets of good Latin and Greek Prose Compositions : they are fond of describing *someone as doing something.*

This does not mean that all Writing or Speaking should describe someone as doing something, for this need not be the ultimate and actual form of Expression ; but *until* you have a clear picture in your eye, you cannot be quite sure that the Expression or Style will be clear. When once you have imagined a picture of 'someone doing something', then your description of that idea is almost bound to be Clear.

So important is this Clearness, that I will suggest to the reader to try to turn the following passage into such English as shall describe someone as doing something.

It is from Gibbon's "Decline and Fall of the Roman Empire" (p. 352 of Vol. I., Bury's Edition).

"The first considerable action of his reign seemed to evince his sincerity as well as his moderation. After the example of Marcus, he gave himself a colleague in the person of Maximian, on whom he bestowed at first the title of Cæsar, and afterwards that of Augustus. But the motives of his conduct, as well as the object of his choice, were of a very different nature from those of his admired predecessor. By investing a luxurious youth with the honours of the purple, Marcus had discharged a debt of private gratitude, at the expense, indeed, of the happiness of the state. By associating a friend and a fellow-soldier to the labours of government, Diocletian, in the time of public danger, provided for the defence both of the East and of the West. Maximian was born a peasant, and, like Aurelian, in the territory of Sirmium. Ignorant of letters, careless of laws, the rusticity of his appearance and manners still betrayed in the most elevated fortune the meanness of his extraction. War was the only art he professed. In a long course of service he had distinguished himself on every frontier of the empire; and, though his military talents were formed to obey rather than to command, though, perhaps, he had never attained the skill of a consummate general, he was capable, by his valour, constancy, and experience, of executing the most arduous undertakings. Nor were the vices of Maximian less useful to his benefactor. Insensible to pity, and fearless of consequences, he was the ready instrument of every act of cruelty which the policy of that artful prince might at once suggest and disclaim."

It may be as well to take this piece and to write a short *abstract* of it, first putting down the *Ideas* as briefly as possible, and in as business-like a form as

possible. After this has been done, the Paraphrasing
may run somewhat as follows :—

By that which he first did, when he had become Emperor, he
showed himself not only able to control himself but also really
desirous of helping his country. For, after the example of Marcus,
he chose for himself as his colleague Maximian . . . but he and
Marcus chose very different men, for very different reasons.
Marcus, in order that he might pay back a debt to a private
individual, chose a luxurious youth as a sharer in the glory
of reigning. Diocletian, in order that he might protect both the
Eastern and Western frontiers of the Empire, chose a fellow-
soldier as a sharer in the labours of governing. Maximian was
of rustic birth and, like Aurelian himself, born in the Sirmian
territory. Ignorant of letters, careless of laws, by his rustic
appearance and behaviour he showed of what birth he was, even
when he had reached the highest position in the State. In war
alone he excelled: for through many campaigns on all the frontiers
of the Empire he had shown himself an excellent soldier ; and
though as a soldier he was more suited for obeying than for com-
manding, and though he never shone as a very great general, yet
by his valour, constancy, and experience, he was able to do the
most difficult things.

Nor did he benefit Diocletian by his vices less than by these
virtues. Being without pity, and without care for that which
would result from whatever he did, he readily carried out every
cruel act which Diocletian, a man of great cunning, first of all had
ordered to be done and then, when it had been done, repudiated.

Let the reader compare his paraphrase with this, and
let him try to find whether his paraphrase or the above
is nearer to the real meaning of the 'Gibbon'.

This piece is often set for Latin Prose, and three-
quarters of its difficulty lies in the fact that it is very
obscure: when once the real meaning has been mastered,
and the personal form of 'someone doing something'
has been found, then the greater part of the work is
over.

There have been those who have spent hours and hours in making sure that their Style was Clear: they would not let their Composition 'pass' until they were quite satisfied that it would be thoroughly understood by the reader or hearer, and *that it would mean to the reader exactly what it meant to them themselves.* One writer used to read out much of his work to his servant; for he rightly supposed that, if his servant understood what he wrote, then people of greater intelligence and higher education would also be certain to understand it.

Another great aid towards Clearness, besides this *inviting of the candid opinion of as many others as possible,* is to take one's Composition and look at it again *after an interval,* and then to criticise it (see p. 335) as if it were the work of one's deadliest enemy.

Yet another help would be to take good Writers, and from them to select the Clearest passages, and then to *Analyse* these passages (see p. 213), and thus to find out exactly what it is that makes them clear.

A few other hints are suggested here.

If your passage should still seem imperfect, if you should have the slightest shadow of doubt about its Clearness, then it may be safer either to alter it, or *to express the Idea in a second way, to repeat it,* putting it perhaps, the second time, in the abstract form as opposed to the first time in the personal form (of ' someone doing something '), or using some *Comparison* or Metaphor which might make the meaning absolutely unmistakable, or some *Contrast* which might bring out just exactly the shade of sense which you wish to convey (see p. 291); it might be as well to express what it is that you do *not* mean. Perhaps after all this may be one of the best Exercises.

As another help (which, however, is a dangerous help), I should suggest *Exaggeration;* it is this which makes *Proverbs* so Clear; three-quarters or nine-tenths of the Proverbs which we hear are Clear because (P. 152) they are gross Exaggerations; and those who are wont to address the uneducated, very frequently sacrifice truth and accuracy for the sake of Clearness: they fear that, unless they exaggerate, they will not be understood.

But, when your general statement is not quite Clear, a safer method is to think of a single *Instance* of the general principle: that is to say, to start with the Instance, and from that to pass on to the general statement; this will be a wonderful help.

To what I have said above, certain Objections may be made. It may be said that the abstract expression is often necessary, and also has the advantage of short-ness, whereas the personal expression (of 'someone doing something') is apt to fix the attention on personal details which are unimportant. In answer to this, I should say that the Concrete and personal *must come first* in the mind; afterwards, if it be thought advisable, the abstract and general Expression may be preferred, or may be given *as well as* the personal expression; but, until the personal form has been found out, few Writers or Speakers can be certain that their meaning will be clear to the *ordinary* reader or hearer.

Secondly, it may be said that the Concrete and personal expression is often *bald;* but no reader of the New Testament could assert that this is necessarily the case, although, almost throughout, the language is personal, and describes 'someone as doing something'. Much will depend on the Order of words, on the Number of words, and on the Rhythm. Much more

will depend on this than on the actual 'Concrete-
ness'; and anyhow baldness is generally better than
Obscurity.

As to the *advantages* of Clearness I need say very
little.

To be certain that you are not misleading your
readers or hearers is in itself a very important consideration. It is true that you may be expressing an
Idea in a way which will not please the most educated
Public, but at any rate you are on the safe side, because
you are appealing to a much *larger Public*, and, provided
that (you practise Clearness as a special Exercise, there
is no reason why your Composition should not appeal
to the educated quite as much as to the uneducated.
At first, of course, it will not do so: the striving after
Clearness will have its drawback.

Those advisers who say to the beginner, "If you wish
to be Clear, be perfectly *natural*", are absolutely wrong:
for imagine anyone having given that advice even to the
learned genius Herbert Spencer (p. 228). He would probably say, "Throughout my works I have been perfectly
natural". I imagine that he wrote down just what it was
natural for him to write down: there seems to be no
conscious effort after Clearness! But, in his case, the
result was something very far from Clearness: it was
often a baffling obscurity. (The fallacy that what is
'natural' to everyone must therefore also be best for
everyone should have been exploded by the history
of past ages.)

Another advantage of Clearness is that it is undoubtedly a very great help, not only in *persuading*
others, but also in *impressing* things on one's own
mind. It is a commonplace that (a person remembers

things better when he has understood them, and that
he can hardly understand them properly unless they
have been clearly expressed.) Therefore Clearness will
help the *memory*.

Lastly, it will encourage what every one needs,
namely *self-criticism*. People need to criticise their
own work as well as the work of others, and every
attempt to make one's Writings or Speeches clear will
be an Exercise in self-criticism and self-correction.
The moral effect will therefore be very considerable.

CHAPTER XLII. **BREVITY AND ECONOMY.**

ECONOMY in Essay-Writing and Speaking is well worthy of consideration: not only must we try to economise space, but we must also try to economise time, and energy.

We must economise space, not by Writing as much as possible on a single page, for this is utterly False Economy, but by cutting off as much as possible, whether we have to cut off unnecessary or inappropriate Ideas, or unnecessary Sentences or Words.

Time is not truly saved by one who writes an Essay or makes a Speech immediately he knows what the subject is, for that again is False Economy of time; he will save time more truly by practising each part of Essay-Writing or Speaking correctly by itself, so that the saving may be not in the immediate and transitory present but in the longer future.

Energy again is not truly saved when the work is done slackly or in a slipshod way or in an unscientific way: for that again is False Economy. Strange as it may seem, we can best save energy in the end by using the greatest amount of it in due season; only we must concentrate it upon the right things, and we must do these things in the right way.

In fact, we may use up a great deal of space and a great deal of paper, we may use up a great deal of time, and we may use up a great deal of energy, in preparing an Essay or Speech according to my method, and in practising each part of my method by itself. And yet in the end there may be a wonderful Economy. The Essay which we shall write or the Speech that we shall make, in a year's time after such practice, will be far better in every way, and, besides this, it will be done with less expenditure of paper, of time, and of Energy; so that we are as it were spending a few pounds to-day that we may save many hundreds of pounds a few years later· In the struggle between Rome and Carthage, Carthage refused to invest a comparatively small sum of money in ships of war : the result was that a few years later she was defeated and had to pay thousands of talents. History presents many such instances of False Economy.

The Law of Economy applies to the whole of the Essay, and to its different parts, the Paragraphs, the Sentences, the Clauses, and the Words. But one point has to be emphasised and never to be forgotten. *For the sake of Brevity we must never sacrifice Clearness, Interest, Proportion of Emphasis, or Variety.* These are four Laws that may contend against the Law of Brevity.

The Law of *Proportion* we have already noticed : according to it, the more important the Idea is, the longer the Paragraph should be, that is to say as a rough-and-ready rule. If we have an Idea which is important, and express it very briefly instead of in a longer Paragraph, then we may be securing Brevity but sacrificing the proper Emphasis : the important Idea will not have its proper prominence and bulk. But, on the other hand, occasionally a very short

Paragraph may be a sign of Emphasis (see p. 312): this, however, is the exception.

It is a safe general rule that *the Essay or Speech should be short*, that most of its Paragraphs should be *short*, that most of its Sentences should be short; and even the Words should as a rule be short. Except in the case of the last three, where, e g., Variety and Emphasis are to be aimed at, it is especially important to notice this need for Brevity *to-day:* for the tendency is for everything to grow shorter and shorter, at any rate in our country and in America. It cannot be regarded as a healthy sign that the great mass of people object to long Books, long Articles, long Chapters, long Speeches, long Paragraphs, long Sentences, and long Words. Nevertheless it is a sign of the times, at least in our country, and as such it must be taken into account; for, as we have seen, the Law of Appropriateness tells us to make our Essay, etc., Appropriate not only to our Aim but also to our readers or hearers.

As a help towards Brevity and Economy, you might, after you have finished the Essay, etc., *analyse* it into Headings, re-arrange these Headings, and *re-write* the Essay, etc., again; count the number of words in the old Essay and in the new. Of course this should be after an interval, and it is a process that can be applied with equal effect, or perhaps with even better effect and certainly with more pleasure, to the work of someone else: take some Writer who is particularly verbose, and treat some of his Writings thus.

While recently editing a German work (especially for the athletic public) I was surprised at the number of words to which the ponderous and inflated Sentences of the original had to be reduced before they could be clear : the German work was (a vast mass of Abstract and impersonal statements.) After *turning the Abstract into the Concrete and Personal* (see p. 233), I found that the language became not only clearer but also far shorter.

But of all the helps few can be compared with *the careful preparation of the Headings and Sub-Headings* themselves. You can prove this in the following way. Do any Essay on any subject just exactly as most people do it, that is to say, straight away : (begin Writing the moment you get the subject, and the moment you have finished Writing consider the Essay as done.) Then take this same Essay and work it out by Headings and Sub-Headings, using the General Lists as far as possible ; Collect, Select, Underline, and Arrange these Headings and Sub-Headings, clearly understanding each of them (for instance, by forming pictures in the mind, see p. 231); then Express them in simple language.

Now compare your former Essay with your present Essay. It is quite possible that you will find your present Essay is no longer than the first, and yet contains twice or three times as many Ideas. It will probably be twice as well Arranged, and much better Expressed.

Above all, do not think that the number of words is of any great importance. I remember one pupil telling me that he was afraid that he would fail in his Essay-Paper in an Exam., because he did not feel that he could write more than fifteen pages on *any* subject. I told him that if he did (a good Essay of five pages it would be much better than a bad Essay of twenty)

R

pages, and would certainly please the Examiner far more ; but he did not seem to believe me. After the Examination he told me that he had only done thirteen pages : there were probably at least eight pages too many.

Yet there is a certain importance attaching to the number of words, especially in Articles for Reviews and Magazines. It has often seemed to me a very iniquitous thing that the Editor of a Magazine or Review should fix a definite number of words for an Article (for instance, three thousand) quite apart from what the subject is and how important or unimportant it is. But still it is customary, and therefore to be taken into consideration.

Among other helps to Brevity and Economy, notice such Rhetorical Devices as

'honest rags' ;
'a cheap market'.   And see p. 299 foll.

These are often helps to Vigour and Emphasis as well.

CHAPTER XLIII. APPROPRIATENESS, OR ADAPTATION; AND UNITY.

THE Composition must be Adapted to the readers or hearers, and to the subject, and even to the different parts of the same subject; for instance, there will not be the same Style for graphic description, for quiet proof, and for indignant refutation. Professor Barrett Wendell's remarks on the subject are admirable.

Adaptation in its widest sense would mean that one must Select one's Ideas according to the readers or hearers, and according to one's Aims. Thus, if one is Writing or Speaking to a popular audience, then there would be very few Ideas.

In the same way, the Arrangement of Ideas must be carefully Adapted to the readers or hearers, to the Aim, and to the Subject. In a popular subject, the Arrangement might as a rule be that which is given on pp. 178, 216, which might be absolutely out of place if one were addressing a number of Specialists.

In this Chapter, however, I only wish to speak of the Adapting of the Expression and the Style, quite apart from the Adapting of the Ideas.

A friend of mine once pointed out a truth very clearly, in a railway carriage. Pointing to the dust on the window-ledge and floor, he said "Dirt is very bad in here, but out there in the farms it is just what is wanted". So, although we might condemn dirt for general occasions, still we must realise there are occasions when it is in place. There are occasions when an Idea or a Style, which is excluded from most Compositions, e.g. because it is too learned or too 'special', must be adopted : it is appropriate just here, under just these conditions.

It is a fallacy, then, to suppose that the ordinary 'Laws' in Composition are Universal Laws.

One might think at first that it was a Universal Law that all Writing or Speaking should be so *clear* as to be transparent. And yet, as we have seen, no reader of Carlyle can doubt that a great deal of his Force would be gone if one made his Writings transparent. If one took some of Carlyle's most typical works and paraphrased them in simple English, the effect would not be a quarter as good as it is.

Once again, one might think that *Economy* was a Universal Law : that it was right always to cut out every word that *could* be cut out. Treatises on Essay-Writing or Speaking usually emphasise this point ; and as a general rule the advice is good. But there are occasions when Repetition is needed, and when the number of extra words really adds to the effect, which effect could not well be produced without them.

And once again, Professor Freeman was never tired of telling people to use *Anglo-Saxon words*. He drags in this piece of advice into all his Books, in season and out of season. And other Authorities also advise people to use short Sentences. And yet undoubtedly there are subjects or parts of subjects where Anglo-Saxon words are not so good as the (often longer) Latin words (see p. 305), and where short Sentences (see p. 319) are not so good as long Periods.

I will give two more instances to show how Laws, which seem to be Universal, are as a matter of fact subject to the higher Law, the Law of Appropriateness or Adaptation.

A smooth *Rhythm* is recommended, and for ordinary purposes it is best. But for the description of a piece of rugged scenery it might be quite out of place.

Many teachers say that slang and vulgar expressions are always out of place in any and every sort of Composition. But readers of Sir Walter Scott *must* feel that he has violated the Law of Appropriateness when he makes the common gardener or workman or child speak in beautiful and cultivated and high-flown language, showing no distinction between this Style and the Style of the most learned Professors. It is a great blot on his work.

The Law of Appropriateness and Adaptation will therefore be one of the most widely applicable Laws in all Composition. And let me repeat that it means to adapt oneself, one's Ideas, and one's Style, to the subject, or part of a subject, and to the reader or hearer, according to what one's Aims may be.

Let us therefore consider the above remarks more carefully.

The Law of Adaptation will override *the Law of Clearness*, when the expression which is not Clear will nevertheless be more Forcible and striking, and will make people think because it attracts their attention and interests them and (see p. 258) makes them rebel: a perfectly Clear statement will not always do this.

The Law of Adaptation will, as we have seen, override *the Law of Brevity and Economy*, when we wish to repeat an Idea, or to introduce Comparisons or

Contrasts, and perhaps to produce Balance and Rhythm. Sometimes, in fact, the Law of Clearness or the Law of Emphasis may be far more important than the Law of Brevity or Economy.   As in feeding, so in Writing and Speaking, it is a mistake to condense always. Occasionally there must be something which does not actually nourish, but gives the Food what we may call material, bulk, or size.

The rule that we should prefer *Anglo-Saxon words* is an excellent one ; only, in Philosophical and Scientific Writings and Speeches addressed to none but Specialists, the Latin words may be not merely a saving of time and trouble, but they may also express the meaning far more clearly and accurately.

The rule of *Short Sentences* may be broken by the Law of Variety, the Law of Balance, and the particular kind of Style which is fitted for the purpose.   If the purpose be to reason quite calmly, or give a quiet narrative or description, then a long Sentence or a Period may be found more Appropriate.

The important Laws, then, are only general Laws for ordinary purposes, for we have seen that there are occasions when slang, or harsh Metres, are strictly Appropriate, and therefore indispensable.

When we ask what *is* Appropriate, we find it easier (as is so often the case) to explain by means of a Contrast (see p. 291).   In an American Novel we find the words " Hast discovered yon traitor?"   "Yes", said he. "Then", quoth his comrade, "hurry up".   Here the Inappropriateness of the "hurry up", or, rather, the Inappropriateness of any word like "hast" or "yon", is very obvious.   I should say that the Inappropriateness was not in the "hurry up" but in the "hast" and the "yon", which are out of place in a Detective-story of modern times. The opposite to Appropriateness will therefore sometimes be Bathos. See p. 260.

N.B.—This Ending ("See p. 260") is probably itself inappropriate, as an Ending to a Paragraph!

Rhetorical Devices, such as Questions, are very well when they are in their proper place, but they certainly have their proper place and are to be avoided elsewhere. Some American Novelists, again, are very fond of introducing them on every possible occasion, using them so often (even in simple quiet descriptions) that, when they come to a place where they need something 'Rhetorical', they find they have exhausted all their devices already. Like the man who got into the habit of swearing without provocation, when the provocation actually comes they have no further weapon to employ.

The general principle then will be, not to use these various devices unless they are really wanted, really Appropriate. It will take a long while to learn where they are, or are not, really Appropriate.

The word 'Adaptation' will apply to the length or shortness of Paragraphs. These should vary in size partly according to the importance of the subject, partly according to the Law of Balance, and partly according to the Law of Variety; but, on the whole, the shorter are clearer and pleasanter than the longer Paragraphs. And the probability is that Paragraphs will become shorter and shorter: there has certainly been a tendency in this direction for some time past. A very good piece of advice, however, is *to summarise a long Paragraph by a short Sentence at the end of it;* by this means the advantages of a long Paragraph (which are considerable) need not be sacrificed. For it is a very great mistake to suppose that short Paragraphs should be used throughout Writing or Speaking : a long Paragraph is one of the best means of calling attention to the importance of an Idea.   Though, once again, Writing and Speaking, and different classes of Writing and Speaking, have different Laws.

The length of *Sentences* also must vary, but here also the shorter are safer than the longer Sentences, especially when they have to be Spoken and then heard, rather than Written and then read.   The shorter Sentences are of course better for a quick narrative, e.g. telling of rapid action, and for passionate reasoning, but the longer Sentences are almost demanded by certain slower and quieter descriptions, and by calm arguments : in fact, if there were not long Sentences, the short Sentences would cease to have their full effect; that is to say, you could no longer denote exciting actions by means of short Sentences if you were constantly using the same short Sentences for a quiet description of scenery.

As to the *Vocabulary*, that also should be carefully Adapted.   There has been a tendency, in the Novels and Stories of late years, to Adapt the Vocabulary to the character, that is to say, not to make all the characters speak in exactly the same Style, generally the best Style that the Author can write.   Poetic Vocabularies may be right for certain kinds of description, and for pathetic passages.   A simple Vocabulary, especially of Anglo-Saxon words, would be best for ordinary Narratives, and for *every* branch of literature if the readers or hearers (or any of them) are uneducated.   If Technical language *must* be used, it should nearly always be preceded by untechnical language, that is to say, the explanation and meaning should come first, and the Technical word may then come afterwards. But, for a learned audience, Technical language and ponderous Words are often the very best. It is quite possible that in a single piece of Composition several different kinds of Vocabularies will have to be used, and indeed, for the sake of Repetition, Emphasis, and Clearness, simple language and Technical language are often to be combined and used side by side.

On page 284 we note that *Comparisons* must be very carefully Adapted to the readers or hearers and their surroundings : the choice of Comparisons will also depend a good deal on how hard the subject is for the readers or hearers to understand, and how important the point is. A Comparison or Metaphor may be excellent in itself, but, when introduced where the Idea would be quite clear without it, and where the Idea is not important, will be a violation of the Law of Appropriateness. There are occasions, however (e.g. see p. 215), where two Comparisons (or even three) will be Appropriate.

Almost exactly the same may be noted of Contrasts.

With regard to *Rhythm* we have already said a good deal. We have seen how a dignified piece of Composition will have long Sentences and long Words, whereas a rapid and passionate piece will have shorter Sentences and shorter Words. In a quiet and ordinary piece, the Sentences and Words may be of average length.

In conclusion, it will be seen that the Law of Adaptation or Appropriateness must run through the whole world of Composition, and that it is a Law that needs very careful attention and study : it forces the Writer to think not only of his subject, from very many points of view, but also of his aims and objects, and of his readers or hearers and their conditions of 'mind, body, and estate'.] It is so general a Law that a great deal which one says about it is bound to be vague. If one says to a cricketer, 'Adapt your batting to the bowler, to the ground, to the state of the game, etc.', or 'Adapt your bowling to the batsman, etc.,' the advice is none the less sound because it is general.

In a small Book like this, I cannot possibly exhaust all the ways in which the Law must be applied. In the above pages I have only pointed out one or two of the applications.

For a good discussion of *Unity*, I may refer the reader to Barrett Wendell's " English Composition ". Besides what I have just said about Adaptation, one or two remarks may be added about Unity.

A compact *Period* may give a good impression of Unity, by gathering together, between its beginning and its end, a number of subordinate sentences or thoughts : the mere sight and sound of the Period can help to give compactness and to weld the whole together.

If, however, a number of Independent Sentences or Clauses are used, then how is Unity to be kept? How can we weld? And the same problem occurs if we have had to digress. A single Sentence at the end of the Paragraph, gathering up the thoughts in a *Résumée* (p. 247)—this may be one of the best solutions.

CHAPTER XLIV. VARIETY.

IF the passage from the New Testament, on p. 212, be very carefully studied, it will be found an admirable instance of Variety. We noticed in it one single Idea expressed in many ways and by many means: we noticed in it Repetition for the sake of Clearness and Emphasis; we noticed Comparisons, Contrasts, and Details; we might have noticed a certain approach to Humour; we noticed also Balance and Rhythm. It has a changing Rhythm, which may not be so remarkable in the Greek as in the English. We noticed also the Question, and many other features as well; and all these in spite of the fact that there was only one Idea, namely, that the really good are those who are good in their inmost selves and at their foundations.

There is Variety also in the length of the Words and Sentences, and, if we study the Sermon on the Mount as a whole, we shall find Variety in the length of the Paragraphs.

In this instance we found the great Variety used for one purpose in particular, namely, for Emphasis; but it will be seen that the Variety serves two other purposes as well: it makes the Idea Clear to the audience, and also Interesting and Suggestive.

The Law of Variety is, like most Laws, subject to the Law of Appropriateness or Adaptation: to take any *unimportant* Idea and to repeat it in all the above ways, by mere Repetition, by changing the Construction, by different Comparisons and Contrasts, and by Questions, would be an instance of Variety which would be wrong, because it would not be Appropriate. Somewhat similarly we see that certain pictures make a great mistake in giving the details of a thing which should by rights be represented very vaguely, so as not to attract the attention at all. And this too holds good even though the Variety in this case may be quite Interesting to the audience: that is to say, it is not enough excuse for altering and changing to say that you are interesting your audience; it is not only the audience that is to be considered but also the relative importance of the Ideas themselves.

Especially deserving of study is *Grammatical Variety.* It is a good Exercise to express certain Ideas in as many ways as possible. To every reader of Grammar, such terms as Sentence, Voice, Mood, Tense, Person, and Number, are familiar; but they probably have for him very little meaning or use. We know more or less what these terms mean, but we cannot employ our knowledge. Now if the matter be carefully studied, and if we express a thing in many different ways, then we shall find that all these words are valuable.

Let us take an instance first. A *Sentence* may be a Statement or a Denial, or a Question (and there are many kinds of Questions), or an Exhortation or Wish, or, lastly, an Exclamation. All these are Varieties of the Sentence, and there are certain Ideas which can be expressed in at least five different ways, namely, as a Statement or a Denial, a Question, an Exhortation, and an Exclamation. I suggest one example here.

1. You ought to go ; it is your duty to go ;

2. You ought not to stop ;

3. Why do you stop? Why do you not go? Why have you not gone? Ought you not to go?

4. Go; I wish you would go; I pray that you may go ;

5. How foolish (etc.) of you to stop!

This has already included certain changes of Mood and Tense, but still more Variety can be introduced: the *Moods* can be varied, and yet the Idea can remain practically the same.

And so also of the *Tenses:* a general truth can be expressed in three different ways. 'Ice is slippery', would be a general statement. 'Ice always has been slippery', would be a 'Perfect'. 'Ice (always) will be slippery', is Future. It is noticeable that the strictly Present Tense, i.e. where you put in the word 'now', or say 'Ice is being slippery', does not give this general sense.

Varieties of *Voice* are worth practising 'for certain purposes: it does not make much difference whether we say 'It has been done by him', or 'He has done it'; for Passives can generally be turned into Actives, except e g. the housemaid's 'It has been broken'! Practice in this Variety of Voice is useful, because one often wishes to avoid changing the Subject of the Sentence if one can help it.

Changes in *Person and Number* are not always possible, except in general statements, and, besides this, it is a pity to change the Subject of the Sentence unnecessarily, as in 'Jack had come home, but when his father had died [better—when he had lost his father] he went away again'.

For an example of an unnecessary change of Words and Construction, I may refer to the Instance on page 325. It will be seen there that the word 'requisite', which is used in the first part, is changed to 'necessary' in the second part; the Number, which is Singular in the word 'the man', is unnecessarily changed to Plural in the word 'boys'; all such changes are to be avoided. They were dear to Gibbon, and they helped to make his Style so exasperating to many of his readers.

A particular branch of such unnecessary Variety is where an Author calls a person first by his proper name, for instance, Tiberius, then by some other term such as 'the luxurious despot', then by another term such as 'the foreshadower of Nero', then by yet another, such as 'the gloomy and discontented monarch'. The general rule would be not to use any such descriptions unless they add something to the sense, or help to explain the particular scene, etc. After a Member of Parliament had been mentioned, he was referred to as 'an indulgent parent'. Now, if he had just passed over some fault of his son, then 'indulgent parent' would be all right, but, if he only (let us say) had had a cup of tea, then 'indulgent parent' would be out of place. It is much better to allude to a person by his name or by Pronouns (e.g. 'he'). Sidgwick aptly calls this allusion to a person by different terms the *Ornate Alias;* it is a phrase worth remembering. Latin Prose Composition is one of the best helps towards the avoiding of it.

Confusion of Metaphors, etc., is another form of bad Variety: the historic instances are, 'It was a mere flea-bite in the ocean', and 'I smell a rat: I see it in the air: but I'll nip it in the bud'.

A WRITER or Speaker often makes a very great mistake in writing or saying things which are Interesting to himself, without first considering whether they are Interesting *to the reader or hearer* also, or even to the reader or hearer only. And, when one advises a Writer or Speaker to keep up the Interest during his Writings, one means the Interest of the reader or hearer, and not merely his own.

Interest is especially necessary at the *Beginning* of a Composition, for we know how often people choose Books and Stories simple by their beginning. The art of beginning in an Interesting way should therefore be very carefully studied (see p. 258); and not only should the beginning of the whole Composition be Interesting, but also the beginning of each Section and Chapter and Paragraph. It is obvious that the Writer or Speaker cannot ensure this Interest unless he has sympathy with his readers or hearers, and adapts himself to their point of view.

There are some things which are of Interest to almost everybody: thus, if you can appeal to the reader's *Emotions* (e.g. his pity, his indignation, or his fear), or if you can point out the *advantage* of the readers or hearers, or how they may help others in some way, or if you can *criticise* a fault, or if you can give a telling Comparison (p. 281), especially one which appeals to the eye, and with which he is familiar, or if you can give him a Contrast (p. 291), you will probably succeed in getting his attention.   And, to some, even a mere Repetition may be Interesting, if it is carefully managed; but one essential in securing Interest is to secure *Variety*, not so much in the subject (see p. 213) as in the way of treating it.

The reader will also probably be Interested if he is able to *apply* what you suggest to other subjects as well, and if he is able to carry out original research; so that it may be often a good thing not to let the Composition be merely the giving of information, but to let it suggest something for the reader or hearer to work out for himself.

A step further is when the Author (by Questions and other means, see p. 296) *asks the reader or hearer for information*, as it were, and seems to draw the answer from him, so that it appears that the reader or hearer is really finding out everything for himself, and even teaching the Author.   In Teaching, it is of course important for the pupils to think they are finding out a great deal for themselves.

Among miscellaneous helps towards exciting Interest we may mention *Humour and Absurdity*, Novelty and Paradox, and the exciting of the *Curiosity*, and of the Reasoning Faculty.

Several useful lessons may be learnt from *Advertisements:* the Advertiser aims at arousing and keeping the Interest of the reader, and a study of Advertisements will therefore be a good study of the means of getting the attention of large masses of people.

Or, again, various *Articles* in Reviews and Magazines, and even the *Titles* of Books and Articles, deserve a very careful examination,

Occasionally a little *Flattery* will excite the attention of the reader or hearer, and put him on his mettle. Instead of saying "This is so", the Author may say "A thoughtful and intelligent reader cannot fail to see that this is so", though one is bound to confess that this method is frequently abused.

Interest cannot be kept up for an indefinite period of time. By Variety, Interest may be sustained for a long time. But, unless you are very clever and ingenious, you had better be brief. Monotony is a great fault, but often excessive length and mass and bulk is a greater fault—as in the case of food.

S

A GOOD deal of what I say here applies not only to the very Beginning of any Composition, but to all the Beginnings of Paragraphs, etc., within the Composition itself.

The importance of the Beginning is well known *in the choice of Novels:* (the Beginning is only one degree less important than the Title, which itself is the Beginning of Beginnings.) And another Comparison would be the Initial, which is the most important part of a name: it can even stand for the whole name.

Beginnings should as a rule be *Interesting:* they should arouse the attention and keep it. Within the Essay itself, each Paragraph should begin in an Interesting way, unless, that is to say, it is to be linked to the Paragraph before, in which case the principle may not be Interest, but rather Connexion.

A *Paradox* makes a very good Beginning. The reader or hearer thinks to himself, 'How can the man possibly say this? what *does* he mean?' His curiosity and opposition are at once stimulated. One of the most excellent examples is the 'Sermon on the Mount', which began by saying that the poor were happy: only of course it was a particular kind of poor, namely, those who were poor in selfish thoughts.

Under Paradoxes might be classed untrue statements, which you then go on to prove untrue; or partially true statements, which you then go on to correct. *To refute a Fallacy* is often the best Beginning, because it is very human to like to hear someone else being 'shown up'. The Section of the 'Sermon' (on p. 212) began by exposing the Fallacy of Appearances.

Among other Beginnings, *a Quotation* is very often found Interesting (see p. 163), or an Anecdote, or a *Comparison*, which is afterwards applied.

A *Question*, for instance one which suggests a problem, will frequently arouse the Interest and attention.

Some people are fond of starting their Essays with a *Scheme* of the Essay itself, showing the scope of it (as Macaulay did in his "History"), the aim of the Writer, the importance of the questions, the difficulties, and so on.

Others again start with a statement of the *Authorities and Evidences* as to the subject, and they say (see p. 140) where these are good and where they are bad.

Practice in Beginnings is of great importance in all Composition, but of supreme importance in Speaking. And a very good kind of Practice is to take the Beginnings of good Books, Chapters and Paragraphs, and of good Articles, Essays, and Speeches, and to see exactly how they manage (or fail) to arouse Interest.

A very easy and a very instructive study (cp. p. 256) is the study of Advertisements. It is the whole aim of the Advertiser to start his Advertisement with something which will attract the reader's notice, and hence, although he goes to an *extreme* to which a serious Essay would not dare to go, yet the general principle is sound. Among various ways of starting Advertisements, one may notice the Quotation (which often has nothing whatever to do with the thing Advertised l). But the methods of attracting the millions are too numerous to be mentioned here: all that one need say is that they are very valuable in showing how to appeal to a popular audience. We might notice here that the Endings of these Advertisements are as a rule singularly uninteresting: the Advertisements are not to be taken as a complete model for Composition! That which starts as if some exciting adventure is to be described, and ends up with somebody's "Blood Mixture" or "Pill", has an interesting Beginning, but an Ending which can only be called Bathos or Anticlimax.

CHAPTER XLVII. **ENDINGS.**

IN many Essays, and (to a smaller extent) in Speeches, the Ending may be written or prepared right at the very outset, and may be kept in view throughout.

The Ending is sometimes even more important than the Beginning, corresponding to the last tastes of a meal, or the last notes of a tune. And, like the Beginning, the Ending applies not only to the whole Ending, but to the Ending of each Chapter and Paragraph.

The Ending should as a rule be *Impressive, or should encourage the reader or hearer to think;* but, within the Essay itself, the Ending of a Paragraph very often is rather to form a *Connexion* between that Paragraph and the next.

The chief faults in Endings are *abruptness and tameness.* The Greeks were very careful here to avoid abruptness or even excitement : they liked to end quietly. This is perhaps not a modern characteristic ; but, as in so many departments, perhaps the Greeks were nearer to being right than we are.

Their finishing Sentences often seem to us to be actually tame and insipid, and this is a fault which we are very careful to avoid. But many analogies (e.g. the analogy of Physical Exercise) would seem to favour the quiet Ending.

If we are trying to make Endings as Impressive as possible, we shall sometimes succeed by *Summarising* ıs̔ the subject, sometimes by pointing out how *important* the subject is, sometimes by suggesting *problems* for the reader or hearer to work out.

But the particular Ending must depend a great deal on what the particular *Aims* may be. They may be to encourage or to frighten, to make people careful, to make them think for themselves, and so on.

The best Practice will again be a careful study of Endings: those of Speeches and of Articles are best worth attention. Advertisements (as was shown on p. 260) generally have very feeble Endings, and they will be studied from another point of view, namely, as specimens of that which is to be avoided.

Among their other faults, besides tameness, they often end in a lot of short words. Had this Chapter ended here, it would have had the same fault. A few long words form a better close, just as Cicero liked to close with such Rhythms as the wonderfully effective 'esse vidcālur'.

CHAPTER XLVIII. CONNEXION AND COHESION.

THE principle of Connexion holds good for the Sections and Chapters of a Book or Speech, and for the Paragraphs of a Section or Chapter or Essay, and to some extent for the Sentence of a Paragraph, and the Words of a Sentence.

The Connexion between one Paragraph and another is that which I wish to deal with here especially. An example is given directly. Each Idea should lead naturally to the Idea which comes next; though this of course is only as a general rule. But what *are* the Connexions between various Ideas?

First of all, both Ideas may belong to the same Class, the same general Heading. For instance, on p. 185 we should say that the Family Organisation, the Political Organisation, the Character, etc., of the Romans would come under the General Heading of ' The Romans considered by themselves', whereas the Alliances and Treachery and gradual Conquests, etc., would come under the Heading of 'The Romans in their dealings with others'. This then will be one principle of Connexion, viz. the fact that certain Ideas belong to a single 'group'.

In the same List (on p. 185), we find Colonies, Roads, and Extension of Rights: these are not only members of the same 'group', but they also have a Connexion *with one another.* The Roman Colonies were situated along the great Roads: in fact the Roads stretched between Rome and her Colonies; the subject of Roads, then, might easily *lead to* the subject of Colonies, or vice versa. What would be the Connexion between the Roads and the Extension of Rights? Obviously the Roads would help to extend Roman influences, and, when Roman influences were being extended, Roman privileges were being extended also. The next Heading is the Allies: what might be the Connexion between the Allies and the Extension of Rights? Apparently there would be very little, but the two could be linked together in some such way as this. The Romans extended their Rights and privileges to those whom they had conquered and to those whom they feared as enemies, but they also often extended them to faithful Allies.

The Connexion, then, besides such a Connexion as where one Idea is *a Cause or Hindrance or an Effect*, would frequently depend merely on some *casual link*. One knows how, in conversation, something which happens to be mentioned in one subject leads people on to quite a new subject: this new subject in its turn leads people on to some third subject, although there may be no *real* Connexion between the three subjects: perhaps the Idea which leads from one to another may have very little to do with either of them. The Connexion, then, may include anything which links one Idea to another. See further "How to Remember" (to be published in February, 1900, by Warne & Co.).

Of course much of the Connexion can be shown by the mere *Arrangement* (p. 172). If the Headings and Sub-Headings are carefully Arranged, each may be made to lead naturally to the next, so that the whole appears as one single chain. If the Headings on p. 185

are written on Cards, each having a Card to itself, and if the Cards are then shuffled, it will be found that there may be little or no Connexion between any Heading and the next before it and the next after it: one will not naturally lead to the next.

Among the different means of Connecting Paragraphs may be mentioned *Comparisons or Contrasts.* You wish to pass from one Idea to another, and you find that you will have to leap or jump; there seems to be no bridge, and the question is how to form some bridge or link. Good Practice for this will be to study Loisette's System of Memory, e.g. in "How to Remember" (see p. 264); in fact Loisette's System might be called the Link-System; and Comparisons and Contrasts will very often be a great help as Links.

The exact Connexion may often be made clearer by *actual words.* 'Then' will give something which follows either in point of time, or as a result or inference from the first Idea ('therefore'), and 'also' and 'while' will give something which happens very often side by side with the first Idea and in addition to it. 'But' or 'although' will give something opposed to the Idea, e.g. as a Hindrance. 'For' or 'because' will give a Reason.

Besides these Particles, the Connexion may be shown by some word in the previous Idea being *repeated,* or else by a *Pronoun* such as 'he' or 'it' or 'this'. The Connecting word need not come in the very beginning of the Paragraph: the Beginning had often better be Interesting: and indeed the reader or hearer may have his attention kept on the alert as he wonders what on earth the Connexion is going to be.

Another means of Connexion is the *Résumée,* an instance of which may be given here. Supposing you have six reasons for something, and you have given four reasons one after the other, perhaps in four consecutive Paragraphs; and supposing the last Paragraph is a long one: let us call these four reasons A, B, C, and D; the fifth reason, beginning a fifth Paragraph, may now be introduced as follows. " But the reason for this was not only A, B, C, and D: there was yet another reason. . . ."; and then one proceeds to give the fifth reason. This method is of great value because it not only serves to Connect the fifth reason with the other four, but it impresses all five Reasons together upon the mind of the reader or hearer.

It is important to notice once again that the Connexion need not come at the Beginning of a Paragraph: the Paragraph may begin with the mention of the subject or Idea of the Paragraph: in fact this is a most useful Beginning for Paragraphs. The beginning of Macaulay's " History of England " is often quoted for this: he mentions the scope of his History.

Or (see above) the Beginning may be decided by the principle of Interest, and the Connexion between this and the preceding Paragraph may come afterwards. Sometimes there need be no Connexion at all: in fact a sudden jerk, a sudden transition to a new topic, will often be far more impressive than any Connexion can be.

Good practice in Cohesion or Connexion will be to take any Article or Chapter or Book or Speech which leaves in your mind a general train of Ideas, and see why and how it is that the Ideas *have* been left behind in your mind in that particular order. The practice will be still better if you take some Writer who is well known for his Arrangement, for instance Burke, and *analyse* on Cards one of his works, e.g. his work on America; then take the Cards and *shuffle* them, and try to re-arrange them in the best possible order, as if you were yourself going to address the House. Afterwards take his work, and see what his order is and why it is just this and not that, and why it is better than yours for his particular purpose.

Another exercise is to *criticise bad order.* Nothing is commoner than a piece of Composition which is a series of jerks: no Idea seems to lead naturally to the next. Take these Compositions, and criticise them; then re-arrange the Ideas so that there will be Connexion and cohesion. In doing this you will notice that a good deal of the want of Connexion is due to the Ideas being arranged in a bad order, and to the Writer perpetually flying off at a tangent, drifting away from the point.

You will learn from this that, if you wish your Ideas to be closely Connected with one another, you must pay great attention to the Law of *Economy and of Unity:* you must not stray away from the Idea which your Paragraph is describing.

As to the Connexion between the various words of a Sentence, I shall leave that till we come to Chapter LIX.

CHAPTER XLIX. EMPHASIS.

As we saw in Chapter 222, Force and Vigour generally bring Emphasis with them. But I shall here treat Emphasis as a special subject, partly because there are other means of Emphasis besides Force and Vigour.

I will assume that you already have a list of the Headings and Sub-Headings which you wish to Emphasise, and there now arises the question of how you are to Emphasise them, and to Emphasise some more, but others less, according to the Underlining (p. 170).

In Speaking, you instinctively speak louder, or you pause more, or you change the pitch or note, and so on. The nearest approach to this in Writing is actual *Underlining*, Italics, and so on.

In considering how to Emphasise any given Idea, let us first of all ask which parts of a word or of a particular Book are noticed most. The answer will obviously be, *the Beginning, and the Ending.* We notice the Title on the cover of a Book, and from the Beginning a good many people are apt to turn straight to the End. Some of them then have the audacity to say that they have read the Book! In a word or name, also, we notice the Beginning, the Initial being most important, and the Ending, because it lingers longest as the last sound we hear. Thus the Beginning and the Ending will be places of Emphasis.

But now let us take another Comparison. Supposing we wished *to hammer a nail* firmly into a board, we should first of all choose the right place in the wood, perhaps preparing the wood e.g. by making a hole in it with a gimlet or bradawl. Then we should get a clear view of the nail, and hit it straight on the head. This by the way would need some practice beforehand. We should hit it with force and vigour, firmly and quickly. We should repeat the blows: perhaps each blow would not be quite the same as the last, but, of course, the heavier the head of the hammer was, the more easily would the nail go into the wood. And it would also be an advantage to draw back the head of the hammer before we struck. Supposing the first nail were not quite secure, we should add another nail or a screw as near as possible to the first, but not exactly in the same place. We might also put the second in at a different angle from the first.

Strange as it may sound, all these processes will find their analogies in the Emphasising of Ideas.

Let us take yet another principle. We can bring an object into prominence by throwing a very strong light on to that object, or by throwing lights on to it from many sides, and especially by throwing upon it an unusual and unexpected light, and best of all by throwing the background into darkness.

It would be a good Exercise for the reader, in working out Comparisons (p. 281), to try for himself how this can all be applied to the Emphasising of Ideas, before he reads what I am going to say now.

※　　※　　※　　※　　※

Let us apply these principles.

1. First of all, corresponding to the Loudness, etc., to mark Emphasis there would be Italics or Underlining, or thick black type, or Capitals.

2. Then there might be *a pause* before an Emphatic point. This would be called leading up to a Climax. The expectation would be raised so that the way would be prepared for the important Idea. By this means Interest would be aroused, and a sense of expectancy. Thus, for example, Emphasis might be prepared for by means of *a Question.*

The right place is of great importance: the Beginning is one emphatic position, and the Ending is another (see p. 261).

The way would be *prepared* by means of a familiar and easy starting-point, something which we know already better than the thing which is to be Emphasised. By this means the point will be clearly realised. A *Comparison* would therefore be useful.

In the expression of the Idea there must be *briskness, Clearness, and Brevity:* the words must sharply hit the nail straight on the head, and this will need considerable practice beforehand.

There will have to be *Force and Vigour* (see p. 222): they are very very hard things to define. Dignity and Rapidity are among the common characteristics of Force and Vigour.

Repetition is the next means, and it is the commonest. We can repeat the exact words, or we can change the words slightly, varying by the abstract, the concrete, or (see p. 273) the very concrete, and varying the Voice, Mood, Tense and the forms of the Sentence (see p. 253).

On p. 266 I have pointed out that the *Résumée Method* is one of the best forms of Repetition: it means the gathering up of all the old before you proceed to the new.

A mass of words (which might be called weight or 'bulk') is often a means of Emphasis: the number of words and the size of words impress the eye, and also impress the ear, and, although this may degenerate into padding, still even padding has its advantages for purposes of Emphasis. If you give an important Idea a longer time in which to impress itself upon the mind, it will impress itself upon the mind more firmly than if it had only had a moment.

Variety in the point of view is of very great value, as we saw on pp. 181, 214. We get to know a place quite well if we pass through it again and again, and not always by the same roads, but from different directions: we get to know each of its features better and better. Hence there must be changes, which will keep the attention fixed, and these can be made, e.g., by means of Parallels, Comparisons, and Contrasts.

Among Contrasts we may include *refutation of the wrong view*. Few means of Emphasising are more important than Contrasts and refutation. To start with the question, 'Is it so-and-so?' and then to prove that it is not so-and-so, then to ask 'Is it this?' and then to prove that it is not quite this, and to go on thus, may help more than anything else to arouse the interest of the reader or hearer, because it will encourage him to think *with* you. Some of the greatest Teachers have used this means, as we have seen in the passage from the New Testament (p. 212), and in the introduction to Guizot's "History of Civilisation".

Another very useful means is (see p. 278) *the throwing of the unimportant parts into the background:* sometimes this can be done by differences of type. This is one of the parts of Composition which people have practised least of all. Some Americans perhaps err most with respect to Emphasising too many things : they suffer in their advertisements and in their notices in certain Papers, because, when they wish to Emphasise an Idea, they have no further means at their disposal : all their best means (see p. 247) have been used up for comparatively unimportant and trivial matters.

That which is *striking* also conduces to Emphasis, as Carlyle's writings show. *Proverb, Paradox, Epigram, exaggeration, humour, and unexpected order of words,* all these can be means of Emphasis.

An instance would illustrate some of these methods. Supposing we wished to Emphasise the division of labour which had already begun in early Rome, we could say that some of the early Romans were engaged in war, agriculture, and politics, while others were engaged in trading and industries. We might emphasise this point by means of italics, etc. We might arouse attention by asking what were the means by which Rome succeeded : this question could come at the Beginning. We might, though this is by the way, Emphasise the Idea by means of a picture or drawing ; and we might also Emphasise it by pointing out how the health of the Romans was promoted by their variety of labour.

A clear statement of the facts would be very necessary, and it is astonishing how much practice is needed before a clear statement can be given. The statement might be made striking, or Brevity might be ensured, by the omission of unnecessary words. Then the exact words might be repeated, or the idea might .be repeated in a more Concrete form. For instance it might be said that the early Romans were mostly farmers, politicians, soldiers, shepherds, traders, and so on. A still more Concrete way of expressing this idea would be " Cato was a type of the early Roman : he was a farmer, a soldier, a politician, etc." This would be nearly the most Concrete form of all. The best method of repeating this idea would be to gather it up at the end, by a *Résumée* (p. 266).

Among other means may be mentioned a lengthy Paragraph (p. 312) in which the Idea is described ; and the use of long words within the Paragraph. English or other Parallels would be good, and Comparisons, such as the analogy of the ants, and their division of labour. Contrasts also would be of service : the Romans might be contrasted with the nomads and barbarians, among whom little division of labour is known. Under Contrast, we might expose the Fallacy that the Romans were mere warriors, or were mere farmers.

The rest of the points which we do not wish to emphasise could be put in such ordinary language that they might attract little attention. This would help to throw up the more important fact that *the Romans had* division of labour. Besides this, Paradox, Epigrams, and exaggeration might be brought into play. It would be an exaggeration to say that in early Rome there was not a single idle man : but it would not be very far from the truth. A humorous description of Cincinnatus might help to impress the Idea upon the mind.

To these we can add yet other means of Emphasis.

We often remember things better when we know what has *caused* them, or what has helped them, and what has been their *effect*. For instance, we should remember the History of Rome far better if we knew the Geography which had helped to make that History, and we should know the Geography far better, in its turn, if we knew its effects on Roman History. And so we should remember the division of labour better if we knew some of its causes, for instance, the fact that the Romans had defences and buildings of stone, and that they were trained by constantly fighting with some of their enemies. We might remember this division of labour better if we remembered its effects, for instance its effects upon health and upon progress.

I began with an illustration, and I will now give another. If some General were attacking an enemy, and wished to succeed, what would be his method? First of all he would have practised a good deal beforehand. Then he would try to draw the enemy on to his own ground, or at any rate he would learn the enemy's ground, and as much about the enemy as he could. He would learn their strong and weak points. Then he would probably concentrate his forces on one particular point, reserving some of his forces however in case this attack should fail. This illustration might be of value towards a study of Emphasis. (If you wish to impress a thing upon the mind, put yourself in the reader's position, and then study his point of view: in order to make quite sure, it is better to approach a thing from too many points of view than from too few.)

A hint may be offered here about *the order of words*. Just as the General must pay a great deal of attention

to the order and disposition of his troops if he wishes
to produce a definite effect, so the Writer must pay
attention to the order and disposition of his words.
A natural order of words in a Sentence would be
Subject, Adverb, Verb, and Object, though this is liable
to many variations. Now supposing we wish to Emphasise the *Verb*, we should not leave it in the middle,
but should put it at the *Beginning*. The Adverb also
may often be put at the Beginning, and the Object as
well. The Subject of the Sentence, on the other hand,
would not be Emphatic if it came at the Beginning :
the Emphatic place for it would be the End.

A very common Greek and Latin means of Emphasis must never be forgotten, viz. the *Anticipation*
of an Idea or Word by a Pronoun like 'this'. We
can imagine the Greek or Latin Speaker using gesture
as well, when he said "But I know *this :* he never yet
has acted save for his own interests" (cp. the origin
of 'that', in of 'he`said that it was so'*) 'They
did it for the following reason : (viz. that) they were
afraid of our power'.

This 'Figure' rouses the interest by suspense : or it
may be compared to a sign-post or to a hand pointing
towards *the* important thing.

The reverse of this would often be less effective,
e.g. 'They were afraid of our power : *this* was why
they did it'.

Closely akin to it is the English 'It was by him
that the Drama was purified', 'It is this that we need'.
The Greeks and Latins could change their order of
words far more freely than we can, since we, for
example, generally have to rely on the order to show

* It has no Emphasis now.

which is the Subject and which is the Object] (in ' The orator abused the general '). Our ' *Circumlocution* ', then, is often almost our only weapon.   It owes part of its effect to the bulk of words, as if one were to say ' By him, by him, by him . . .'

It is curious that Emphasis may be given both by many words and by few words : the many words (even if not well chosen) are to some extent like the large-headed hammer (see p. 269): they have mass and ' bulk ', and the eye and ear are arrested for a longer time ; the few words (if well chosen) are more like the straight and well-aimed blow with the smaller-headed hammer : they arrest the understanding, which unconsciously blesses them for being brief and business-like.

Connectives also may be many ·or few : there may be the slowly and carefully uttered items (' beef and bread and cheese and beer and tobacco '), or the short sharp incisive list (' beef, bread, cheese, beer, tobacco '). The latter is rather more appropriate to exciting passages.

The reader should take Bain's " Rhetoric and Composition ", and study and practise the many means of Emphasis which he suggests : my Book does not deal primarily with details of the kind.   Let the reader notice the effect of such ' Figures ' as the following.   See further p. 299.

(*a*) Inversion, e.g. ' life eternal ' ;

(*b*) ' Metonymy ' etc., e.g. ' sail ' meaning ' ship ' (' Part for Whole '); ' red tape ' meaning ' official formalities ' ('Accompanying sign '); ' linen ' meaning ' linen sheets ' (' Material '); ' the pen ' meaning ' written words ' (' Instrument '); ' Bradshaw ' meaning " Bradshaw's Guide " (' Agent '); ' the purse ' meaning ' money ' (' Contents '); ' the bright death ' meaning ' the weapon ' (' Effect '); and so on.

Some of the above may become quite commonplace, and may lose their Emphasis altogether.

(*c*) '*Chiasmus*', e.g.

'here to-day, to-morrow gone'.

(*d*) *Word-play*, e.g.

'what I have written, I have written' (quoted by Bain : here the second 'I have written' means 'I have written once for all : it is final').

These are but a few of the means of Emphasis : but I do not wish to make this Chapter too bulky by a fuller list. The reader who wishes for further information may study the Chapter (p. 299) on Rhetorical Devices : nine-tenths of them may be used (partly) in order to draw the attention to some important point. But the above means will suffice for ordinary purposes : only the art of Emphasising must be practised all by itself. It is not acquired in a day.

Note.

This Chapter is badly put together. After I had written it, I came across several useful books that I had not seen before. Instead of re-writing the Chapter, I thought I would leave it for the reader to Analyse into Headings, and then (see p. 172 foll.) to Arrange, with special attention to the Order and Connexions.

To emphasise an Idea is much easier (if the art has been practised) than to state an Idea without Emphasis, or rather, to throw it into the background. So it is often necessary to practise self-restraint, and to make some Sentences purposely unemphatic or even weak, if the Emphasis and Vigour is to have its full effect when it is really needed.

I have already spoken of Advertisements, especially some American Advertisements. What a great deal is needed before the attention *is* arrested and fixed. This is because the attention has so often been arrested and fixed where little or no attention was deserved.

Purposely to weaken an idea is a hard art. But a few hints may help.

The unemphatic position in the Essay or Paragraph is generally the latter end of the middle: here should be put some of the 'bulk' of the food, as it were, the fibrous matter, as opposed to the appetising elements.

The Idea should be expressed once only, in simple language, with no striking words or order of words or Rhythm. There should be no Rhetorical Question, no forcible Comparison or Contrast, no Epigram.

A good Exercise might be to read a Daily Paper, or an American Paper, and re-write it, taking care that Emphasis shall fall only on what you consider to be the really important points.

CHAPTER LI. **PARALLELS.**

In this Chapter I shall say very little, leaving most of my remarks for the next Chapter (Comparisons).

Parallels (in spite of what many Authorities say) must be worked out separately. In an Essay on Cicero, for example, it will not do to trust to some Parallel 'presenting itself naturally to you' (see p. 174). This may do well enough for the genius, but for the learner it may mean that no Parallel *will* present itself. For the learner a better piece of advice will be 'Search if you wish to find'. It may be some little time before e.g. Demosthenes and Gladstone 'present themselves'. And, even when the names are chosen, that is not all: it remains to be seen how far each of these Orators *is* 'parallel' to Cicero, and how far he is to be contrasted with Cicero.

Nor is even this sufficient. For Cicero was not only an orator: he was also what we should call a 'gentleman': here we might compare Xenophon with him. As a letter-writer, he suggests comparison and contrast with Pliny; and so on.

In fact, unless this branch of Essay-writing be worked out by itself, it will be done badly. And, as we shall see (p. 284), it is a very important branch: for it gives Variety, it gives Interest, it gives Emphasis, and it may give Clearness. It *demands* much care and labour.

For what points are we to find Parallels? For points which we wish to emphasise (see p. 170), and for points which we wish merely to make clear, and (occasionally) for points which we wish to make interesting. If we have to consider certain characteristics of Philip of Macedon, or Julius Caesar, we should find that a Comparison (and Contrast) with Napoleon might serve all these purposes.

CHAPTER LII. COMPARISONS, ANALOGIES, ETC.

OF Parallels we have already said a few words : we saw how, if one wished to show that Philip of Macedon was a great General, a great Nation-maker, and an unscrupulous Diplomatist, the bare statement might not be enough : one might have to try to find some Parallel in order to make these three points *clear*, and to *Emphasise* them. And we found, as a Parallel, Napoleon. We know that Napoleon was a great General, relying as Philip did on the charge of his cavalry, we know that he was to some extent a Nation-maker, or at any rate a 'welder' of the Nation, and we know that he was also a Diplomatist.

We now come to something rather wider than the Parallel, and that is the Comparison or Analogy or Illustration.

It is a great mistake, a great fallacy, to say to Speakers, or Essay-Writers, or Writers generally, "*Do not* search for Comparisons, but only use them if they come of their own accord : otherwise your Comparison will be forced and unnatural." This is all very well for the genius or for the experienced Writer ; but just consider my own case. When I began this Book, I wanted to make it clear to the reader that Essay-Writing was a very difficult and complicated art : but no Comparison or Illustration of this occurred to me at once and naturally. Is it then true that I should have used no Comparison at all ? Of course not. I had to search and

think of something which would illustrate my point,
i.e. make it clear and emphasise it.   After a while it
occurred to me that Building was one appropriate Comparison (see p. xv), and that the playing of Games was
another (see pp. xiv, xix).   The latter I chose because
it came within my own experience, the former I chose
because it was very easy to understand.   I ask the
reader to read once or twice the passages referred to,
and then to decide whether or no these Comparisons
or Illustrations helped to make my meaning clearer.
Possibly the reader may be able to see that the Comparisons have been worked out separately, that they did
not come to me uncalled-for and unsought.   But I think
that if they emphasise the complexity of the art, they
are better expressed than unexpressed, even though
they have some disadvantages.   The 'joints' and the
'mechanism' may appear, it is true, but it is better that
they should appear than that the writing should be
obscure, or the point passed over unnoticed.   Moreover,
with careful practice, the 'joints' will come to be covered
over, and the 'mechanism', though it may not be quite
hidden, will at any rate work more smoothly and easily:
the clumsy laboriousness in the early stages is almost
bound to disappear and to give way to neatness and
skill.

It is for this purpose that I suggest the special
Exercises at the end of this Chapter.   After the reader
has seen what the advantages of Comparisons are, he
will be able to judge whether these Exercises are
worth trying or not.

Before I begin pointing out the uses and values of
Comparisons, let me give one or two more instances.   Let
the reader look at p. 269.   He will see that Emphasis is

the subject. I wished to make clear to the ordinary reader, the idea of Emphasis and the means of giving Emphasis. I therefore chose the Comparison of the hammer and nail, and the light.

Supposing, again, I wished to make clear the Roman system of Roads and Colonies, and to show what they were like, how they were placed, and what effects they had, or what was their relation to Rome itself, I might give, among other Comparisons, that of the spider and its legs. I might say that the legs of the spider go out in various directions from the body, that they are all attached to the body, that the blood circulates from the body to the legs and back again. I might say that the feelers at the end of the legs are far off from the body, and in various directions, and that yet they depend on the body for knowing what to do, and for being fed and protected, while the body itself could not easily reach in various directions and far off without these feelers.

It stands to reason that, if the subject is well known, the best Comparisons will come more easily and more rapidly, so that the greatest help in finding Comparisons will be to learn the subject thoroughly, and to study it from many points of view.

As to the numerous uses and values of Comparisons, they depend on these Comparisons being used in the right way; and the first point to notice is that they must be perfectly *clear* not only to the Writer but also *to the reader*. The Writer has to put himself into the position of the reader before he can be sure that the Comparison is the right one.

It follows from this that those Comparisons which appeal to *most* people will be the best for ordinary purposes : see p. 236.   It will be necessary to start with what the reader knows, and with what is familiar to him, before one proceeds to the new point which one wishes to make clear and to Emphasise.

The great secret in working out Comparisons, then, is to try to find what is familiar to the average reader.

(1) Comparisons help to make the points *clearer*. One simple way of expressing an Idea may fail to attract some reader's attention, and the Comparison may just supply this want. It is for this reason, namely, the value of Comparison for Clearness, that they *must* be used in Teaching, or at any rate in the early stages of Teaching.

(2) Comparisons, if they are well chosen, arouse *Interest*, partly because they are understood, and partly because they are striking.   They often actually give a feeling of *pleasure*, or at any rate of satisfaction.

(3) They therefore help the *Memory;* for it is easiest to remember what is understood and what is interesting. Moreover they often serve as links, and improve the power of associating Ideas.

(4) They encourage people to use their reasoning powers, and to draw *Inferences*.

(5) *Repetition* is often needed throughout life, but mere Repetition is apt to be tedious. Now a Comparison is a kind of Repetition, while not appearing to be one. We see this in the case of Philip and Napoleon (p. 281), and in many other cases as well.

(6) For this cause, Comparisons are an excellent means of *Emphasising*, for, as we saw on p. 216, Emphasis can be given by Repetition.   If, therefore, a Comparison is a kind of a Repetition, then it can also become the means of giving Emphasis.

(7) The great advantage of a Comparison over a mere Repetition is that it ensures *Variety*. The idea may be nearly the same, but *the point of view* may be changed.

(8) In Comparisons also there is some scope for *Humour*, which is generally excluded from the more serious Essay, and perhaps rightly so.

(9) More generally speaking, Comparisons encourage *originality, and observation ;* and, in our present Educational System in England, originality and observation are not much encouraged : they are generally sternly crushed. Every now and then one notices how apt a little child's illustrations are, and how they describe an idea far more neatly than a grown-up person is wont to. There is a great deal to be learnt from this and, among other lessons, the fact that this power of Illustration is not cultivated nearly enough as life advances. The little girl who said that after influenza her legs were very "giddy", was using (unconsciously) a most vivid Comparison, and it would be impossible to think of any better means of describing the feeling.

(10) Comparisons will encourage very wide *learning* and studying, especially the studying of Nature and human nature. They will give a fresh interest to a walk in the country or in a town, if one knows that the walk may supply illustrations which will help one's powers of Writing or Speaking.

(11) For Comparisons help to connect the various Sciences, and the different departments of life, with one another. In fact, they counteract one great fault in our Education, namely, that so many studies are carried on quite separately. By Comparisons one learns to see that the various studies are closely connected

with one another. Indeed, there are certain principles which apply to almost every subject, and, if we can learn them in the case of any *one* subject, and can also get the power of Comparing things, we can easily apply these same principles to other subjects also.

(12) Thus the power of comparing things may *save a great deal of time and labour*, besides being a little Education in itself.

(13) The person who can Compare things and work out Analogies readily will be able to *use masses and masses of information* which otherwise he would never use at all. In the lumber-room of his mind he will find thousands of odds and ends which will no longer grow dusty from not being employed, but will be taken out and applied for valuable purposes. For example, he knows much about Games, and, when he has acquired the power of Comparing things, he will be able to use Games to illustrate great principles such as (see p. 289) Co-operation, etc.

(14) Thus *every subject*, however great or however small, will be made interesting and useful.

(15) *Sympathy* with others cannot fail to be increased in the person who is constantly asking himself: "What will the average reader most readily understand? What is there in his mind, already, by means of which I can describe this new Idea to him?" And this is not all, for

(16) Comparisons *suggest many new points*. Take an example. You wish to find out and you try to work out what are the Bonds of Union between England and her Colonies. You arrive at certain Ideas, after a long time. But supposing you ask yourself another question, viz. "What are the Bonds of Union between two members

of one family?", then you could easily work out the answer, because you would be starting with something familiar to yourself, in fact, part of your everyday experience. This second question would suggest many Ideas (see p. 112) which would not occur to you at all if you considered the first question all by itself. And the same would apply if you first considered the advantages of an Absolute Monarchy in a State, and then the advantages of the Family being ruled by a good father.

(17) Comparisons and Analogies are also valuable *Evidences*. Perhaps they rather suggest things than prove them, but still they are somewhat of the nature of a proof. The mere fact that the Family succeeds under the government of a good father is a kind of a proof that a State might succeed under the government of a good Monarch.

(18) For Literary purposes, Comparisons may form transitions and links between one Paragraph and another, or between one Sentence and another.

For the Classes and Uses of *Metaphors* and other 'Tropes', I must refer to special works on Rhetoric. Metaphors, etc., may serve much the same purpose as Comparisons, and had very similar origins, though now many of them (such as 'I see and understand and grasp what you're hammering into me') have passed or are passing into our everyday language. They are losing their vividness, and becoming commonplace and regular means of expression.*

But, even when they have almost passed into this language, even then they must not be '*mixed*' rashly,

* See "How to Learn Philology" (Sonnenschein), p. 223.

as on p. 254, or even as in the sentence bracketed above. In such cases it is safer to appeal to the most refined and particular ear ; so that, if it is felt that '*under* these circumstances' (see p. 207) might offend him who remembers that circumstantia were *once* 'things that stand around', the word 'under' should be avoided, and perhaps the phrase 'under these *conditions*' should be substituted.

CLASSES OF COMPARISONS AND ANALOGIES.

The different classes of Comparisons or Analogies cannot all be mentioned here. It must also constantly be remembered that no Comparison is an exact Parallel : things can only resemble one another *partially*. But, in the choice of Comparisons, there is one principle which is almost universal, and that is *to describe what is not well known by what is better known*, especially by what appeals to the senses of *sight*, hearing, touch, and taste. And in each case the thing which is Compared must be better known, and more familiar, *not only to yourself but also to the reader or hearer*.

The best Comparisons and Analogies are from *Nature*, the plants and their seeds, the animals, the 'elements' of Nature, such as heat and light : all these have formed the stock-in-trade of Writers and Speakers, and many of them have passed into the class of everyday words. Indeed, Language has been called a storehouse of faded Metaphors.*

Family life, again, gives many useful Comparisons (see p. 286), and so do the various *occupations* in life, e.g. not only feeding but also the more serious

---

* See "How to Learn Philology" (Sonnenschein).

occupations, such as business—and athletics. In fact, all that men do, all, that is to say, that appeals to the public, can be made a means of Expressing and Emphasising a new Idea. For instance, on p. xv, we alluded to the art of Building, and, on p. xiv, to the art of learning Games.

The New Testament should be very carefully studied, as it gives a good idea of the best Metaphors and Analogies for Literary purposes. Matthew's Gospel alone would be an admirable field for research, and this I should suggest as the first kind of Exercise, namely, to go through various Writers and to see what Comparisons they use (p. 214), and what are the most effective Comparisons.

There are two other kinds of Exercise as well. A Class of boys at School, for example, might be asked what lessons Football teaches, what it illustrates. This form of Exercise would be *to take something which is familiar, and then to find out for what Comparisons it can be used:* or in other words how to apply an Analogy which is already given to them. Thus Football might illustrate Co-operation, Specialisation, and the effects of Practice; it might illustrate Endurance, Promptitude, and Pluck, and also Competition in its best form, and the value of government by a single person: and many other things from the list above can be treated as Exercises of the same kind.

The third Exercise would be to ask, '*How can one illustrate something which is less well known* and less familiar to the reader or hearer?' Using the above instance, if one wished to illustrate Co-operation to boys one would ask what thing there was which

U

was well known to boys, and which would illustrate this principle; and a good answer would be a Game of Football or Cricket.

Undoubtedly this last Exercise would be one of the best for Teachers, for it would force them to ask themselves a question which they may often have asked themselves in their daily life, but may seldom have troubled to apply in teaching, namely, '*What do the learners already understand? what is familiar to them? on what foundations can I build up the new Ideas which I wish to describe to them?*'

CHAPTER LIII. CONTRASTS.

CONTRASTS are very like Comparisons in their effects and in their value: indeed, what I have said about Comparisons will apply almost without exception to Contrasts. These two great helps to Clearness, and Interest (and Pleasure and Satisfaction), and Variety, and Emphasis, can be used as alternatives, or, in special cases, can be used side by side to supplement one another.

In each case it is for the Writer to judge whether the Clearness or Emphasis can better be given by a Comparison or by a Contrast.

If Freedom were to be described, probably it would be better to describe it by its Contrasts, Slavery, etc. We cannot properly realise what light is unless we also consider darkness. Pleasure would not be pleasure if we are always in the same state : before we can realise what pleasure is, we must have either the condition in which we feel no pleasure, or (better still) the other extreme, pain. A holiday, again, has no meaning for a person who never works: at least it has no real meaning.

To show the value of Contrasts, I can take an instance very near home. If I wish to teach the art of Essay-Writing, I can do my best to show how the art might be acquired, or how it would not be acquired: I can say what is right, or what is wrong ; what is a merit, or what is a fault. If I wish to make anything particularly Clear or Emphatic, then I shall probably use both means. I shall advise the reader to notice what is bad as well as what is good.

A special branch of Contrasts is of great value for the beginning of a Book, or of an Essay, or of a section of an Essay, or of a Speech; and this is the plan of excluding and *Rejecting*. Guizot began his "History of Civilisation" by asking what Civilisation meant : he said, 'Does it mean this?' and the answer was 'No; not only this.' Then he said 'Does it mean a second thing?' and the answer was 'No, not merely this second thing.' Finally he said what Civilisation *did* consist of, after he had paved the way for it and excited the reader's attention and had cleared the ground by his statements as to what Civilisation did not consist of. We have seen a similar instance in the New Testament example (on p. 212): in order to describe who *are* really good, it was necessary to say who are not really good, for instance, those who merely say good words or who look pious.

Another branch of Contrast would be what may be called *Parallelism.* It will be seen very well in the same passage (p. 215), where the house on the rock is Contrasted with the house on the sand; the perfect balance between the two descriptions cannot fail to give us a kind of *pleasure*, which can only be realised if we alter the description of the second house so that it shall no longer correspond. This might be done by taking for this the version on p. 214; and the sense of discomfort produced by the change of words would be very considerable.

I need not say very much here about the different *Uses* of Contrasts, because what I have said about

Comparisons will apply almost throughout. I shall simply repeat here that Contrasts, like Comparisons, are useful for many purposes. The reader should work these out, with his own instances.

(1) Clearness;

(2) Interest given to the subject in hand;

(3) the helping of the Memory;

(4) the helping of the Reason and the power of drawing Inferences;

(5) Repetition (which should not seem to be Repetition, see p. 216);

(6) Emphasis;

(7) Variety (not so much in the Idea as in the way in which one looks at it);

(8) Humour;

(9) Originality, and Observation;

(10) the use of wide learning and study (see p. 286): masses of information, which might otherwise be unused, become valuable;

(11) the Connexion between various Sciences and other subjects (p. 285);

(12) the fresh *interest* given to every subject, and to daily life;

(13) (to a less extent than with Comparisons), *Sympathy;*

(14) the *suggestion* of many new points;

(15) *Evidences.*

A word may be said about this last point. We have seen (p. 149) that one special branch of Evidence is called the Evidence of Omissions. Supposing someone is looking at a Testimonial and he finds that in that Testimonial the person is said to have certain merits, but that one or two of the merits which he requires are not present; he begins to feel (that is to say, if he is used to dealing with Testimonials) that these merits may be wanting in the person; for he says to himself, 'If they had been present, they would have been mentioned.' But he does not decide immediately: if he can, he gets other Testimonials and sees whether the same omissions occur in them. If a Testimonial of someone, who wishes to be a schoolmaster, omits some important characteristics of a good schoolmaster, and if all the Testimonials without exception omit this same characteristic, the Evidence is almost conclusive. At any rate, even if the Contrast does not prove anything, it may suggest a great deal which may be worth following out.

In History-topics especially, where the Evidence is often very meagre, we have to work a great deal by means of Contrasts and Opposites. If we wish to judge of the effect of a certain Drug, we cannot judge properly simply by administering the Drug and noting what takes place afterwards. A patient has fever, and takes a Drug, and, after a week, the fever disappears. Now it does not follow that it is the Drug that has removed the fever; for someone might say that the fever would have been removed without the Drug: perhaps he might say that the fever would have been removed quicker without the Drug. To judge of the real effect of the Drug one would have to take two very similar cases. In the first case one would let the fever continue without the Drug, and one would note what happened; in the second case one would administer the Drug, and also note what happened. If the cases were really similar, then the Contrast between the two would be Evidence. And so it is with History: if we wish to work out what the effect of some King of Spain was upon Spain, we had best work out this not merely by reading what the Authorities tell us, but also by looking at the state of Spain before and after this King had ruled it.

Contrasts, in fact, will suggest new features and will sometimes be actual Evidence.

But, as with Comparisons, so with Contrasts, we cannot say that all the above results will hold good unless the Contrasts are used properly. For instance, to use Contrasts for every Idea throughout the Essay would be monotonous, and inappropriate, and would also offend against the Law of Proportion : for it would make all the Ideas of equal importance. We must reserve the Contrasts for special occasions. In using Contrasts, no less than in using Comparisons, there is a certain self-restraint necessary.

Exercises are ready to hand everywhere: any statement can be taken, and the opposite or opposites to it can be worked out. Abstract terms can also be taken, such as *honour*. We cannot really define the word *honour* until we know exactly what the context is, and even then the best way will often be to say that of which *honour* is the Opposite, e.g. obscurity, or disgrace, or shame.

There is hardly any Speech or Essay-subject which does not demand the use of Contrasts and the study of Contrasts as a special Exercise. In fact, if I were asked to say which departments of Speaking and Essay-Writing had the greatest educational value, I should certainly mention Comparisons and Contrasts, when worked out as separate Exercises, as *among the three best.*

THERE are probably very few who realise what is the nature of an ordinary Question. It is a kind of subject without a predicate: for instance, if I say 'Where is Jones?', it is not a complete Sentence, but only the beginning of a Sentence: I might just as well say 'Jones is ——': the Sentence will not be complete until the answer has been given, e.g. '—— in town'. And this can be proved by the raising of the voice during a Question: we know that in an ordinary Sentence the note on which we speak goes lower and lower: we begin on a high note and finish on a lower note, and the Sentence itself does not seem to be done until this lower note has been reached. A Question, on the other hand, does not reach this lower note, that is to say, it is like an unfinished tune: the answer will finish off the tune by ending on the lower note.* This only applies to the ordinary Question. For there are other Questions which are really Statements or Denials, or have other meanings: for instance, "Is it not so?" can be nearly equivalent to "It is so", and "Is it so?" can be nearly equivalent to "It is not so".

But here I shall speak chiefly of those Questions which are of the nature of true Questions, especially those that ask for information.

The great advantage of a Question is that *it may*

* See "How to Learn Philology" (Sonnenschein), p. 192.

——— ————

encourage the reader or hearer to think for himself, and prepare the ground for what is coming. There are certain Questions, also, which are much better than Statements, because they practically force the reader or hearer to *admit* a point before one proceeds to base some argument upon this point: a good instance will be found on p. 292.

Questions are also useful for the purpose of *excluding* views which are wrong: a stock instance would be "What went ye out for to see?" there comes a list of Questions which 'expect', or rather practically contain, the answer 'No'.

A Question may serve as a mark of *Emphasis:* it calls attention to a particular point as deserving special attention. It may serve to Emphasise what follows very much as a pause might. Being thus a mark of Emphasis, it should not be misused: it should not be employed where no Emphasis is wanted.

Open-air preachers are very fond of perpetually asking Questions of their audience, trying to keep the attention of their audience thus: but then, when the answer comes, the point is often found to be quite unimportant. This Question-asking becomes a bad habit; these preachers avoid saying anything directly, and always lead up to it by a Question: the result is that, when they have something which they really ought to Emphasise, one of their great means of Emphasis has lost its capacity.

Lastly, Questions introduce a certain amount of *Variety,* and occasionally they form a kind of rest: a series of Statements is apt to be somewhat wearying.

But Questions themselves can be wearying also, and can be singularly unnatural and 'didactic'. Thus the stock Question 'Who blew what how many times round the walls of where?' is almost as great a misuse of the art of Questioning as the words of the little prig, in the old-fashioned " Teacher's Guide": 'Oh mamma dear, is it true that in the year 63 B.C. Marcus Tullius Cicero was Consul and spoke against the arch-Anarchist Catiline?' The Answer of Mamma is 'Yes, my dear'; it should have been something else.

CHAPTER LV. OTHER RHETORICAL DEVICES.

FOR Rhetorical Devices I must refer to special Books on Rhetoric (e.g. Bain's); though anyone who really 'feels' his Ideas is likely to use the right 'Devices' as naturally as an Orator who really 'feels' his Ideas is likely to use the right expression and 'gestures'.

We cannot tell how far the greatest Orators introduced these 'artifices' consciously or instinctively: but, supposing that *you* do not use them instinctively, then it may be as well to study their use and to practise their use. Demosthenes, Cicero, Burke, and Macaulay, might be among the Text-books.

The means are not to be employed haphazard: to use them for a quiet narrative would be a mistake, an offence against *Appropriateness* (p. 243). At first, i.e. until the use or non-use becomes half-automatic, you will have to be constantly asking yourself, ' Is this means necessary or useful just here?'

To distract the attention and emotions by 'Figures of Speech', as it were by vivid colouring or minute accuracy of detail, to the wrong things or to minor points, is a thing to be sedulously avoided. To lash oneself into 'Declamation' over mere trifles, as some Satirists have done, belongs more to the province of Comedy and Tragedy. The 'habit' of Declamation and Ranting is to be kept under.

Among Rhetorical Devices might be classed

> Questions (p. 296),
> Repetitions (p. 216),
> Contrasts (p. 291),
> Comparisons (p. 281).

Many names are given to the Devices, such as the name of 'Similes', 'Metaphors', and 'Tropes' to the different kinds of Comparisons.

Balance, Parallelism, and Antithesis are very common Devices. We saw an instance of Balance on p. 215, where the 'house on rock' balanced the 'house on sand' by way of Contrast. The Psalms are full of Parallelisms also, the sense of the first half often being equivalent to the sense of the second half.

> 'Who will lead me into the strong city: and who will bring me into Zion?'
> 'Hast not thou forsaken us, O God: and wilt not thou, O God, go forth with our hosts?'

Indeed, this was an early feature of 'Poetry'. Here the correspondence is one of sense, or of mere words. Thucydides and Tacitus were very fond of using words which seem to be Contrasts, and to balance one another, but which really did not do so.

'Balance' of Sound of course often appears in Metre, and in Rhyme, and in actual Music. The sense of Balance and Correspondence leads us to *expect* and wait for certain sounds. The Balance gives satisfaction.

'Contrast' in Sounds is a point well worth study. We shall soon speak of 'Alliteration' (p. 304), but it probably has its opposite, in Sounds that are not in the least like one another.

Besides the Balance or Contrast of Sense, of Words,

of Rhythm, and of Sounds, we may notice *Exaggeration* (or Hyperbole). It abounds in Proverbs, and in the New Testament, and indeed among Southern and Eastern Nations* generally. See p. 160.

The *Epigram* ('his success was built up on the most solid foundations, that is, on failures') is frequently in the nature of an Exaggeration.

'*Interjections*' are another Rhetorical weapon. Carlyle should be studied here, as also for his *apostrophising* (e.g. 'O happy king, whom . . .').

Unnatural and *striking* phrases, orders of words, etc., were another feature of Carlyle's Rhetoric.

He also used *Humour*, generally a severe kind of Humour. Humour is to be classed as a Rhetorical weapon, and indeed as one of the most powerful.

Bain gives a good List of Devices in his "Rhetoric and Composition". He mentions, for example,

Irony, or saying "the contrary of what is meant" (e.g. 'You *are* clever!');

Innuendo, or "implying instead of stating plainly"; but this cannot be altogether distinguished from the understating of the truth, (which is called Meiosis or Litotes), as e.g. in the slang expressions 'just a little', and 'rather', meaning 'very much so'.

> 'His honour rooted in dishonour grew,
> and faith unfaithful kept him falsely true',

would be an example of verbal Paradox or *Oxymoron*.

Climax, i.e. the leading up to the strongest point, is familiar to everyone (e.g. 'That deed was great, heroic, godly').

Its opposite, *Anti-Climax or Bathos*, is useful especially when one wishes to throw scorn or ridicule upon a person or an idea, as in 'he marched, with his arm̀ed legions, with the troops whose ancestors had won the world, against the fierce Barbarians who had defied his power : at length he came within reach of the enemy, and began his work in earnest. Single-handed he carried it out, and returned to celebrate his triumph in the great Capital.

* See "The Teaching of Jesus To-day" (Grant Richards).

Yes, he had done well, and with him alone rested the glory—*of having picked up a few shells upon the seashore !*

Among Rhetorical Figures may also be classed such phrases as :—

'he is *a Croesus*' ;

'he lets *the brute* get uppermost in him, and lets the angel fall' ;

'let not *ambition* mock their useful toil' ;

' Phyllis is my only *joy*' ;

' I hate *red tape*' ;

'a *restless pillow*'.

See further Bain's "Rhetoric, etc.", from which some of the above instances are taken.

CHAPTER LVI. **RHYTHM.**

RHYTHM, in its wider sense, includes something more than mere sound : for instance, there is a certain *balance of sense* as well as a balance of sound. It is often quite as important that the sense should correspond as that the sound should correspond. We have seen an instance on page 215, where the house on rock 'balanced' the house on sand.

But undoubtedly the Music and Rhythm of sound alone, in Essaying-writing and Speaking, are quite a power in themselves. We could scarcely realise what the oratory of Gladstone or Canon Farrar would be without its Rhythm. We may well doubt if it would then hold its hearers or carry them along. A (Conservative) Member of Parliament once said that he did not like listening to Gladstone's Speeches because they so often carried him away and 'convinced' him without giving him any idea as to any particular meaning. He said that, even as he read the Speeches in a paper, a similar effect was still perceptible. Had he analysed them, and considered the Ideas as Ideas, I doubt if the effect would have been anything like this.

One of the secrets of Rhythm is *Variety*. This does not mean so much that the Rhythm should differ in an unscientific way, merely for the sake of difference, but that each particular Rhythm should be *appropriate* to its subject. In Poetry there was no poet who could use his Rhythm so well as Vergil. The mere sound of some lines has been known to convey the general meaning even to those who understood no Latin at all. This is really a very great test. In Prose, perhaps De Quincey has come as near to this effect as anyone else, and there is no doubt that Prose has its metres as well as Poetry. Of course Prose has nothing quite so fixed as, for instance, the Latin Hexameter metre, but yet there is a certain metre or Rhythm demanded for certain passages and certain positions in the Paragraph or a Sentence: Cicero's *esse videātur* was decidedly a good finish up to a sentence.

The ancient Writers and Orators among the Greeks, and among the Romans in their train, paid far more attention to the Rhythm than we do. Especially did they avoid harshness and jingle, although they were not averse to Alliteration.

Alliteration has a great deal of effect on Rhythm: how much effect we seldom realise, because Alliteration is *not always obvious* on the surface. Professor Barrett Wendell gives the following quotation, "Quietly rested beneath the drums and tramplings of three conquests". Here the casual reader may not notice the perfect Alliteration, forgetting that *t* and *th* and *d* are all letters of the same class, namely Dentals, and that *r* occurs once or twice, and so helps the Alliteration.

The letters *p*, *b*, *m*, *(f)*, *v*, all are Labials; *t*, *d*, *n*, and *th* are Dentals; *k*, *c*, *qu*, *g*, *ng*, and to some extent *w* are Gutturals; and *r* and *l* are Liquids.* It will thus be seen that Alliteration is something subtler than the mere putting together of a number of words which begin with the same letter, as in combinations like

* See "How to learn Philology" (Sonnenschein).

'Little Liver Pills', 'Rhyme and Reason', 'Deadwood Dick's Big Bonanza'.

A still subtler form of Alliteration, and one little studied, is that between Vowels and Consonants. For Vowels also can be classed as Gutturals, etc.* A special branch of Alliteration would be the Rhyme; and Onomatopoeia may be mentioned also.

As to general principles, it may be noticed that a quick Rhythm is suitable for a quick narrative, especially for exciting scenes, and for impassioned oratory, whereas the slower Rhythm may be better for a quiet narrative, and for calm and logical reasoning. Shortness, again (the Words or the Sentence or both of them being short), will be suited for quick narrative and impassioned argument.

Of course Rhythm can also give the effect of suspense, and the effect of majesty.

Striking Ideas, again, can be expressed by a striking and unusual Rhythm.

Closely connected with Rhythm is not only the length of the words, but also their *origin*. *The choice between a Latin word and an Anglo-Saxon word* will often make a considerable difference to the Rhythm, and the effect on the shortness or length of Sentences is considerable. Notice also how a long word at the end of a Sentence or Paragraph (p. 262) will do much to prevent 'tameness'. The choice between many single clauses and single complicated Paragraphs is intimately connected with the Rhythm also.

And so is Punctuation, though Punctuation and Rhythm are seldom mentioned together. A badly punctuated passage rarely reads well: the unsatis-

---

* See "How to Learn Philology" (Sonnenschein), p. 204.

X

factory feeling which it produces cannot be overcome by the otherwise excellent swing.

As to Practice, the Old Testament, and the New Testament in the Authorised Version, will always be models for Rhythm; and almost by their side will stand the Translations of the Iliad and Odyssey by Butcher and Lang, and by Leaf, Lang, and Myers. The New Testament should be analysed, and the secrets of its Rhythm should be discovered, especial attention being paid to the length of the words, to the length of the Sentences, the absence of harshness, and the occasional (and often veiled) Alliteration. Not only should the passages be copied out, but they should also be *read out loud*. I believe that a *Phonograph* would be a very valuable help, and before long we shall see it introduced into Education.

A word of warning is necessary here. The ancients studied Rhythm so carefully that they often took little pains to study the sense. The Athenians and the Romans listened for the sound and expected it to affect them in certain pleasing ways, as music will do, and, entranced by this pleasing feeling which it produced, and by the emotion which it aroused, they too often failed to demand good sense or even truth: they sacrificed the Ideas to the Expression. And this is what many Writers have done again and again after their time, and many Speakers. The criticism passed on thousands of Writers and Speakers must be: "Their Style is beautiful, but their Ideas are meaningless or execrable, and so is the Arrangement of their Ideas".

Yet, in spite of its misuse, Rhythm is a factor that must not be neglected in Writing and Speaking. Often, even when we read to ourselves, we cannot possibly fail to notice the Rhythm; it is bound to affect us.

And so, in revising the Composition, we should (see p. 330) give one special revision to the Rhythm: we should read the Composition out loud so that we may study and criticise that alone. And particular attention should be paid to the Rhythm at the end of every Paragraph and at the very end of the whole Composition, where, as we have seen, it is as a rule bad to end with a few short words, and better to end with longer words, forming a Rhythm marked by dignity, smoothness, and tranquillity. With rare exceptions, it is wrong to end up with a quick sharp jerk like this.

CHAPTER LVII. CHAPTERS.

THE Chapter of a Book may be compared with an Essay: like the Essay, it has Paragraphs, Sentences, Clauses, and Words.

But there is a difference: for the Essay may be complete in itself, even if it suggests problems for research; whereas the Chapter is only a part, and, however important a part it may be, and however complete it may seem, it should stand in a certain relation to the other Chapters or parts. If I may use a Comparison, the Essay is like the player of a Single at Lawn-Tennis: he plays for himself and by himself. The Chapter is like one of a Football team: he should play as well as he can so far as his own part is concerned, but he should play with reference to the other members of, e.g., the Fifteen: he should help them and in turn expect their help. If he is a Half-Back, he should often 'feed' the Three-Quarters, but should expect the Forwards to help him to get the ball.

On the one hand, then, the Chapter should be perfeet, and should have Unity: it should deal with a special subject or aspect of a subject. This might be called *Specialisation.* But, on the other hand, the Chapter should be connected with the other Chapters, and should lead up to their work, help their work, and supplement their work, expecting similar services in return. This would be called *Scientific Division of Labour, or Co-operation.*

The Chapter, then, is to the Book very much what the Paragraph is to the Chapter, or (to a smaller extent) what the Sentence is to the Paragraph, or (to a still smaller extent) what the Word is to the Sentence.

For example, as the *length* or bulk of a Paragraph (when compared with the other Paragraphs) should greatly depend upon its importance (the word 'mass' is aptly used by Prof. Barrett Wendell), so the length of a Chapter (as compared with the other Chapters) should greatly depend upon its importance also.

Again, as the Paragraphs should vary in length, so should the Chapters.

Once again, as the Paragraph should, as a rule, begin with what is *Interesting* (e.g. the scope and subject of the Paragraph), or with what will *Connect* it with the previous Paragraph, so the Chapter should, as a rule, be guided by a similar Law.

In fact, the various Principles which we apply to the Paragraph should be applied to the Chapter also.

A PARAGRAPH is a part or member of an Essay or a Chapter or a Speech. A Paragraph is made up of Sentences, and these are made up of Clauses or Words. Apart from the relations of the Paragraph to the Essay, and of the Paragraph to the Sentence, it is very hard to say what the Paragraph is or should be, but a good general description would be this. A Paragraph should be capable of being summed up in a single Sentence or as a single Idea. Professor Wendell's remarks are far the best that I have ever read on the subject: he shows that, among the best Paragraphs, are those in which the first few words and the last few words will give the general Idea of the whole.

The *first* Paragraph of an Essay should be Interesting, the *last* Paragraph should generally be Impressive. The *middle* Paragraphs should be connected with one another, that is to say, as a general rule, each should be a link between the one before and the one after. This does not mean that the last Sentence of one Paragraph should necessarily be linked to the first Sentence in the next, and the last Sentence in this to the first Sentence in the next, and so on: for the Connexion can come in the middle. It is *possible* to write an Essay or make a Speech of twenty Paragraphs, such that each Paragraph shall have an Interesting Beginning and an Impressive Ending, and the Connexion between each Paragraph and the next shall come in the middle of the Paragraph: in other words, as we read a fresh Paragraph we shall be Interested in its Beginning, but perhaps we shall not see its Connexion with what has been said before until we come near to the middle of it.

But it would be a mistake to arrange a whole Essay or Speech on this plan: here as elsewhere there must be Variety. Sometimes the Beginning should be Interesting (see p. 258), sometimes the Ending should be Impressive; but at other times the Ending of one Paragraph and the Beginning of the next need not be impressive and interesting, but may merely be (see p. 263) linked together in some way or another.

Each Beginning should, as far as is possible, arouse the attention, but there should also be as much Variety as is feasible; the Ending should never be tame, and it should never be of such a kind that you can cut it off without losing anything from the sense. Frequently it is true that, the greater the Climax, the better the Paragraph. The Latins were particularly careful to avoid Endings of a tame or unnecessary kind: they often kept their Verb till the end of a Sentence, so that, until the last word had been spoken, you could not say that the sense was really finished. Nevertheless they broke through this rule for the sake of Clearness, Emphasis, Interest, Variety, or even Connexion.

Not only should there be Variety in the Beginnings and Endings, but *the length should be varied also:* some Paragraphs should be longer and others shorter (p. 247). Much will depend upon the *importance* of the Idea which lies inside the Paragraph. If it is very important, then the Paragraph should as a rule be long: among other reasons, it may have to contain Repetition, Comparisons, and Contrasts: this in itself will make the Paragraph longer. Nevertheless, a Paragraph of a very short kind is often even more impressive than a very long Paragraph. One of the most impressive in the whole of literature is a Paragraph or Sentence of two words, "Jesus wept". On the average, and for ordinary purposes, short Paragraphs are better than long.

We said at the beginning that the Paragraph should often admit of being summed up in a single Sentence, or *as a single Idea*: so that, besides the Beginning the Ending and the length, which must secure Interest, (often) Impressiveness, Connexion, and Variety, four great principles of Composition, we have to consider the fifth principle, namely, *Unity*. Anything which throws light on that Idea (e.g. the details on p. 212) will not violate the Law of Unity; whereas anything which goes apart from that Idea and outside it but does not throw light upon it, nor yet serve as a Connecting link between that Idea and another, will violate the Law of Unity. It will be seen, then, that the principle really is to some extent *Economy*: we must cut off whatever is unnecessary, that is to say unnecessary and inappropriate to the Idea of the Paragraph.

For the use of the *Résumée*, in case we are forced to digress, see p. 266.

Such are a few of the principles with regard to Paragraphs: for further details the Reader is referred to Barrett Wendell's book on English Composition, which will supplement what I say here.

As to *the writing-out of Paragraphs*, it is a good rule, especially if they are to be Type-written or printed afterwards, to write out each on a separate piece of paper, at any rate for the rough copy. A friend of mine, who has done a good deal of Writing, told me that he had to write the first three pages of one of his Essays over and over again (I forget how many times); and this must be a very common experience. He said that, after much experience, he had taken to using scissors and paste and cutting out that which he did not wish to alter. Obviously he had made two faults : first, he had not prepared his Essay, or at least he had not prepared it on a good plan (e.g. by the "Card-System"), and secondly he did not know of the value of writing out each Paragraph on a separate piece of paper. Yet the value is obvious.

When you have three Paragraphs on a single sheet of paper, if you have to re-write the second one, this would naturally entail the re-writing of the first and the third as well, if my principle were not adopted. A Publisher once told me that it would be misleading for the Printers ; but this is quite wrong, as I know from experience, *if* you give them clear instructions to the contrary ; for, as we shall see on page 378, before anything is sent to be Type-written or printed, instructions should be given which are to apply to the whole of the Composition ; and it was a great error to suppose that Printers like to have a large page full of writing : in fact once, when printers were doing some things for me in a hurry, they actually cut up my manuscript almost into shreds.

Two more words may be said here.

Each Paragraph should begin a little *inland*, a little to the right of the left-hand side of the page, so that the reader may easily see where the fresh Paragraph begins ; this is called *Indentation* and is most important :

many books have so slight an Indentation that they look almost as if each Chapter were one single Paragraph.

On page 362 I said that an Analysis might be given in the margin of a Book or Essay, or else a Scheme might be kept quite separate: perhaps the best way would not only be to do the Scheme before you do the Essay, and perhaps to give it up with the Essay, but to do the Analysis in the margin after you have done the Essay, so that you may not only see where you violated the Law of Unity (p. 250), but may also show the reader the contents of each Paragraph, in case he wishes to look back and read any part over again.

As practice for improving Paragraphs in various ways, it might be as well to study those of the best Reviews, such as the " Nineteenth Century " or the " North American Review ", and to Analyse the Paragraphs, making notes of their Beginnings, their Endings, their Length, their Unity, and their Variety. Occasionally you might write a short Paragraph or two, for instance to local Papers, if you can find anything that they are likely to put in.

CHAPTER LIX. SENTENCES.

THE units in a Sentence are Clauses and Words. Of course Sentences vary very greatly from one another: one may have a single Clause, another may have two Clauses side by side, joined together by some word like 'and' or 'but', and another may have a Period made up of several Clauses. For instance "he went" would be a single Clause; 'he went and saw', would be two Clauses side by side (or Co-ordinated); "he went in order that he might see" would be one Clause as a Principal Clause, to which the other is Subordinate and on which it is Dependent.

We have seen that a Book is composed of Chapters, that each Chapter, which may be something like an Article or Essay, is composed of Paragraphs, that the Paragraph is composed of Sentences, and that the Sentences may be composed of Clauses, and that the Clause is composed of Words. We have seen also that for the Chapter and Paragraph and Sentence and Clause certain general principles hold good. Some of these general principles will be applied here to a Sentence.

First of all, the Sentence is to some extent a single thing or *Unity*, a complete whole, which should admit of being summed up as a single Idea.

But, though it is complete in itself, to some extent it is also *helped by other Sentences, and it helps them in turn.* Just as each person is dependent on other persons, and helps them, and is helped by them, even while to some extent he lives his own life, so it is with Sentences. Each is not merely an Individual, but also a member of a whole, of which other Individuals (his 'neighbours') are members also.

The *Connexion* between one Sentence and the one before it, and the one after it, is not wont to be much studied by itself. Attention is so often fixed on the Grammar and on the Vocabulary that little of it is left for the order of Sentences and their relation to one another. But of these relations we have already spoken in the Chapter on Connexion.

The *Order of Words in a Sentence* is now studied far more carefully than it used to be. The natural Order (as in 'he goes') is the Subject and then the Predicate. The Predicate may consist of a Verb, an Object, and an Adverb : for instance, 'he did it well' illustrates all these. But this is not the only type of Sentence : some Sentences have no Subject or no Predicate expressed, e.g. Exclamations.

There are many deviations from the above order : thus, in 'this man was Julius Caesar', the subject comes last ; sometimes the Adverb or the Object may come first.

The Order of Words will depend partly on the topic, partly on the aim of the Writer, partly on the need for Variety, and Interest, and partly on the Connexion of the Sentence with other Sentences, and the Connexion of its various parts with one another, and partly on *Emphasis*.

This Connexion of the parts of a Sentence with one another deserves special attention : *those parts which are most closely connected with one another in meaning should be closely connected in order also.*

Professor Meiklejohn, in his "Art of Writing English" (p. 277 foll.), gives some very useful Instances of bad order, e.g.

'Five pounds reward is offered for the discovery of any person injuring this property by order of the chief of police'.

'This monument was erected to the memory of John Smith, who was shot, as a mark of affection by his brother'.

I offer a few other instances: most Public Notices should be carefully studied from this point of view!

'The Reader in Comparative * * ology will be glad to see any students who think of reading for Section E of Part II. of the Classical Tripos at his rooms in * * * * College between 10 and 11 on any of the following days: Saturday June 10, Saturday June 17, and Monday June 19.'

'The love which, perchance, follows some when they are dead to that place where a human testimony will not be in vain.'

In the last two passages it is to be noticed that the mistakes in the order of words *can often be remedied by Punctuation*. 'The effect of walking on the heart and lungs' reads very badly, and, if the Construction is not changed to 'the effects which walking has on the heart and lungs', the words may be punctuated thus: 'the effect, of walking, on the heart and lungs': the order of words does not here strike one as being so wrong: at any rate the proper meaning is clear. *The very severest test of the right order will be the removing of all stops:* it is too severe a test and one which legal documents and Latin will stand, but which very few ordinary English writings will stand.

Another common fault, besides that of putting a word in its wrong place in a Sentence, is that of using the same word in different senses: but for this, and others, I must refer to such works as Professor Meiklejohn's.

We have seen above that the most important parts of a Sentence are the Beginning and the Ending. In the Beginning will often come that which will *link* the Clause with the Clause which comes before. The Ending should not be tame—often a long word will do much to redeem the tameness—but should as a rule give something without which the Sentence is not quite complete. As a rule the reader should be listening and waiting for the Ending, his interest and attention being kept up till the Sentence is actually finished. Another common Ending, however, is one which prepares for the next Sentence, and which is a link between the two Sentences.

So we see that, besides the *natural* order of words, at least two principles are to be considered :—

first, Emphasis, which e.g. may make the Subject come at the end, or the Object at the beginning ;

secondly, the Connexion of a Sentence with the Sentence before and the Sentence after.

Yet another principle would be Economy, the cutting out of what is unnecessary ; but of this we have spoken on p. 239.

As to *the length of Sentences*, it should vary very considerably, partly to ensure *Variety* and Change and to prevent monotony ; partly also for the sake of *Proportion*, an important Sentence often being longer than one which is unimportant ; but, partly also *according to the subject* and the 'mood', rapid and exciting descriptions and passionate arguments requiring shorter Sentences than quiet descriptions and quiet arguments.

A series of 'loose' Clauses, following on one another without Conjunctions, is best for exciting and (certain) emotional passages; such a series *with* Conjunctions (e.g. 'and', 'for', 'but') will be less 'excited', but still may be good for rapidity; the compact Period, however, especially when the climax, the main Clause, is reserved till the end, and when there are Subordinate Clauses (like these last two Clauses) by which the interest and suspense are kept up, may be better for quieter narrative and quieter argument. The 'suspense' should not be overdone: if there is any danger of this, sum up the gist in a few short sharp words at the end.

There is another point also to be noted about Sentences, and that is their *Construction*. A Sentence may be put in many forms, such as (see p. 273) Abstract and Concrete and very Concrete.

Again (see p. 253) we may have a Statement, a Question, an Exhortation, or an Exclamation. The Writer or Speaker often has to choose which form he will use, and here again he must be guided by the subject he is writing about, by his aim, and by his readers or hearers. In oratory he will be far more inclined to use Questions and Exclamations and Exhortations.

As safe general rules about Sentences, one might say 'Keep them rather *short* usually, but occasionally vary their length and vary their characteristics: connect them one with another; and, while ending the Sentence itself, pay great attention to the order of the Words and to the length of the Words.

IT is not the purpose of this Book to say much about Grammar (Syntax). But one rule is worth bearing in mind constantly, and that is: KEEP ON THE SAFE SIDE.

While you do not sacrifice Clearness or Simplicity, avoid what would call down the criticism of the *strictest* critic, or even of the grossest pedant. If you can, you had better steer clear of criticism.

Hundreds of critics get a reputation for accuracy because they insist on some 'rule', as they call it. They may be quite forgetful or ignorant of the fact that the language may be changing—that what *was* a 'rule' fifty years ago is ceasing to or has ceased to be a 'rule' to-day. Prof. Barrett Wendell justly calls attention to the fact that a great deal of what was *not* 'Good Use' some time ago, is becoming or has become 'Good Use' to-day. Fashions change.

Now among the growing Constructions of to-day, which will probably grow over and under and through the severe critic's wall, several are especially noticeable, viz.

(i) 'He was going *to just look* inside', which is called a '*Split Infinitive*'. 'To' and 'look', says the critic, must come together, and must not be divided by an Adverb. Nevertheless I prophesy that before another century has passed some 'Split Infinitives' (not all) will be as 'regular' as 'that he might just look inside'. The

Analogy of this latter Construction is almost bound to be at work. This will be so because masses of educated people have felt the Construction to be *natural*, and in spite of the fact that critics tell them it is *wrong*. Anyone who studies Historical Grammar will find our language full of such Analogies. Thus 'under the circumstances', which sounds so familiar and so natural, was once wrong : and even now (p. 207) the critics pounce on it. But are the critics to lay down a law, admitting 'under the conditions' but forbidding the *Analogical* Construction 'under the circumstances', though 'circumstances' no longer mean simply 'things that stand around' (circumstantia)? We shall probably live to see the millions push many a Construction into 'Good Use', unless the critics exert their every effort against this perfectly natural tendency to Analogies.

(ii) We can say : 'Seeing that this is so, it may be said . . . ', for 'seeing that' has become almost equivalent to an indeclinable 'since'. But how often we read : 'Knowing the truth of this, it is obvious that the following holds good'. The 'free' Participle in *-ing* is also a growing Construction. I read in a Daily Paper " My house was struck a few years ago, taking off the roof."

Now in all these cases, where there *is* a doubt, keep on the safe side, and say : 'He was going *just to look* inside', 'Knowing the truth of this, we see clearly that the following holds good', 'A few years ago the lightning struck my house, taking off the roof'.

The other ways are not yet 'Good Use'. Till they *are*, avoid them.

(iii) The commonest source of error is what may be called *Blending* or Contamination.

"He supplies no plan of the Pompeian house, and does not mention the upper story which remains in one of *them*" appears in a well-known Paper. If the writer had said "he supplies no plans of Pompeian houses . . . of them", *or* "he supplies no plan of the Pompeian house . . . in one of the samples", he would not have been criticised; but, as a matter of fact, he here *blends* these two Constructions, and the result, the Mongrel as it were, is so natural that few would notice anything wrong as they read the whole paragraph.

To show how common the tendency is, and how natural the result appears, I suggest a few instances for the reader to consider: let him find the two regular Constructions of which each of the following Constructions is a Blend or Contamination.*

1. "The subject is rarely handled in books, and still less rarely from the pulpit." (This is, I think, the only mistake of language, in the whole of that book).

2. "The house . . . was in the best condition of any . . ."

3. "The subject is of less importance in their estimation to the handling."

4. "Ah! there was 'side' amongst the conquerors in those days, just as Baron de Browne or Smythe puts on now with their subordinates."

[The three last passages are from a single Novel by a well-known writer: 4 contains two 'Contaminations'].   .

*

---

* See "How to Learn Philology" (Sonnenschein), pp. 69–70, 145.

1. 'still less often'+'still more rarely';
2. 'in the best condition of all'+'in a better condition than any';
3. 'is of less importance than . . .' 'yields, in respect of its importance, to . . .';
4. 'just as B. or S. puts on side'+'just like the side which B. or S. puts on';

'B. or S. puts on with his subordinates'+'B. and S. put on with their subordinates'.

I could quote thousands of examples, but these will suffice: the Construction is 'wrong' in itself, but is a mixture of two Constructions which are both 'right'.

'He didn't make more mistakes than he could help' is a 'Contamination' which not one in a million would notice: in fact, it has become 'Good Use'. It will surprise the reader to find, when he *analyses* the words, that 'than he could *not* help' would be more accurate, technically. Mr. G. A. Falk called my attention to this instance.

'*Whom* say ye that I am?' is another case where 'Good Use' would probably lend her queenly sanction.

(iv) "A bachelor's room, who was fond of shelves". Here the order of words is unsatisfactory: 'the room of a bachelor . . .' would be all right.

Whenever you come across such mistakes in your reading, stop and correct them by (*a*) changing the Construction (this is generally easy), and, if possible, by (*b*) changing the order of Words. But alter as little as possible: this will make the Exercise the very best practice.

CHAPTER LXI. **WORDS, OR VOCABULARY.**

I SHALL say little here, except that what Prof. Barrett Wendell calls 'Good Use' is to be considered, i.e. what is recognised not by one good writer only but by the generality of good writers *at the time being*. For 'Good Use' varies.

But here, as in the sphere of Syntax, I would say KEEP ON THE SAFE SIDE. There may be some slang word which has *almost* become part of the Literary Language of to-day : but, unless you are an 'Authority', you had better wait, and use an older and safer word.

This does not apply universally. If, for example, you are writing a Novel, it is 'inappropriate' to make all your characters speak in the same style, as Scott does. The Coster and the Cockney have Dialects of their own, and it would be unfair to accuse them of speaking as if they were Penny-a-liners.

Flaubert used to take enormous pains over his Vocabulary, so that it should be not only *pure* (i.e. free from slang and from whatever was not 'Good Use'), but also the exact expression of his meaning and not of any other meaning. The words must convey one Idea clearly, and *one Idea only*.

Of Obscurity I need not speak here : I shall simply refer to p. 228 foll., where I show how the Technical and Abstract terms account for a good deal. The *Double Entendre* also (intentional or unintentional) is too familiar to need much illustration. Supposing that " Money returned if not satisfactory" followed an Advertisement for some Cure, then, when people demanded back their money, it might be answered that "the money was *quite* satisfactory". A certain orator's speeches were full of Sentences which either had no clear meaning or had two possible meanings. Of course there are occasions where a Double Entendre is *intended*, and therefore 'appropriate' to the Writer's aim.

If only for the sake of the jingle of sound, it is well to avoid that common error of first using a word and then, directly afterwards, again using it [or some word of the same family] in a different sense, as in 'We cannot make out why he makes this distinction', 'he felt that there was no ill-feeling'.

An undoubted difficulty is to steer between Tautology and needless Variety. I have purposely left pp. 310-311 just as I had dictated them, so that the reader may notice the bad effect of the repetition of the word 'Paragraph'. For a specimen of the reverse—a change of words where the idea is unchanged—see p. 254. This example also deserves study :—

"Every quality that is requisite in a man to make him completely and honourably prosperous is *necessary* to *entire success* in the games of boys".

A needless alteration in the Construction of a Parallel or Balancing Clause (p. 292), or in the Subject of a Sentence, is also to be avoided. It is here that a Classical Education is almost bound to tell.

For Latin and Anglo-Saxon Words, see pp. 244, 305.

CHAPTER LXII. WRITING, SPELLING, AND PUNCTUATION.

I SHALL only offer a few notes here, and shall refer to the Books which deal with these subjects.

As to *Writing*, it should above all things be clear and legible, with enough *space* between the words and between the lines. The latter is the more important in one way, viz. that it is easier to insert additions if the lines are further apart. Lately I have taken to writing (for the Press) on every other line instead of on every line. There should also be *Margins* (see p. 362).

Type-writing (see p. 369) is becoming more and more commonly used, and for certain purposes it is indispensable. But here also spaces should be left between the lines, as well as Margins at the sides and bottoms of the pages.

Fresh Paragraphs should begin to the right, i.e. a little *inland*.

For the question of *Underlining*, see p. 270; and, for the Marginal Analysis, p. 362.

As to Capital Letters, it will probably be thought that this Book has far too many: at any rate, I think it marks almost the extreme limit to which one may go.

The position of the body while you are writing is a matter of very great importance. I do most of my MSS. (and of my work generally) standing at a high desk. For details I must refer to " The Training of the Body" (Swan Sonnenschein).* Here I will just mention that, if one is sitting, the seat should have a back and should not be too narrow, nor should it be too far from the table or desk. The paper should be fair and square before one and should not go across to either side, but the desk itself should slope down towards you. Be sure to have a good light, rather behind you and to the left.

Do not sit for too long at a time, but walk about, or work standing, for a change. I like to do some work sitting, some standing, and some lying down. Much depends on the subject. It is worth while to notice that one can do some subjects better in certain positions than in others (and at certain times of the day also).

Of course it is a mistake to work directly after a heavy meal, for then the blood is needed in the digestive organs and should not be drawn away from them to the brain. But it is also a great mistake to work hard directly after severe exercise, or to take severe exercise directly after hard work. Intervals of gentle exercise (such as walking, or kicking about) are quite a different thing: they may help the brain-work very considerably.

Spelling.

Here 'Good Use' is most important, and also the principle of keeping to the safe side. Such spellings as 'develop', 'labor', etc., are growing upon us rapidly: are they 'correct' yet, or do they still have a *soupçon* of America such as the severest English critics object to? If so, then at present 'develope' and 'labour' are safer.

Only let us remember that fashions *do* change.

---

* In the press.

Punctuation deserves a little volume to itself.

To say that a piece of Composition should be clear even if one removes the stops is to demand too much: yet to write such a piece is excellent practice, and of course in Latin this test may constantly be applied.

As it is, Punctuation is a great help to clearness (see p. 317), and to Emphasis (cp. esp. the Note of Exclamation).

The commonest *Faults* are the following.

(i) Too few Commas:—

'And when he had said this, he lay down' is a type of Sentence where I should prefer to punctuate

'And, when he had said this, he lay down'.

But there are many who prefer the former method.

In the following instance, a Comma should most certainly have been inserted after 'can', 'We who can go to the country', and probably after 'we' also. I may remark that, for a Sentence like 'Those who can, go to the country', neither this Punctuation, nor this with an extra Comma after 'those', nor the absence of Commas, gives an altogether satisfactory result. It is something like the choice between 'The cause is sheep' and 'the cause are sheep'. A change is needed, e.g. to 'sheep are the cause'.

Another doubtful case is where there is a 'triplet': some prefer to write

'his father, mother and children ...'

Personally, unless the 'mother' and 'children' are *meant* to go more closely together than the 'father' and 'mother', I should write

'his father, mother, and children . .'

Now, suppose we go on to say

'his father, mother, and children (,) were at the station to meet him',

shall we put a Comma after 'children', or not? This again is a vexed question. There was one learned English Professor who would have always written

'his father mother and children were at the station to meet him'.

(ii) Commas instead of Semicolons.

(iii) Colons or Semicolons instead of Full Stops.

(iv) Too many Notes of Exclamation.

(v) Omission of the Note of Interrogation, ?, especially after a long Sentence.

(vi) One Printer's fad that I can never understand is the order of the underlined marks in such a Sentence as

"Where is he going?" "Oh, he is going to the 'Parks,' to meet his cousin."

Why should we have 'Parks,' and not 'Parks',? Some Printers almost invariably alter my MSS., but I cannot believe that the custom has a scientific basis.

Correct Punctuation can be best practised in Letter-writing, or in the correction of Letters which have been written by others.

CHAPTER LXIII. REVISIONS.

1. It is needless to say that others will generally be able to Revise your Compositions better than you will, if you are willing to let them do so and if they are willing also.

2. But, if you are going to Revise them for yourself, be sure to leave as long *an interval* as possible; for, after an interval, what you have written will become something alien to you, as it were, and you will be able to read it more impartially. Besides this, new Ideas may have been thought out in the meanwhile, and unconsciously you will have corrected certain faults.

3. While Revising, you must think of your Composition as if it were the work of your deadliest enemy, and *criticise it very severely.*

4. The Ideas, that is to say, the Headings and Sub-Headings, should have been Revised already before the Composition is written out. In fact, all the Collection, etc., of Ideas will have been finished before you Write a word, except perhaps the Beginning and the Ending.

It remains for you therefore to criticise and Revise the Expression of Ideas; and at first you must not do this by a single process. This is why I use the word Revisions instead of the word Revision, for there are many things to be Revised, and they cannot all be considered at once. It would be too much to expect that anyone would Revise his Composition, let us say, ten times, looking out for something fresh each time: for instance, looking out at one time for ' *Obscurity* ', at another for *Prolixity*, at another for *Dulness*, at another for *Want of Connexion*, and so on. But there are one or two points of view which should be treated separately.

5. You should *read the Essay or Speech aloud*, if you can, with a view to correcting the *Rhythm;* and a special Revision might also be given to the Grammar and Punctuation, and perhaps even to the choice of Words.

So a really important piece of Composition will have to be Revised at least four or five times.

PART IV.

PART IV. **HOW TO TEACH, LEARN,
AND PRACTISE COMPOSITION:
WITH GENERAL HINTS.**

CHAPTER LXIV. **HOW TO CORRECT COMPOSITIONS.**

THE pupil benefits little if the Teacher simply takes a *'general impression'* of an Essay, and says that the Essay is worth so many marks, or reaches a certain standard. This may produce quite a fair estimate of the Essay, in fact in some cases it may give the very best idea of the relative merits of a number of Essays, but for the pupil himself it is next door to useless.

Nor is it much good to *underline individual mistakes*, and yet to fail to point out *why* they are mistakes, what is the principle underlying them, and *how* the mistakes might have been *avoided*.

Unless the Teacher has *the natural gift* of Correcting Essays, he must *analyse* the Essay, in order to criticise the *Ideas* and their *Arrangement*. But it is much better that this should be done by the Essay-Writer himself, and that the *Scheme* should be given in together with the Essay.

The first thing to do will be to criticise *the Ideas* (see p. 54), e.g. their Collection, Selection, Proportion, and Arrangement; and then to criticise their *Expression*, for instance to call attention to the obscurity of the language, its monotony, its harshness of Rhythm.

With each individual fault should be pointed out *the underlying principle:* the fault should be Corrected (if possible) by the Essay-Writer himself, and, above all, he should be made to *take Notes of his commonest faults*, and he should be told the best Exercises by which he may amend them.

A special Note-book might be kept in which the mistakes would be written down under their Headings, for instance under such Headings as Clearness (or Obscurity). With each mistake should be noted what the mistake is, why it has been made, and what would have been better, or (to put it in the language of School-books) what would have been the right answer.

The attention of each individual pupil should be devoted to Exercises on those special points in which he is *weakest*. He should be made to correct a number of faults of the same kind *in the Compositions of others*. A teacher of thirty pupils very seldom remembers that, in the thirty Compositions, he will probably have *examples of nearly every kind of mistake*, and that he has at hand a number of Exercises in criticism, which he may with great advantage set before his pupils, while the subject is still fresh in their minds.

The Teacher should not leave *too* long an interval between the writing-out and the correction of the Essay : he should correct it while the pupil still remembers it.

A good plan is to make a Class practise *Speaking*, either after or without preparation : those who are not Speaking should note the faults, and each Speech should be criticised directly after it is finished. The Teacher can be at hand to see fair play, and to supervise and direct. Notes should be made by each Speaker, after the criticism. The subjects should of course be of interest to the pupils.

CHAPTER LXV. HOW TO TEACH COMPOSITION.

THERE are many reasons why Books and Teachers so often fail to Teach.

First of all they may be too fond of *abstract phrases,* and may not suggest nearly enough examples and instances to make their meaning clear. I have (on purpose) left an instance of this on page 178 : it will be found that what I have written there is not nearly so clear as it would have been if I had given examples.

Teachers and Books frequently omit to explain the subject as a whole, and to *show how extraordinarily difficult it is.* They plunge straight into the intricacies of the subject, as if it were likely to be as simple to the pupil as it is to the Teachers.

Such Teachers will not at the outset lay any firm foundations on which to base their later teaching. They do not pay attention to each difficulty of the subject in turn, so as to [*concentrate their attention on* *each part of the subject in turn*] rather, they spend their time as it were in *polishing the surface.*

Again, I have noticed many Teachers at the University who have criticised, in precisely the same way, the scholar who is likely to get a First Division of the First Class, and the scholar who will be only too thankful if he scrapes into the Third Division of the Third Class. The polishing of the surface, and the attempt to remove little tiny faults or blemishes, may be quite

Z

appropriate for the already skilful and advanced pupil, but for the beginner such a polishing is quite out of place. It would be equally wrong to begin the details of a picture before you have sketched its outlines.

Once again, Books and Teachers *seldom point out the real interest and value of the subject.* They begin to *Teach* at once, whereas they ought first of all to show that the subject is worth teaching : either they do not realise its importance themselves, or, if they do, they do not insist on their pupils realising it also.

One great branch of Teaching they too often exclude : they do not give the pupil nearly enough *criticism* to do. We enjoy finding fault with someone else ; and, so long as this habit of criticism is kept within due limits, it is not only a good method of learning, but is also indispensable as a habit to be carried into every department of life. A pupil should certainly spend a great deal of his time in finding out and correcting faults in the work of others : those who would refuse to work hard in any other way can thus be made to take an interest in the subject at once. Give a boy a bad piece of Composition, and tell him that he is to be the critic and to find out the faults in it, and to show *why* these faults are faults, and the boy will not fail to learn a great deal. As it is, he does not take nearly as much interest in his work because he is always trying something himself and seeing *his* faults called failures.

More generally speaking, *every pupil should be made not only to criticise and correct, but also occasionally to Teach. In learning, there is nothing, absolutely nothing, that can take the place of the attempt to Teach others.* It ought to be made an integral part of the Class-work, at any rate in the higher Classes, that each pupil in turn should Teach the form for a short time every week or even every day, and then should be criticised by the rest of the form. It will be the master's duty to see that the criticism is fair and not unkind. The boy who is to give an account of the subject to nearly thirty boys, of about his own age, will be almost sure to be put upon his mettle and to do his level best. He will not be keen to make a fool of himself, and he may even get answers ready for the criticisms which may be made. The rest of the boys will be kept awake by this, far more easily than if the master went on talking and asking questions the whole time.

There is not time to mention all the faults of Teaching, but a certain one cannot be passed over, and that is that the pupils are not given nearly enough *choice.* Very often one single subject is set for an Essay, and that subject is supremely uninteresting or unpractical, perhaps for every single pupil: occasionally, at any rate, the pupil should be allowed to choose his own subject absolutely freely, or else within certain limits. He may (see p. 14) select out of a large list.

Teachers have undoubtedly many difficulties to contend against; most of them find little time for special work with *individual* pupils; a great many of them have never learnt the subject themselves: having done it more or less *by the light of nature*, they either still do it badly themselves, or else do it well enough but without the ghost of a notion as to how a beginner should set about doing it. It is not too sweeping a statement that in England few Teachers know how to Teach *anything*, except the art of being true gentlemen and true 'sportsmen'. Teaching does not come to most by nature, and it has not come to them by art. Of all subjects, Essay-Writing is that which they most lamentably fail to Teach.

The Examination-System throughout our country is about as useless for Teaching purposes as it could well be. Let us consider how valuable it might easily be. We may take for granted that in an Examination the person does his best, that is to say, the *incentive* of getting marks (or whatever it is) makes him put forth every effort. We may therefore presume that his work is nearly as good as *effort* can make it, and yet *what happens to his written work*, presumably his very best work, when it has been looked over and marked? *In nine hundred and ninety-nine cases out of a thousand the work is never looked at again.* This error is singularly stupid, for, if the papers were taken and if they were gone through and corrected soon afterwards by the Teacher with the pupil, they could be made a most splendid means of pointing out the faults as well as the merits. Every Examination Paper that is worth the name should not only be answered, but should be *gone through afterwards;* then the right answers should be given and learnt, and the wrong answers corrected.

Only a few more suggestions can be offered here, and for details I must refer to the Chapter on 'How to Correct'.

At the very outset the *difficulties* of the subject should be explained, and also the various *processes* which are involved ; thus in Essay-Writing the pupil should be made to understand the difficulty of Collecting Ideas, and then of Selecting and Rejecting, and then of Underlining the important Ideas, and then of Arranging the Ideas. He should be made to feel that *all the processes are very hard,* even when taken separate'ly. He should also be made to feel the difficulties of Expressing Ideas, and this should include the difficulty of Clearness, Emphasis, Variety, Rhythm, and so on.

He should also be told *why the subject and all its processes are interesting, and why they are valuable*, not only for Essay-writing, but also (e.g. see p. 400) for other purposes as well.

Then he should have *Exercises on these various separate processes*, one at a time: e.g. for Comparisons he should have at least three different classes of Exercises (see p. 289). The Exercises might take these forms:—

(1) What things do you understand best? The answer will perhaps be some Game or form of Athletics.

(2) What lessons can you draw from this Game (or whatever it is that you understand well)? The answers will perhaps be 'obedience to the Captain's orders', etc. (pp. 289–290).

(3) Find something which you know well, and which will illustrate the following principles:—Co-operation, Division of Labour, etc.

The learner should have practice not only in *doing*, but also (as we have seen above) in correcting. He should learn to correct the mistakes of others, as well as his own, and to see exactly where the faults lie, and then he should be made to *re-write* correctly that which has been done incorrectly.

When he has read anything in his work, he should (if possible) be made to put his acquired knowledge to the test and to apply it: he should never be allowed to learn anything that is *worth* learning, without going through it again to see whether he really knows and understands it, and, if possible, doing some Exercise to see whether he has really mastered it. He should be made to look at the same point in many different aspects.

Even while he is still young, he should be allowed to some extent to *choose* his own subjects, and to do *these especially*. This should be *at intervals*, the rest of the time being spent in practising weak subjects and weak departments of his Composition, such as the Arrangement of Ideas (p. 172), and (p. 227) the power of Expressing them clearly.

A great deal should be done *vivâ voce*. The pupils in any subject, whether it be History or Geography, should (as far as is feasible) be made to try the subject before they read or learn about it; after the lesson they should be made to try it once again, writing down the Ideas *as Headings*. The Teacher should help and direct them in finding out these Ideas for themselves, for instance (see p. 287) by means of Comparisons and Contrasts.

With regard to *Style*, as well as Ideas, *the New Testament should certainly form the basis of study:* see p. 217. It is a fault, if not a positive sin, to use the New Testament only for the purposes of teaching boys, e.g., that St. John was confined in the castle of Machærus, and never to teach them any lessons either of morality or of the kind which I have alluded to on page 217. I am very strongly of opinion that whatever *can* be taught from the New Testament *should* be taught from it. We cannot easily teach such subjects as Anatomy, Physiology, Euclid, Algebra, or Latin Grammar, from the New Testament, but we *can* teach much of the art of Composition from it.

Every now and then, *Time-Essays* should be given, that is to say, an Essay should be set which has to be done within a given time ; this makes a pleasant change, or an unpleasant change, but anyhow it *is* a change and it must quicken the pupil's powers and improve his promptitude. *For the pupil should aim not only at correctness and soundness, but also at rapidity.*

Debates and short Speeches are also an admirable Exercise. Forms and Classes at Schools ought to have plenty of Debates, and, to give the subject some interest, the pupils might even take various characters, e.g. represent various statesmen. No pupil should be allowed to read out his speech : at the most he should be allowed to refer to Headings which he has prepared beforehand. During the Debate, criticism of course should be allowed at the end of each Speech, and the master should also criticise, but the most important thing is that, at the end of the Debate, every pupil should write down the main Ideas on both sides of the question, the 'Pros and Cons', and the master should then go over them on the Black-board, and, after rubbing them out, he should make each boy reproduce them. Before each fresh lesson, the chief Ideas of the old lesson should be repeated.

Of course all this means a great deal of time and trouble and preparation, and a great deal of thought and tact on the part of the Teacher as well as of the learner, and of course such labour will be very slow and difficult at first. But no success can be expected without such labour, and, if this system were introduced into our Schools, we should be fitting every pupil to become in his turn a Teacher, if ever the opportunity should arise.

As it is now, *we send out our millions of young, not*

only badly taught, but with not the slightest notion of the right methods of Teaching, whereas the boy who had tried to Lecture, if only for five minutes, before a class of twenty-five other boys, would at least have realised that Teaching is a very difficult art; at least he would have had his interest aroused, and he would have had the advantages of practice.

Let me finish by *exposing that terrible fallacy that, if you cannot Teach naturally, if you are not a born Teacher, you will never be a Teacher at all.* Not one person out of a hundred or a thousand is a born Teacher, but there is no reason on earth why every one of the thousand should not master certain elementary principles of the art of Teaching, such as the following :

to find why the subject is interesting or useful, and to show the pupils why ;

to put himself into the position of the pupils, and to ask himself 'What do they understand already, and by means of which of these things, that they understand already, can I best Teach those things which they do not yet understand?

to make the pupils correct faults, helping them to see *why* faults *are* faults ;

to make them practise each part of the subject *per se*, by means of special Exercises ;

to make the pupils practise Teaching ;

and so on.

These are a very few of the many principles which every Teacher should know. He may not be able to teach perfectly, or even well, when he has tried to put them into practice, but at any rate he will not teach quite so badly as he would probably have taught by the light of nature.

IT is a very great error to suppose that the Teaching of any single subject should have only one single Aim and Object, unless indeed we define this Aim and Object as "true development and improvement".

But what is *true* development and improvement? It is the highest development and improvement of each individual, through his own efforts, so that he may help others to develope and improve similarly. The Americans might call this 'Teaching each individual to become as good a *Citizen* as he can'.

1. While having this as its Aim and Object, the Teaching should be as *interesting* and as *pleasant* as possible.

2. It should also be of the greatest possible *advantage* and profit, to the individual's 'mind, body, and estate'.

It is not enough that the individual should absorb a mass of 'information', or even that he should be skilful and successful in his own department (e.g. Essay-Writing). If this is all that the Teaching has done, then it has, to some extent, failed.

It should have taught the individual, for example,

(*a*) how to use this information, as well as to understand it ;

(*b*) how to study other subjects besides his own ;

(*c*) how to teach his own subject and also other subjects ;

(*d*) how to improve himself all round.

345

Such are a few of the Aims of Teaching : in other words, those who teach Essay-writing should of course try to help their pupils to prepare and write good Essays, and should put into their hands the means of self-correction, and the means of teaching and correcting others ; but they should also try to exercise and develope the mind and character of their pupils in all the best possible directions.

CHAPTER LXVII. **HOW TO PRACTISE.**

THE Habit of Practice is one which is very seldom acquired in early years, but it is among the most valuable habits of life. Benjamin Franklin was one of the few who understood how to acquire it. I cannot but think that, if it were once acquired, that is to say if a correct and scientific and interesting system of Practice were once acquired for any *one* subject, it could easily be applied, *mutatis mutandis*, to practically any other also.

Here, as elsewhere, we may begin by a few words on the *wrong method* of Practising.

In Essay-Writing and Speaking it is wrong Practice (at any rate at the outset) simply to try to do Essays, or make Speeches, to try, that is to say, to do the whole Essay or Speech as a single piece of work, and not to divide it into parts (see p. 45), and to Practise each part by itself. Why should this be wrong? One reason is that your Essay or Speech is certain to have many faults, and, unless you take these faults one by one, you will never really correct any single one of them. You cannot correct any one part properly when you have to be attending to ten other parts at the same time.

It is a mistake also *not to make notes*, i.e. always to be *doing*, and never *correcting;* never to analyse one's merits or faults, or the faults or merits of others, and never to find out the causes and underlying principles.

As to *the right way of Practising*, many of the above

Chapters will suggest methods for each particular department. Thus on page 63 foll. will be found a way of Practising the Collection of Ideas, on page 172 foll. a way of Practising their Arrangement, on page 231 a way of Practising Clearness ; and so on. For example, Bacon's Essays could be Analysed, and the Headings could then be reproduced from Memory (after an interval), then corrected, then re-arranged, then corrected again, and then Expressed.

One rule may be of great use. When I was treating of the choice of subjects I said that, if the occasion were an important one, such as an Examination where success was the main object, then it would be as well to choose one's strongest subject; but for ordinary occasions, where improvement should be the object rather than success, it is better to choose one's weakest subject. *In practice, then, go for your weakest points, but in emergencies use your strongest points.*＊

Practise *simple things first,* and Practise them if possible *in their right order.* The order has been given in the previous pages of this book (see p. 36): for instance, the Collection of Headings, and then of Sub-Headings, should go before Selection, and this before Arrangement, and this before Expression, and so on.

Each part must be Practised by itself, and some parts, such as the use of Comparisons and Contrasts, require (see p. 289) three separate methods of Practice.

To quote an instance, we have seen that the Arrangement of Ideas should be taken as a separate Exercise, and that either the "Card-System" should be used, or the division of Ideas into " 1, 2, 3, *a, b, c* ".

The Realising of Ideas has already been treated

＊ Cp. the advice in " Lessons in Lawn Tennis " (Upcott Gill).

(p. 231); but it is so important, so essential, that it needs a special word here.

Drawing, and the use of Diagrams, are of very great value: we are apt to learn far too much by *words*, and far too little by clear Ideas and by sights. A Diagram, or a Drawing, or a mental picture of a thing, will often help to make it very clear when nothing else will.

Paraphrasing is also valuable. Poetry should be paraphrased into Prose, and Prose into Poetry, and, at an advanced stage in Essay-Writing or Speaking, various styles might be imitated. At any rate, various forms of Expression should be studied side by side, for instance the Abstract and the Concrete. Supposing, for example, that we took the phrase " Wisdom brings happiness ", this would be Abstract: a Concrete expression would be " Wise men are happy ", a still more Concrete expression would be " Socrates, who was wise, was happy ", and one still more Concrete " Socrates, whenever he had done some wise thing, was happy ". Personification would give the same idea, e.g. " Happiness is a daughter of wisdom ". Cp. p. 273.

As we have seen on page 243, it is essential to consider the point of view of the reader or hearer rather than merely one's own point of view: in other words, *one must understand the mind of the reader or hearer.* Hence anything which encourages *sympathy* with others must be good for the Essay-Writer or Speaker, and it is the best Practice for him to be always asking himself ' What interests A or B ? ' and ' What is well-known and familiar to him ? ' in other words to take stock of other people's minds.

Indispensable, in Practising, is the art (or the trouble) of *cutting out* afterwards whatever is unnecessary or bad, and of freely criticising one's own work. It is almost as good Practice to do this to the work of others. Excellent Books for this purpose can be bought on Bookstalls at a halfpenny each : the cheaper they are, the more useful they are likely to be! One can often take it for granted that a Book which originally cost six shillings, and is now offered for a half-penny, contains materials for criticism. Only it must not always be other people that you criticise : it must *sometimes* be yourself.

A special Exercise is to find out *why you have failed :* not merely to say that so-and-so is wrong, but to find out *why* it is wrong, and how the mistake might have been avoided. And then it is very necessary to *register* the faults under their different Headings, and to Practise these especially. In order to analyse your mistakes, to make notes of them, and to watch your progress, you should constantly keep at your side either Note-books or Cards.

One or two really good samples, for instance the passage on page 212, should be gone through and read out loud again and again : I know one passage in which I found five new points even after I had studied it twenty times.

A few words may be added in conclusion.

While you are Practising, or rather before you begin to Practise, be sure that the work is made as *interesting* as possible (see p. 255). There must be *some* drudgery, but probably, the less there is, the better the work will be done. The notion that Practice *must* be unpleasant is gradually being done away with in Education.

Secondly, always *use effort and put your energy into the work. If this is done in the first stages, it will save*

time and energy in the long run. This does not mean
fast work: it means energetic work. They are two
very different things.

Thirdly, *when the attention begins to flag*, then, if you
are not too tired, turn to *something else.* Practise some
other thing: for instance, a change from Collecting
Ideas would be to paraphrase Abstract Language
(see p. 233). But, if it be possible, almost directly a
thing begins to tire you, avoid going on working at
it. You may, for instance, try to Collect (by yourself)
Headings for some of the Essay-Subjects in 'Pros and
Cons', and then refer to the book itself. But, directly
your Ideas cease to come, rest, or change your work, or
else do some other part of it: e.g. draw a Map, or else
read the Authorised Version for the sake of studying
the Rhythm.

CHAPTER LXVIII. HOW TO READ.

PEOPLE are often told *to read*, or they want to read, and they are often told or they decide for themselves *what to read*, but they are seldom if ever told *how to read*: the result of it is that most of them do it in quite the wrong way.

I may as well begin, therefore, with a few words as to how one should *not* read.

One should not attack a Book or Article, etc., before one has carefully *thought out the subject for oneself*: this does not apply to Novels and Stories, though even to them it might also apply occasionally.

Secondly, one should *not begin by reading only a part of the Book, etc., and mastering that*: the whole should be read through quickly first.

Thirdly, one should not simply read a Book or Article once, and then *put it aside* for ever. To do this is almost as bad as, or even worse than, the second fault of beginning some single part very carefully before one has grasped the general ideas.

Fourthly, one should *not analyse a Book, etc., page by page*, or Paragraph by Paragraph, or Sentence by Sentence. It should be analysed *in Sections*, probably in Chapters, and the Analysis should not be put aside when it has been made: it should be reproduced and studied.

Last of all, when a Book, etc., has been read, the information should not be left unused. It is a bad thing to stock oneself with information which one never uses. The mind in such a state has been compared to an overloaded stomach.

I can now say a few words about *the right way of reading*, taking it for granted that the Book, etc., is *worth reading*.

It should not be in bad print : never has there been a time when to use bad print would be such false economy. Books are cheaper now than they ever were, and to injure the eyesight and much more besides for the sake of a few pence is wretched policy. This does not mean that one should altogether give up small pocket editions of books : these are very useful for travelling, and many of them are excellently printed on excellent paper.

1. Before reading a Book, etc , be sure to *think out the subject first for yourself:* write down your own notion as to what the Book, etc., should tell you, how it should arrange the Ideas, what Comparisons and Contrasts it should use, and so on. Put yourself into the Writer's position and think of the readers for whom he has written. This preparing of the ground is absolutely indispensable.

Then read the Book itself. I think that, if it is really worth reading, it is worth reading three times.

2. *For the first time, read it very quickly*, so as to get the general sense and drift ; perhaps the quicker you read it the better, just as, in Drawing, the quicker you do the outline, the more correct it is likely to be *as an outline.*

2

3. *In the second reading, study the Ideas more in detail.* Chapter I., for example, should be read through slowly : the Ideas should be written down as Headings when you have finished the Chapter, but not before. Either an ordinary piece of paper or Cards (p. 186) may be used; then look again at the Book and fill in what you have omitted. Write out the Headings once more in a Note-book of your own, or on Cards.

4. It is important to write these Headings under one another, and not consecutively, and to leave spaces between them so that you may add fresh Ideas in the future. The Headings might also be marked 1, 2, 3, *a, b, c,* etc.

5. When you have finished Chapter I., try Chapter II. in the same way, but, before you begin Chapter II., read through the Headings of Chapter I., or, better still, first try to reproduce them for yourself. Then, after Chapter II. has been done, proceed to Chapter III. Chapter III. should not be begun until the Ideas of Chapters I. and II. have been gone through again.

6. Continue this *Résumée*-method,* and then, before you have reached Chapter X., you will have learnt Chapter I. ; and at the end of the Book you will have learnt practically all except the last two or three Chapters, and these can now be learnt in a very few minutes.

7. During this reading, notice any suggestive passages, and make notes of them, either on Cards or in a Note-book ; an A B C (Where is it ?) Note-book is the best. Be sure to give references to the original Book and its pages. These Notes should include notes on good subjects for Essays, on good Ideas, on good

---

* See "How to Remember" (to be published by Warne & Co.).

Illustrations, etc., and they should be carefully catalogued or arranged at intervals.

8. The third reading should again be a slow reading, and in this you should study the Ideas no longer, but rather the Expression and Style. This may not be perfect: in fact, part of what you should do now is to criticise. Throughout this reading again write Headings on Cards or in your Note-book, and write out good passages under their various Headings (such as Clearness, and Emphasis). Try to imitate these passages in your own writing. As to how to find out exactly in what the Style consists, see page 211 foll.

9. From what has been said, it will be clear that as you read, at any rate during the second and third readings, you should keep either a Note-book or paper or Cards *by your side.*

10. Nowadays, also, a piece of advice can be given which would not have been so much in place years ago, namely, to *mark* the Book, *if* the marking of a Book is any help to you; for to-day Books are so cheap that one can afford to mark them. By marking I do not merely mean underlining or adding lines at the side, but I mean also the writing of marginal notes or the making of notes at the top or bottom of the page. Personally, I write a great many notes at the end of the Book, making references to the pages. Then, at intervals, I classify these. For very important works, Interleaving is a good thing; such a work as Buckle's "Civilisation" might well be interleaved.

11. When you are considering the Ideas, and their Arrangement, and the Expression and Style, *do not consider them only with a view to imitating the Writer.* Imitation (see p. 219 foll.) is a very good thing if you wish

to become a writer of parodies, but otherwise it is apt to be a mistake; for you will be very liable to imitate the eccentricities rather than the merits.

12. With regard to the notes that you make, you should label them and catalogue them and as it were *take stock of them, at intervals;* and, when you are taking stock, you will often find that you have a good deal that you can add.   Such notes, especially if they are done on the Card-system (see p. 186) will be of the greatest value to you.

13. [cp. 8.] Do not be afraid of criticising: this is important to remember.   Besides this, the *occasional* criticism of Books is far more interesting than constant imitation: it gives you more chance of working independently.

14. Keep a list of the Books and Articles which you read, and of the dates at which you read them, and perhaps of your general impression of them; and keep a second list of the Books etc. which you ought to read.

15. It is a good thing to read a little every day, keeping the lighter works for after meals or for the short time before you go to sleep.   It is worth while to map out the Books etc. according to the time of day to which they will be most suited in *your* case.   Anyhow, keep as great a variety of suggestions as you can. This is essential for travelling.   Sir John Lubbock points out how many people err in taking a single Book for a long journey; it would be worth while to take ten minutes, before such a journey, in choosing what half-dozen books it would be best to take.

16. And not only should you think out the question for yourself: you should also ask for advice.

Above all, I cannot repeat too often that the notes

which you take should be read again and again and not merely put aside.

Of *the advantages of Reading*, a great deal has been said by many writers. A very good collection of passages referring to this will be found in Mr. Shaylor's excellent little book on 'The Pleasures of Literature'. He gives quotations from many writers.

And as to *the best Books* for reading, the New Testament, the Speeches of Demosthenes (in English), and the Speeches of Burke, may be among the most useful for anyone who wishes to study Style and (see p. 299) the artifices of Style and 'Persuasion'. As to the best Books for subject-matter, those are best which *suggest* most: for instance Buckle's " History of Civilisation in England" would be good for this reason, that it sets one thinking and makes one work out ideas for oneself. For the same reason one could recommend Stout's " Psychology", Hogarth's " Philip and Alexander of Macedon", Cunningham's " Western Civilisation," and hundreds of other well-known works. The lists of " The Hundred Best Books" will suggest others.

CHAPTER LXIX. **HOW TO LEARN FROM LECTURES, SPEECHES, ETC.**

IT is a great mistake to listen to a Lecture or Speech *without previous preparation*, for in such a case it will be like sowing on ground that is not ready for the seed.

A second great mistake is *to write down every word which is said, and afterwards never to look at the notes again;* this mistake is very common at Schools and at the Universities : I have many such note-books!

Still further, it is a great mistake to write down the Ideas, or to listen to them without writing them down, and then *never try to reproduce or apply them afterwards.*

The great difficulty and *problem* is this. If at a Lecture I write down what I hear, I shall not be able to attend properly ; if I attend properly, I shall not be able to write down what I hear. The difficulty is solved if the Lecturer or Speaker, e.g. after the Lecture is over, presents his hearers with a Scheme or Syllabus of the subject-matter. But few are energetic enough to do this, and as a rule the listener has to do what he can, all by himself.

The following piece of advice is most important.

As with reading, so here, *the subject must be worked out beforehand.* What will the Lecturer say? how will he Arrange his ideas? what Illustrations and Contrasts will he use? how will he begin the Lecture, and how will he end it?

The advantages of working this out beforehand are almost too obvious to need mention. When the Lecture comes, it will be of far greater interest to you ; it will have given you a chance of working out the subject for yourself, that is to say, a chance of originality and self-activity. And not only this, but the ground will have been prepared : you will have a smaller number of Ideas to pay attention to, and to absorb and assimilate. Your power of criticism will undoubtedly be improved, and, if by any chance you have thought of a number of good Ideas which the Lecturer has not mentioned, you will gradually acquire more and more confidence in your own powers, and you will be greatly encouraged to go through the same labour again.

When the Lecture begins, either jot down the Ideas at the time, and try to reproduce them afterwards, and then correct and re-write (in your Note-book or on Cards) what you have tried to reproduce, or else write down nothing at the time, and try to reproduce the Ideas afterwards; most of this latter reproduction might be corrected afterwards either by a Book or Books, which are sure to contain most of the Lecturer's Ideas, or by a report in a newspaper, or by a friend's notes, etc.

The third method, which is especially valuable if you can take Shorthand notes, is to write down the Lecture word for word, and then to copy it out afterwards and read it as a Book or Essay.

Much will depend of course upon how good the Lecture is, and on how important the subject is.

CHAPTER LXX. GENERAL HINTS AND HELPS.

THE reader should consult the Chapters on "How to Learn" (pp. 23, 358), and "How to Practise" (p. 347).

1. For the Collection of Ideas a very great help is a knowledge of *History*, and not only of its main features but also of certain Periods in detail; and a knowledge of Biography is invaluable : such men as Watt and Carey and Algernon Sidney are well worth following through their career.

2. Of more general subjects, *Sociology* and *Science* may be mentioned, but it is of little use to read these subjects in the wrong way (see p. 352): they must be read with very careful observation, and must be thought over beforehand, and thought over and reproduced afterwards.

3. *An occasional walk* in the country or in a town may be made a very useful means of Collecting or Revising Ideas : see for instance the Chapter on "Comparisons" (p. 288). It will also secure that very important element, change.

4. In fact, the subject should be *changed directly one begins to feel tired*, and great care should be taken to apportion the special subjects to the special times at which you can do them best. Keep the easiest subjects for the times when you feel least inclined for work.

5. The *memory* should be carefully cultivated and exercised (see "How to Remember", to be published by Warne & Co.); for without a good memory your Compositions will be pretty certain to fail.

6. Memory in its turn depends largely upon *health*, so that health should be a very important consideration for Essay-Writers and Speakers.

7. Without health it is almost impossible for most people to *concentrate and focus their attention* for long periods of time together, and we have found that, in order to succeed, the Writer or Speaker *must* focus his attention not only on the work as a whole but on each of its parts in turn.

8. Moreover, it requires very great *effort of will* to keep the general Idea of the Essay in the mind at the same time that one is attending to each part.

9. Another help towards this concentration is *Interest*. Of Interest we have already spoken on page 255: the preparation of the Composition will have far more Interest if one takes a little trouble about such things as *timing oneself* (e.g. seeing how long it takes to write an Essay of 3000 words), or if one keeps records of improvement, or if one asks for criticism from others, and so on. With a little care the work may become very interesting for *many* reasons.

10. *Practice*, again, we have seen to be quite essential to progress, that is to say if at first it be correct and slow, and if it be persisted in ; it *is* essential, in spite of the fact that the success may not be immediate. One of the best kinds of Practice is Précis-Writing (p. 183): it can be done by the " Card-System ".

11. Another form of Practice is *to take passages*, and first of all to analyse them and find the Ideas they contain, and the way in which those Ideas are Arranged, and then (p. 211) to find the peculiarities of Style. In fact any *good* passage should not only be read, but should also be analysed in this way, so that whatever is good may be found and noted.

12. But many passages will not be nearly as useful as they might be, unless you *read them aloud.*

13. It is a good thing to take a general subject (like 'Slavery', or 'Athletics') and first of all to do it with the 'General Essay Headings' (p. 92), and then to treat some one of these Headings (e.g. 'Changes', or 'Results') as a separate Essay all by itself. For this the Period-Headings (p. 83) will be of use.

14. In the Composition it may be useful to put in a few simple Diagrams or Maps : this is very seldom done in ordinary Essays, and yet how often we see an Essay or Article in which a simple little Diagram would explain an Idea far more fully than a whole page of description. At any rate during the preparing of many Compositions such Diagrams are indispensable.

15. Whether or no one should *write an Analysis* in the margin of the Composition, or should give a separate *Scheme* quite apart from the Composition itself, is a question which has often been discussed (see p. 314). There are many who say that the plain Essay should appear without any running Analysis in the margin, and without any Scheme. I think this is quite wrong, because the Analysis certainly helps those who wish to refer to any particular part again, and the Scheme helps those who wish to rush very quickly through the whole Composition again ; and if, on the other hand, people do *not* want the Analysis or the Scheme, they are quite at liberty to take no notice of it.*

16. This piece of advice is part of a more general principle, namely, *adapt yourself to the larger number*

* With regard to printed Books, etc., it may be noted that the (indented) running Analysis in the Margin is a very expensive item, though undoubtedly a wonderful help to the reader.

of readers or hearers, and especially to those who demand most.

Let your Essay be clear for the benefit of the ignorant and unliterary; let it be short and interesting for the benefit of the lazy and unenthusiastic; let it be correct and polished to satisfy the scholars and pedants, and let it have in it some personal elements to satisfy the young—and females. And perhaps let it have a little flattery in it to satisfy nearly everyone: for intance (see p. 257) "the sensible reader must be aware that . . .".

17. When the Essay is done, it must be *revised* once or twice at least, after an interval if possible. See p. 330.

18. Above all things, *never over-economise in paper,* because paper is as a rule cheaper than time and labour.

19. The need of a *change* of subject has already been mentioned. There is also need of another change—a change of position: you should read a good deal standing instead of sitting. I believe that certain subjects are best read while one is actually lying down. Another change will be to read out loud (see p. 307), at first very distinctly and carefully.

PART V,

PART V. **HINTS ON WRITING FOR THE PRESS,
SPEAKING, AND LETTER-WRITING.**

CHAPTER LXXI. HINTS ON WRITING FOR THE PRESS, CORRECTING PROOFS, AND INDEX-MAKING.

In the first place, there should be *no economy of paper*. It is one of the greatest mistakes that Writers make, to waste an hour of time so as to save a farthing's worth of paper. Time is worth more than a farthing an hour, at any rate to most of my readers.

In Writing for the Press, the methods which I have already described (p. 36) should *always* be used. Especial care should be taken over the *Scheme* and its arrangement.

After the Scheme has once been prepared, a long *interval* should be left. Supposing that the Scheme is done on the Card-System (see p. 186), then put aside these Cards for let us say a week. They should be put where they can easily be got at and added to. During the week the subject will be (often unconsciously) turned over and over in your mind, and at the end of the week you will have certain additions, corrections, and alterations.

When the Composition has been written out or Type-written, you should (after the interval) criticise it *part by part*: that is to say, you should criticise the Ideas and their Arrangement etc. by the Scheme itself; you should criticise the Expression and Style by the Essay or Article; and then you should criticise the Rhythm separately; reading aloud is almost the only means of doing this.

Unpleasant though it may be, yet *the criticism of a friend,* or (better still) of an enemy, is invaluable: there is scarcely one person in a thousand who can look at his own productions with an unbiassed eye. As the mother is wont to think all her children quite perfect, and will not be convinced that they have any faults, so the Writer is apt to think his own Writings perfect. It is only a second person who has the power of criticism; and, the more critics you can get, the better it will be.

When criticism has been offered, it should not necessarily be accepted and acted on, but at any rate it should be considered with an open mind, and the suggestions should be noted down for future use, for instance in an 'A B C' Note-book. In the same way you should make notes of any suggestions by Editors or Publishers, though unfortunately they are not easy to get. I suppose the Editors or Publishers dread a long letter of self-defence.

When an Article or Book has been written, it must be *type-written* before it is sent to the Editor or Publisher, that is to say, unless it has been ordered beforehand or unless you are well known. The reason is not simply that Type-writing looks better than ordinary writing, and that it is easier to read, but it actually is a fact that few Editors or Publishers will *read* anything that is not Type-written. It is much to be lamented for many reasons, but still it is a fact to be remembered.

Yet Type-writing has more advantages when one looks into the matter: it is fairly cheap, of course far cheaper than print; and it gives a fair idea of what the work will look like when it is in print. It is seldom remembered that there is a great distinction between a thing which is heard, and a thing which is read in ordinary writing, and a thing which is read in print. In fact these differences almost necessitate certain differences in Style. Now Type-writing is far nearer to print than ordinary writing is.

But this is not all, for Type-writing, if done by some other person, ensures an interval during which new Ideas may occur to you. Without such an interval it is quite possible that the work would have been sent straight off to the Publisher in an unready condition; after it had been sent, you would think of something that you would wish to alter. Very few have the strength of mind to keep back for a whole week a piece of Writing which they have finished. Type-writing sometimes necessitates this interval, or at any rate a certain interval.

A novice who has written anything for a Publisher or Editor must be prepared to *wait:* a novice has not the *smallest* conception of how long the waiting may be. A short time ago I sent an Article (with a stamped and addressed envelope) to a certain Editor: not hearing from him for a few weeks, I wrote and enclosed another stamped and addressed envelope, and asked him to send me a word to say if there were any chance of his accepting the Article. After three such letters (each very polite and with its envelope), I eventually received my Article back; the Editor said that if I had been content to *wait for a little* (this was after five weeks), he would have put the Article in! This delay is not exceptional.

Another Article I sent to a Paper, and after *twenty* weeks, and after many letters (which enclosed stamped and addressed envelopes), I was told that the Article was unsuitable for the Paper.

2 B

The reader must not think that these are at all unique cases. The other day a friend told me that a well-known Editor had kept an Article of his for three years, and had then offered to exchange it for another (perhaps because it was no longer up to date).

Therefore, even if you write the politest letter in the world, and enclose a stamped envelope for reply, you must not expect to have an answer for some weeks or months or even for a year or more.

There is *some* excuse for the Editor whose numbers have to be prepared weeks and months beforehand: spaces are left, it is true, but these are either for special topics of the day, or for Articles by regular Contributors. Moreover masses of contributions are wont to be sent in daily.

But in my opinion nothing can excuse the laziness of a great number of Editors. When the Writers are poor and have staked a great deal on their Writings, then the laziness is simply disgusting: in fact, it amounts to cruelty. It is concerned with some of the very saddest tragedies that the world has ever seen, and I only mention it because it is very common and because it is as well that the novice should know what to expect.

The following point is very little considered, but still its consideration might have saved thousands of disappointments. *The right Editor or Publisher* should be selected. The Writer whose best work has been once or twice refused is apt to despair, but the reason is not always that the work is bad. I would not for a moment encourage worthless Writers, but at the same time it is as well that a Writer should be given every chance. Putting aside the laziness of the Reader or Publisher, or his bias in favour of the most orthodox and customary views, it is quite possible that the (Reader or) Editor or Publisher may be of the wrong kind for your particular work. Your work may be on a subject which he does not care for, perhaps on a subject outside his 'line'. For Publishers have lines. Or it may be too long, or too short, or the subject may not be treated according to his views of what is right. I have found that what one Publisher has rejected with scorn or even with abuse, another (and perhaps even a superior) Publisher has actually welcomed. Possibly the second Publisher is less wise than the first: but the point which I wish to emphasise is that *he may accept* what the first has rejected. This has held good not once only within my own experience, but many times. In the case of one of my works it was refused at first by an inferior Publisher, then by a better Publisher, then by a still better Publisher, and then by a still better Publisher, and was finally accepted by one who stood very near the top of the list!

For this reason, and because no Writer can be expected to know *what* particular Publisher or Editor will be likely to accept his work, I should suggest the advantage of a good *Agent*. Not only does he save you bother, but he may save you time, and disappointment. Instead of your offering the work to ten people, he will say at once "This is something for A or B; if neither of these two will accept it, probably no one will."

As to *the sending of your Manuscript,* you should have on it your name and address, and the Number of Words (this is very important), and the Date. The Manuscript, as we have said, should be Type-written, and should be paged, and the pages should be fastened together; the whole should be carefully packed, and with it should be sent a stamped envelope addressed to yourself, so that the receiver may return it if he will. If you write a letter to the Publisher, let it be very very short: do not write an Autobiography.

Though I believe it is not often done, still it is extremely useful to send a *Scheme* of the work with the work itself, so that the Reader can see at a glance, not only the subject of the work, but also the way in which the subject is treated.

In fact, probably numbers of Editors would be glad to receive, in the first instance, a Scheme along with perhaps one paragraph or two as a specimen of the Style of the whole. With the Editor's (real or imaginary) pressure of work, this may save many minutes. The Scheme and the specimen together might be two pages, instead of perhaps fifteen for an Article, or two or three hundred for a book. You could write, with them, a short note to this effect :—

Dear Sir,

I enclose a Scheme and a specimen. Are you likely to accept the work, provided that it is done to your satisfaction, and on the lines shown in the Scheme, and provided that it has about [3000] *words? If not, could you suggest any alteration which might incline you to accept it?*

The great advantage of this will be the saving of time for you, as a Writer: and the saving of trouble and of disappointment, and also of expense, if the work is going to be Type-written; the waste of money and time are chiefly to be considered in case the work should *not* be eventually accepted. It is needless to say that you will save the Reader a great deal of time and trouble, and Readers (being human) will be likely to be pleased if you do this for them.

The chief merit of the method is this. The Reader will easily judge of the Ideas, and of their Arrangement, by the Scheme which you send, and of the Style and Expression by the specimen which you send. If he is likely to accept the work *at all*, he will be just as likely to accept it when he sees the Scheme, as when he sees the whole work without the Scheme—in fact, far more so.

There is another reason also. When you have sent your work, and before you receive an answer, there is sure to be an interval: it may be only a few days, it may be many months. During that time, your views and ideas are more than likely to change. Supposing you have only sent the Scheme, and in fact have only *done* the Scheme, then it will be very easy to add to or alter that Scheme. But, if the whole work has been already *written out*, it will be very tiresome to have to add to it or alter it. While to alter the Scheme would take perhaps only two minutes, to alter the work itself might take as long as two hours.

In Writing for the Press, the *length* of the work is of very great importance. An Editor is little likely to accept an Article of ten thousand words, and the present tendency is for Articles, and for Books, to become *shorter and shorter*. As we said, the length of the work should always be quoted as so many Words. The best way is to count the number of words in a line, taking an average of say fifty lines ; and then to count the number of lines on a page (in Type-writing they will generally be the same number); and then to count the number of full pages; by this means, multiplying the average number of words in a line by the number of lines, you will get the number of Words quite near enough for practical purposes.

The *Title* of the work is almost of more importance than even the *Beginning of* it (p. 258), though that of course is itself a part that is worth much time and attention. The *Ending* is more difficult than the Beginning, but *possibly* it is not always of so great importance. When you Write, you must constantly take account of the rapidity with which your work is likely to be read; we might almost say not only the rapidity but even the carelessness. If you were an Editor and wanted to judge of a Composition within two minutes, you would consider three things: the Title first, the Beginning second, and the Ending third. By the first two (and perhaps the Illustrations) people are wont to choose Novels. For one Book which I wrote I had to suggest nearly twenty Titles before I could get one that would satisfy the Publisher. The Publisher, as I now realise, was perfectly right.

A few details may be of use. You should keep an abundant supply of good paper and of paper-fasteners; your Cover should be carefully prepared; and the paper itself should have wide margins.

One or two words may be said about *Dictation.* Some statistics as to time are given on page 191. If you can afford to dictate and to have the notes Type-written afterwards, you may be able to do the work in perhaps *one-sixth of the time;* and the advantage is not only this saving of hours and hours, and the saving of the (almost mechanical) drudgery of copying out notes, but it is also most excellent practice for the Speaker. To have notes before one, merely consisting of Headings (p. 63 foll.), and to be able to turn those Headings at once into Sentences, at the rate of as many as six thousand words an hour, must not only improve your mastery of language, but must also help you to express yourself at a moment's notice (for instance in an after-dinner Speech or in a Debate). Besides this, many realise their faults and failings better when they are speaking out loud to another, than when they are writing on paper.

The Phonograph is to be recommended, but there is a certain amount of mechanical work in attending to it.

If you wish to decide whether it is worth your while to dictate to a Shorthand-writer, or whether you ought rather to write out the work for yourself, you will have to consider *how much your time is worth per hour*. If your time brings in, let us say, ten shillings an hour, and if the dictation for one single hour will cost five shillings and will save you five hours of mechanical work, then I unhesitatingly say 'Dictate'. It is true that you will be spending five shillings, but you will be saving five hours, which will mean the possibility of earning fifty shillings. If you have very little time to spare, and very much money, then by all means dictate.

If, on the other hand, you have a great deal of time to spare, but very little money, then write out the whole thing for yourself, or Type-write it if you can.

It is left for each reader to find out the right mean between the two extremes—that is to say, to find out whether his time is more valuable to him than his money. The question is one that is well worth a very careful calculation.

Why Publishers etc. do not accept Compositions.

When a Composition is not accepted, it may be the fault of the Author (or perhaps of his Agent), or it may be the fault of the Publisher (or of his Reader). Or, again, the fault may lie with both parties, or the fault may lie with no one at all.

Supposing the Composition itself is bad (I use the word 'bad' in its widest sense), supposing it has bad Ideas, is badly written, badly Arranged, badly Expressed, and so on, or supposing it is too long, or supposing it is not in the Publisher's 'line'—for Publishers *have* 'lines'—then the fault may lie with the Author (or with his Agent).

But the fault may lie with the Publisher or Reader, supposing that the work is not looked at or is not read (and this is the case occasionally), or supposing it is read carelessly, or supposing it is read carefully but the Reader refuses to open his mind as it were, or supposing (as I have known to be the case once or twice) the Publisher or Reader has some personal prejudice, or takes offence at something that is said.

Supposing again that the Publisher or his Reader expects that the work will not sell, then the fault may be a fault of judgment, but anyhow it is not always one for which the Publisher or Reader are to be blamed. Thousands of gross errors have been made for this reason, and many of them may be put down to the fact that (unwilling as one is to say it) Publishers and their Readers have seldom received the right kind of education to fit them for their task. The education for such a task should be of the very widest kind, and yet of the most special kind. I do not think that England at present offers any such education.

Where the fault lies, when the Writer has not yet won a name, is very doubtful, for the Publisher can hardly be expected to publish a work which he thinks that no one will read, and, on the other hand, the work itself may be well worth reading, especially if its 'public' can be found.

It is no one's fault if the Publisher has no time to publish; his year's List may be quite full already.

HINTS ON CORRECTING PROOFS.

To begin with, one may say that there should be some clear understanding, or rather some *written Agreement*, between the Writer and the Publisher, stating how much per sheet (of 16 pages) the Author is to be allowed for Corrections: it may be 4*s*., for instance. For, on the one hand, it is ridiculous that the Author should never be allowed to see his proofs at all (this was the case with one Article of mine) ; and, on the other hand, it is still more ridiculous that the Author should be allowed to make Corrections which amount to two or three hundred pounds, as I believe was the case with a certain well-known work. The Corrections were not only huge but also extremely silly ; evidently the book had been carelessly prepared. A couple of perusals of the MS. may save pounds of expense in Corrections.

A great deal of trouble I have found to be saved, if, with the Manuscript, there are sent *instructions to the Printer*, pointing out, for instance, how the Type should be altered, and that Capital Letters should be put in where they occur in the MSS! But anyhow the Author should notice where the Proof differs from his Manuscript: he can hardly be called upon to pay for any Corrections of this kind.

Much has to be left to the Publisher. But, if there are going to be *heavy* Corrections, the Author should suggest that he should have the Proof in 'Slips' before he has it in pages. The expense of heavily correcting print when it is in Slips is very much less than that of correcting print when it is in pages. For, if you add three lines to one page, that will affect the following pages—perhaps as many as 15 pages. On the other hand, the turning of Slips into pages is itself a very expensive process.

In these Slips always ask for wide Margins, for the printers have no right to economise in paper: the paper of their Proofs is often quite inferior enough already.

When the Proofs come, look through them immediately, especially if they come in Slips; but do not send them back at once; if you can, keep them for a day or two, or even for a week, especially if you are going to look through them only once: the Punctuation alone may require a separate reading.

The following remarks may be commonplaces to a great many of my readers, but I feel bound to mention them here.

Write in ink, unless your pencil is very black.

Learn and practise very carefully, one by one, the

different signs for changes. Underlining a word or words means *italics;* a double line may mean capital letters or thick type.

The following little passage will show what the commonest signs of correction are.

To these remarks I may add a few extra hints.

When anything has been omitted it is as well to insert it by means of lines, and to put the new words in the Margin.

When there is anything to be noticed, for instance when the type is not quite straight, then a little mark in the Margin should be quite enough to call the attention of the printer to the fault.

When there is a large Correction, it may be as well often to re-write the whole sentence ; the printer may be able to use some of the old type again, and thus you may save expense.

But, when there is a large addition to be made, then it may be better to write it on a separate piece of paper and to pin this on to the Proof, marking very clearly, in the Proof itself, the place where it should be inserted.

The above Corrections and Hints should be practised carefully, one by one. A very good opportunity for doing this is an ordinary journey, especially in the train : many minutes can be spent most usefully in this way.

But, after all, you will save much trouble in correcting the Proofs if you take great care with your original Manuscript. Indeed, when I prepare works by the Card-System, I find that instead of having to correct, let us say, twenty words on a page, sometimes I only have to correct one or two words on two pages. Not only should the Card-System be used, but the Manuscript when done should be laid aside for a time and then looked at again; a week is almost the smallest time which should be allowed. As I have shown (on p. 369), Type-writing will help in this direction: the delay which it ensures will mean far fewer Corrections when the Proofs arrive.

HINTS ON MAKING INDICES.

The importance of an Index, for nine books out of every ten, is undoubted. There are some people who do little or nothing else but prepare and write Indices, and whether you give up the Index to one of these workers or do it yourself is again a matter of money as compared with time (see p. 375). It will also depend on whether you think that the Index-maker would understand your work sufficiently well to make an Index which would satisfy you. The following remarks are intended only for those who mean to do the Index for themselves.

Read through the work carefully at least once, and try to put yourself in the average reader's position, asking yourself what things he or she is likely to wish to refer to.

While you are reading through the work, make 'cross-references', and write down on a sheet of paper the most important pages, especially those where (so to speak) two or three roads meet, that is to say, pages which contain allusions to a large number of topics which will come in the Index. On the same principle, if you were studying the Geography of a country you would have to make a careful note of the chief towns, and of the places where many roads met.

It is better of course to have the Index too full than too empty: to refer to a word or idea two or three times, than to refer to it only once. A great difficulty of Indexing is that there are in our language many Synonyms (such as Wealth and Riches); if one chooses a single word, it is quite possible that the reader will look in the Index for some other word; it is therefore better to write down both words. Practice in *Paraphrasing* (see p. 252 foll.) will come in useful here.

The Card-System, with small Cards or pieces of paper, is essential; and it is also essential *not to write more than one Heading on a single Card*. It is the greatest mistake, in doing an Index, to write down ten Headings on a single piece of paper. You may have to add some very important new Headings, and the putting-in of these Headings may make the paper in a terrible mess. If you write each Heading on a separate piece of paper, it becomes very much easier to arrange these pieces in alphabetical order afterwards; in fact to re-arrange and alter and add would be no difficulty at all. The following Diagram will show the contrast.

Here, as elsewhere (p. 367), there must be no sparing of paper: paper is very cheap.

| a b c |
| a h i |
| a j k |
| a n o |
| a l m |
| a d e |
| a f g |

(1.) Card-System : the wrong order can easily be remedied if each Heading is on a separate Card or Slip.

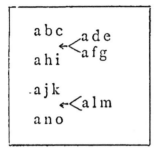

(2.) Page-System : the insertions are clumsy, especially if a d e happens to be a large Heading (e.g. of 10 words).

Besides paper, you may need paste and long strips on which to fasten the various separate pieces.

You also need *a very large table,* on which to arrange the pieces of paper, or else a Holder like that which is described on p. 187. Do not let anyone 'tidy' your papers!

In the Index itself, the references and cross-references might be *to pages* rather than to Sections. To refer to Sections is very easy for the Writer, and is good especially when the book will run to a second edition, but it is generally exasperating for the reader. I know of one book where on one page there are five Sections, whereas another single Section lasts for 25 pages! The reader wastes no end of time owing to this want of uniformity, whereas, with references to pages, an idea can be discovered almost immediately.

An Index can be accumulated by degrees, especially if the Card-System is used. Mr. Swan Sonnenschein kindly told me of an excellent plan. Instead of putting all the Cards for the letter C in a mass under C, divide them into CA—CE—CI—CO—CU—: each will include all the words in which C is the first letter, and A etc. the first vowel : e.g. CA would include Cats, Crassus, and Classics. These can be sorted afterwards.

Index-making is work which one does best if one does it for long stretches of time together.

CHAPTER LXXII. SPEAKING.

THERE is a very great difference (see p. 19) between Speaking and Writing. But the difference is not always appreciated. A Lecturer, for instance, very often writes down his Lecture beforehand, and then reads it out from his paper when he comes before his listeners. What may be clear to *him* as he reads the written Lecture may be very far from clear to those who have to listen. Of this I shall speak below.

Speaking demands a considerable effort of *memory* ;* of course I am not treating here of Speaking in the sense of reading a Speech from a paper or book, which is the worst form of Speaking. Not only should the Speaker remember the Ideas, their right Order, their Importance, and their Connexions, and the Comparisons and Contrasts by which he shall make them clear, or Emphasise them: not only should he remember the whole Beginning and the whole Ending of his Speech (the Beginning being interesting, and the Ending generally impressive) ; but he must also remember a certain amount with regard to the way in which these Ideas are to be Expressed. The Practice of Speaking, therefore, will be a first-rate exercise for the memory, putting it to an extremely severe test.

The Memory, as well as the power of Speaking, will depend a good deal not only upon the general *Health*,

* See " How to Remember " (to be published by Warne & Co.).

but upon the *food* which has been taken beforehand. There are some who cannot Speak well after a heavy meal, and there are some who cannot Speak well except after a heavy meal! See 'Muscle, Brain, and Diet' (Sonnenschein).

There are many *different classes of Speeches*, from the Technical Lecture addressed to Specialists only, and the Debate, which may be more or less Technical, to the popular subject, which must appeal to a number of people of all sorts and conditions, including people of very small intelligence and with very few ideas.

As contrasted with print, and especially with the excellent modern print of Books and Articles, Speaking should be *shorter than Writing;* this applies particularly to *Sermons*, which are often stupendously long. The clergyman who has written out his Sermon has no idea how dull it may be when he comes to speak it.

With regard to *Lectures*, so great is the strain of listening to a Lecture for many minutes together, even if it be simple and popular, that it is a wonder that more Lecturers do not have *intervals* in their Lectures, e.g. intervals for *Music*. I am sure that the Lectures would be twice as pleasant and only half as fatiguing. The interval would of course drive some of the Ideas out of the listeners' minds, but, after it, that which had been said before could be gathered up in a short *Résumée*. The same will apply to Sermons. I am sure that the Sermon of more than twenty minutes, unless it be exceptionally good, produces such feelings of fidgetiness and discomfort (if it does not succeed in producing sleep) that the good effects are entirely outweighed. Whereas, if the clergyman *really* has so

2 C

much to say, there is no reason why the Sermon, like the Prayers, should not have intervals of Music. The principle is a very wide one, and, if only the subject be gathered up in a few sentences when the Lecturing is re-commenced, there seems no objection to such interludes.

Not only must Spoken words be shorter than Written words, but they must also be far *clearer*. A useful hint for those who are Speaking to a mixed audience is: "Make your language as simple and clear as possible, and *appeal to the very lowest intellect, as a general rule; but, just occasionally, throw in some little remark or suggestion which might appeal only to the more intelligent or learned.*

It will be found that this was the method which a very great teacher used to adopt. Most of what he said appealed to the lowest intellects and to the interests and points of view of the great majority of human beings; but occasionally he gave little touches which must have been absolutely beyond the understanding of the majority: these were addressed to the more learned and clever.

Of Clearness we have already spoken on page 227. We have seen how the *personal language*, describing someone as doing something, is a very important factor in Clearness, and also how a *Repetition* or a *Paraphrase* may help much, and *Comparisons* and *Contrasts* still more. These latter, the Comparisons and Contrasts, make the Speech more interesting as well; and this brings us to the third point of difference.

A Speech should be *more interesting* than a written discourse. It should have far more *Variety* and change, and there might be more *Humour* in it. An instance should be given now, and now a general principle, and now (see p. 178) another instance. Wherever it is possible, the subject should be relieved by *Illustrations.* The Blackboard should be used far more often than it generally is, especially at Lectures. Open-air teachers have one very great advantage over most other teachers: being in the open air, they can usually take Illustrations (see p. 288) from the surroundings.

In a long Speech it is very important that the hearers should have *a general* notion *of the subject as a whole;* and for this purpose, unless a very clear *Summary* can be given at the beginning and at the end, it is important to provide the hearers with a short Scheme of the subject itself.

It might be suggested that *such Schemes should be used in the House of Commons.* If Speakers would make a Syllabus or Scheme of their Speech before they gave vent to it in the House, a great deal of time might be saved and the Ideas would be far more thoroughly impressed upon the members. At the same time, the faults or the worthlessness of a bad Speech would be exposed. A collection of such Schemes would form a very valuable education in political life. Anyone who collected, and arranged properly, a series of them, dealing with the topics of a single year of the House of Commons' existence, would not only be able to educate the Public on matters of importance, but would also be able to show those who were not in the House how their affairs were being understood and discussed. The same will apply to other Meetings, and even to Debates.

Some Speakers write down the whole of their Speech, and then learn the whole of it off by heart. For this purpose it is very necessary to *know how to learn by heart* (see p. 87 foll.), for most people do it in the wrong way. It would be far better merely to learn the Scheme, and to get that thoroughly into one's mind, and then to learn by heart only a few of the more important passages, such as the Beginning and the Ending.

As to other differences between Speaking and Writing, the *Pauses*, which are so hard to represent in Writing, can be represented in Speaking by actual pauses, or by what is called "*Padding*". It is a mistake to keep the attention of the audience on the full stretch during a long Speech, and so "Padding" has its value if it is used for this purpose, namely, as a relief. Speaking has the extra advantage of *gesture, etc.*

But it labours under one disadvantage, namely that, *unless the words are distinct and well spoken, the Speech may be a failure.* I remember two political Speakers whose Speeches both appeared in the Paper the next day. The one 'read' as if it were exceptionally common-place and silly, the other 'read' as if it must have been a prodigious success: the Ideas and their Expression seemed perfect. Someone who was present, however, told me that the first Speech had carried the whole audience with it, because it had been spoken so clearly and so well, the elocution being perfect and all the 'devices' being employed in just the right places. The second Speech had fallen quite flat: everybody had fidgeted and talked throughout, because the Speech had been badly delivered. It was delivered or read almost inaudibly, and in a dull, monotonous voice, and without any feeling, and without **any** gesture, except such as a penny toy might make. The Speaker, then, should at any rate master *the elements of Elocution*, and a little Book published by Messrs. Drane can be recommended for beginners.

A Speaker also should have a great deal of *sympathy with the Ideas* about which .he is Speaking; and he should thoroughly understand them. *It is far easier for most people to seem to understand and feel a thing when they Write it than when they Speak it.*

The Speaker should also have one or more *objects and aims* in view.

He should *understand human nature*, and its interests, and especially the nature and interests of his particular audience.

He must also take into account *their surroundings and their conditions*, so that he may use the right Comparisons and Contrasts. One of the most striking features of open-air speaking and preaching (e.g. in Hyde Park) seems to me to be the utter failure of the Speakers to use the Illustrations and Comparisons which abound all round them, the sky, the sun, the flowers, the trees, the people themselves and their occupations. All are wont to be ignored, just as if the Speaker were Speaking to dummies in a bare Lecture-room. How extraordinarily these open-air mob-orators have failed to study the best model (see p. 214). There seems to have been nothing in the surroundings which is not seized on at once, as an Illustration of that which is being mentioned. Of course if the Speaker does not *see* the Comparisons and Contrasts in the things around him, there is only one course to adopt, and that is to practise finding and seeing these, as a special Exercise.

CHAPTER LXXIII. LETTER-WRITING.

THERE are very many kinds of Letters, but here I shall be treating chiefly of ordinary Letters.

1. The first piece of advice is *not to economise paper.* Lines put closely together, and, what is still worse, lines written across the writing, are to be utterly avoided. As we have often said before, paper is so cheap that there is no need for such economy.

2. I should suggest that as a rule, before the writing begins, the *Ideas should be Collected by the " Card-System "*, or at any rate should be jotted down on a piece of paper, not close together and in a single line, but underneath one another and with intervals between.

The advantages of taking this great care about an ordinary Letter are as follows. You will have records of what you have written, and records of the most convenient kind. You can prepare your Letters any-where, even in the train, and so save a great deal of time ; and it may be noticed here that the idleness of people, during that great portion of their lives which they spend in travelling and waiting, can easily be avoided in this way. There is a third advantage, and this is that in the end you will save time by this method : among other reasons, your Letter may be only half the length that it would otherwise have been. You will be far less likely to leave out anything of importance. And, besides this, the Letter will be pleasanter to read. Lastly, it will be very good practice for *any* kind of Composition or Speaking.

There are some who shrink from the drudgery of practice *as* practice, but who would not shrink from practice of this kind, where an immediate purpose is to be served.

3. *The interest of the reader* is to be considered above all things by Letter-Writers; they should put themselves into the position of the reader, and imagine the reader's feelings and thoughts; and of course they will enter into these more fully if before Writing they read through previous Letters from the reader. I might mention, by the way, that to analyse previous Letters as they come, and to keep this analysis carefully catalogued (in a Book or on Cards), will be very good exercise in the Collection, Selection, and Arrangement of Ideas.

4. *Business-Letters should be as short as possible*, and (as we have seen) this shortness can be helped by a careful Collection, Selection, and Arrangement of Ideas by the "Card-System". These Cards should afterwards be kept for reference (see p. 187), and they also should be carefully catalogued.

The Paragraphs of all Letters should be far shorter than the Paragraphs of Essays; the Sentences also should be shorter, and as a general rule Brevity should be aimed at. This is not merely in order to save time, but also because a short Letter is more likely (on ordinary occasions) to hold the attention and interest of the reader.

5. If there is any doubt about Clearness, however, either the passage should be *re-written*, or there should be *Repetition* (see p. 270); and perhaps occasional

Comparisons and *Contrasts*. It is a mistake to let any
Sentence of doubtful meaning, that is to say a Sentence
which might mean nothing, or might mean either one
of two things, pass by itself. A Repetition of the Idea
in another form would be almost sure to put the actual
meaning beyond doubt.

6. But for Clearness and for Interest there is no
greater help than (see pp. 231, 349) *picture-painting in
the mind.* In Letters there is a good deal of description,
and, if you can imagine to yourself the actual scenes
about which you are writing, the Ideas are far more
likely to be clearly and vividly expressed. An occasional Drawing or Diagram is a considerable help.

7. The Law of *Relative Importance* is to be observed
in Letter-Writing as carefully as in Essay-Writing.
The main Ideas should be made to stand out prominently, either by Repetition or by some of the other
means suggested on page 268 foll.

8. *Humour* is of course far more in place in a Letter
than in the more serious ·Essay; at least this is the
general opinion.

9. After the Letter has been done it should be
read through, and should (if possible) be *read out loud,*
and you should ask yourself, as you read it, whether
it is *clear,* whether it is *fair and true,* and (last but not
least) whether it is *kind.* Putting it in another way,
you might ask yourself, ' What will the person feel and
think on reading this?' or, 'Should I eventually be
sorry to have received such a Letter myself?' or, again,
'Should I be sorry to have written it, say a year
hence?'

10. For *it is better to presuppose that every Letter you
write will be kept:* **you** must not rely on any Letter

being thrown away or destroyed directly it is read. It is this that makes it worth while to take ever so much more pains over Letters than people generally do.

11. If the Letter is important, especially if it be a Business-Letter, there should be *as long an interval as is feasible* between the writing and the sending off. There have been many who have never written Business-Letters of any importance (and especially Letters in which they find fault with anyone) without keeping them back for a day.

12. *Records of Letters*, giving the gist of them, with the date, etc., would be always at hand if you prepared the Ideas before writing the Letter. The Writer would find that this would soon become quite an easy and almost an automatic task, though at first it would be somewhat difficult and slow, and would demand much conscious effort.

13. It is as well to have *some fixed time of the day for Letter-Writing, and*

14. *to keep ready at hand a list of those Letters which you have to write.* A still better method is to address envelopes or postcards beforehand: this is far the neatest form of Memorandum. If you have to write a Letter to H. Jones, it is safer to address an envelope to H. Jones, Esq. (there is no need to write the address now), than to write down H. Jones on a piece of paper which you might forget to look at again. Such envelopes and postcards can be kept in some special place.

As I said above, Letter-Writing is very good practice for Composition, or rather it *should be* very good practice, and can easily be made so. It gives you facility in Collecting Ideas, in Arranging them, etc.

and in turning them quickly into English, and in criticising this English afterwards. Undoubtedly, if Letter-Writing be done in the right way, it will increase your sympathy with, and your knowledge of, those to whom you write, as well as your kindness, and prompt and business-like habits, which are indeed an integral part of kindness itself.

A few miscellaneous Hints may be added.

15. Each Letter which you write should contain your home-*address*, and also (if necessary) the address to which an answer should be sent.

16. It should have the date, namely the day of the month and year.

17. Enclosures should not be omitted (though they frequently are).

18. On the envelope the time of posting might be mentioned. It is very frequently the case that Letters are late, sometimes a day or two days late, and in applying to the Post Office it is very convenient to show that the Letter which was posted at ten a.m. on a certain day arrived at least three days late.

19. As to the different ways of signing oneself and of addressing Letters, etc., I must refer to the cheap manuals which are published in large numbers by various Publishers.

In conclusion, let me repeat, Letter-Writing is a thing worth spending a long time over, not only for its own sake, but also because it will be the best possible Exercise in all kinds of Speaking and Writing. For it is seldom easy to get any kind of Exercise which is itself of great use in the immediate present. Most Exercises are chiefly means to an end; few are also an end in themselves.

Part VI

PART VI. ADVANTAGES OF THIS SYSTEM, WITH ANSWERS TO OBJECTIONS.

This Method of preparing Compositions will only have its full advantages if it be begun carefully and with patience. If the reader be too hasty, and try to do the whole Essay at once, he will get very little advantage, whereas, when the different parts *have* been steadily practised one by one, then an occasional Essay, to be done in a given time (see p. 343), will have its peculiar value.

The advantages of my Method will include all the 'advantages of being able to write Essays, etc.' (p. 3 foll.), as well as the advantages of each particular part of the art, for instance, the advantages of the "Card-System" (see p. 192 foll.), and (see p. 284 foll.) of Comparisons, and Contrasts.

The advantages of a *Scheme* need not be entered into here : but it is worth remembering that, if you have not had time to finish writing out your Essay in an Examination, it may be as well to show up the Scheme. It is not every Examiner who will see the point of this : but, obviously, every Examiner ought to be able to judge of your Style well enough by what you *have* written out ; all your Ideas and their Arrangement he will be able to see in the Scheme : he can therefore easily gather what the whole Essay would have been. But it must be admitted that an Examination should also test each pupil's power of mapping out his time scientifically.

The chief advantage of a Scheme I should consider to be that it enables the reader or hearer to get a bird's-eye view of the Ideas and their Arrangement.

One very great merit which the Method has is this. The ordinary Essay-Writer, when he is learning or prae- tising, does, let us say, an Essay on Caesar, another on Napoleon, another on Gladstone, and so on. Each one is done separately, and helps the others very little indeed. But, with my System, the Writer or Speaker has a certain set of Headings and Sub-Headings for *all* Essays on Persons (p. 93): these he has to change, to a certain extent, for each particular person, but the foundation and plan of all may be similar, so that, after doing half-a-dozen Essays on Persons, he gets the Scheme of an Essay on *any* Person well into his mind.

And not only this, but he finds that very much the same Headings will be useful or rather necessary when he comes to do an Essay or to make a Speech on a topic of apparently quite a different kind, e.g. (see p. 92) on Government, or Slavery, or War.

Once again, supposing he has to deal with a wider kind of Essay or Speech, one in which it will be necessary to take a glance at a whole Period in all its important aspects (such as Government, War, Religion, Education, Commerce, etc.), he might, in the ordinary way, prepare or read twenty Essays or Speeches of this kind without improving very con- siderably: he might not yet see that there are a number of Headings which to a certain extent apply to *all* Essays like this (see p. 83). According to my Method, he will *already have* these Headings and Sub-Headings, and can then *apply* them to a number of separate subjects (such as the Age of Pericles, of Alexander the Great, of Cicero, of Louis XIV., etc.). After a certain number of such Essays or Speeches, this List of Headings will also be firmly fixed in his mind.

And not only this, but here again he will find these Headings useful for other types of Essays, such as the *Causes* of War; the *Results* of War, the Results of Religion, of Slavery, of Naval Power; the *Sphere* of Government (or, as Herbert Spencer would call it, of Government-Interference); and see further page 133 foll.

In other words, he will have acquired a number of more or less General or Universal Headings, which will help *to draw out* what he already knows on any subject, and *will show him what he does not know,* and will thus tell him the best topics for research and special study.

Another advantage of my Method is that it shows that Essay-Writing or Speaking is not only a difficult art, but a very *complicated art, since it comprises a number of departments which are almost distinct from one another.* It is, in fact, an art which includes many arts.

For this reason I have given a general view of the processes of Essay-Writing: I have shown (that which really must often have shown *itself*) the difficulty of the art, and then I have taken *each part or process* in the art, and have explained it by itself. I have shown what the chief *faults* are, and how these faults may best be avoided, and how *excellence* may best be acquired. I have tried to give the reasons for each *Exercise* which I have suggested.

Two or three of the *qualities which will be developed* by this Method may be mentioned here.

First of all will come *quiet and calm reflection and work.* The Writer or Speaker will get into the habit not only of *doing* things in the 'right way, but of thinking them out logically and from many points of view, before he proceeds to say, or even to *do.* This cannot fail to affect his everyday life: not only in what he writes and in what he says, but even in what he thinks, he will learn to gather together what he knows *on both sides* of any given question.

If, afterwards, he shall study *politics*, he will be able to judge of the merits or faults of political proposals; he will not (as so many politicians do) look at the immediate effects of any proposal, but will look at the effects upon (see p. 125) the subsequent period also. If a Poor Law is proposed, he will not simply say 'This will help the poor to-day', but he will consider the effect on future generations of his countrymen. Such a training is very necessary indeed for some Members of Parliament, who at present are ill-qualified for deciding in favour of or against a proposal by the mere fact that they possess a certain amount of money.

The study of *the New Testament* in Schools (and indeed elsewhere) is at present extraordinarily unsatisfactory, if we judge it by its results on the daily life: and that is really the only way in which we *can* judge it. *Considering the time spent on it*, we must decide that there are few branches of study which are less fruitful. My Method would insist on a study of the Ideas of the New Testament (see p. 213): the Writer or Speaker would have to go through the best parts and to pick out the real meaning, the real sense, apart from the language. At present very few people seem to work this out: they are quite content to read or to hear a Chapter of the Bible every day, or every now and then ; and even if three-quarters of the Ideas are ill understood and ill realised, they think that they will be heard for their much reading.

The New Testament, again, must also be studied for its Expression. The advantages of this I have pointed out on page 215 foll. For the reasons given there, if we study it for its Expression and Style alone, we shall learn more about Expression and Style than by any other means, and we shall be *forced* by the way to consider the Ideas as well.

My Method is also especially intended *for Teachers as well as for learners.* Thousands of Teachers, who can write Essays or make Speeches themselves, confess their utter inability to teach the subject at all. Those who do not confess this are often condemned by their learners : few of their learners can write good Essays or make good Speeches. This Book gives some of the reasons *why* this *must* be the case, if learners are taught the art of Essay-Writing and Speaking simply *by* Writing Essays and making Speeches. It is shown here that many special Exercises *must* be carefully practised one by one.

The System also includes *a scientific way of reading and of listening.* Ninety-nine people out of a hundred read and listen without Method or System, and the result is that the Ideas, by which they might have been improved, are either not absorbed at all or, if absorbed, are just about as useful as lumber in a lumber-room. As in Essay-Writing, so in reading and listening, there must be a certain scientific system and method for beginners : and this method cannot be easy to acquire. At first it must be acquired by very great effort and conscious exertion,

2 D

I have also suggested *means by which the Ideas which are absorbed should be put to some use,* and not only be thoroughly understood (see p. 349) but also made material for further use: for instance see p. 289, for Comparisons.

In the Book itself I have called attention to *the Interest* of Essay-Writing and Speaking as a subject, quite apart from its many advantages: see p. 150. I feel sure that one of the greatest mistakes in our Education is that we give people things to learn in which they take not the slightest interest, although just a few words or a few minutes of explanation would show that the subject was really interesting and valuable. I can never see that a subject is likely to produce any the worse effects because the learner is told that it is interesting and valuable!

The Processes also I have tried to make interesting. Thus I fancy that there are very few who would not find the use of the "Card-System" (see p. 186) very engrossing.   It makes Essay-Writing or Speaking almost as much a game as Whist, for the arranging of the hand at Whist is very similar to the arranging of the Cards for Essay-Writing or Speaking.

The use of Comparisons, again, cannot fail to be interesting: it will be encouraging for the reader to know that there is scarcely anything that he himself understands which he may not be able to use as an illustration or as a means of explaining something which is far harder.

In conclusion, one may say that there is scarcely a good mental quality or faculty which will not be improved by my System, *if* the System be properly used. A methodical plan of doing *anything*, patience in the doing of it, without the demand for immediate results, ⁓ the spirit of fairness, and a sympathy with all sorts and conditions of men—these are a few of the qualities which cannot fail to be developed. Others have been pointed out in the course of the Book itself.

It is not claimed that the Method will be a complete Education : very far from it. But at least *it will show the advantage of every other branch of learning and Education*, and in fact (see p. 285) will call in those other branches to help it. And it will give a System which can be applied to almost any other subject.

But I cannot finish without a word as to its incompleteness. It is probable that the advantages of some Method which will be like this, but very much superior will be far beyond any advantages that I have claimed for my Method. Moreover, there are certain faculties which I believe will chiefly be acquired through Athletics and Games ; among these would be pluck, and perhaps mutual help and co-operation.

But, in so far as any subject (apart from Athletics and Games) *can* approach to a complete Education, I think that this may be claimed for the scientific prepar- ation of Essays and Speeches.

CHAPTER LXXV. OBJECTIONS TO THIS SYSTEM, WITH ANSWERS.

ONE of the chief Objections to my Method will be that my *General Lists* of Headings and Sub-Headings (pp. 83, 92) are a kind of 'Cramming.' As a matter of fact the Headings, for instance those from which one may choose in writing an Essay or in making a Speech on any *Person*, are not Cramming at all: they really ask a series of questions (see p. 73), saying to the Writer or Speaker, 'What do you know about this question, and about *this*, and about *this?*' To try the Essay or Speech without such a List would be something like trying to do an Examination without a paper of Examination Questions. If the Writer, therefore, will only remember that each Heading is really not a piece of information but a question to draw out what he already knows, or to call his attention perhaps to something which he ought to know, then he will not accuse the Headings of being anything like Cramming.

Again, it may be said that there are *too many Headings* and Sub-Headings: that they are not all needed for any given Essay or Speech. I freely grant that in an Essay on the Age of Augustus, for example, all the Headings on page 83 would not be needed.

But on the other hand I find that, without such a List, people are constantly forgetting to make mention of something which they actually know: in fact when, in looking over Essays, I have asked the Writer whether he ought not to have mentioned such-and-such a Heading, he has nearly always said 'Yes, but it did not occur to me'. Secondly, such a List is very easy to learn, especially if it is in a Rhyme (see p. 83); and thirdly, when once it *has* been learnt, it is very easy to pick out just those Headings and Sub-Headings which one wants, and to reject the rest. Fourthly, to have a ready-made List like this saves a great deal of time and trouble, and produces a much better result: it calls to the mind of the Writer or Speaker a great many topics which he really knows, and suggests to him others which he ought to look up for himself. Above all, it gives him the power of rapidly forming an opinion on any general question. Few things are more striking and more lamentable than the narrowness of the point of view of most English people. If, however, such Headings as these were to be constantly used, these people would very soon acquire the *habit of looking at questions from many points of view*, and not from one only. There is yet a sixth point, and that is that every year we see more and more subjects included in the list of 'things worth mentioning'. Contrast the " Daily Mail" of to-day with an old-fashioned paper, and you will see how much that was utterly ignored years ago is now thought deserving of a whole column. Then, again, such Lists gives a fairly good order for general purposes. For the other advantages, see page 73.

But the real test of whether it is good or not is to try an Essay like the 'Results of Geography on English History', first of all *without* any General List, and then *with* the Lists on pages 83, 107: compare the Scheme which you get by the one process with the

Scheme which you get by the other process, and *then* decide whether the general List is really worth learning or not.

It may be said, however, that such Lists would do away with *Originality*. But, as a matter of fact, there will be plenty of room left for Originality (see p. 219) in the Selecting and Rejecting of Ideas, in the Underlining of Ideas, in the working out of Comparisons and Contrasts, and in seeing each Idea clearly as a definite picture in the mind's eye: all this gives scope for Originality. And, besides, if the Essay-Writer or Speaker is provided with ten Headings, instead of the eight which he would think of if he were left to himself, then surely he has more chance of Originality in working out the ten Headings than he would have in working out the eight. He has a far wider sphere within which to work.

If it should be thought that it is an error to make *the various processes of Essay-Writing or Speaking mechanical and conscious ;* that the 'joints' will appear, and that the mechanism will stand out ; then I reply that this is the only way for those who do not do the thing correctly by nature and by instinct. It is all very well for the genius *himself* to write a good Essay or make a good Speech straight off, and then to lay down the universal Law that the right way of making an Essay or Speech is simply to make it at once, and not to trouble about processes : when he comes to teach a Class of various pupils, his theory will prove to be a dead failure. Personally, I have found very few Honours men at Cambridge able to write a good Essay even on an easy subject: they have no method at all. In such cases (where, if anywhere, one might expect success) it is necessary to begin at the beginning again. But how much better it would have been if the beginnings had been got through and the foundations laid *during School-life.* It seems to me that there must be something radically wrong with our School Education if it does not teach the average boy or man to write a fairly good piece of English Composition or to make a fairly good Speech. That which is neglected at School seems to be beneath the dignity of the University to trouble about, and hence as a rule the real processes are never taught at all.

It is true that the 'mechanism' may appear at first: the result will be something stiff and unnatural. But, after the various processes have been steadily practised one by one, especially those processes in which the individual is weakest, the processes will work far more smoothly and easily and rapidly not only by themselves, as special and isolated Exercises, but also in combination within the Essay or Speech.

It is said that 'Correct Reasoning cannot be taught': I think that the right way of expressing this would be that "hitherto a large number of learned people have failed to teach average individuals to reason correctly". If the processes of correct reasoning were taught very carefully and slowly and in the right way, and if they were afterwards practised (e.g. see p. 150 foll.), then it could hardly be denied that the power of correct reasoning would be enormously *improved.* We may not be able to help some (who are called 'duffers') to do things perfectly, but we *may* be able to put them in the way of doing things *better* than they do them at present: as it is, we tell them simply to 'practise', whereas we ought first of all to show them *how* to practise. The secret of practice, for duffers and indeed for most learners, is to practise, at first, not the whole process, but its various *parts*, one by one, correctly, slowly, and again and again, until each has become half automatic.

I grant that it is a pleasure to read an Essay by a genius, but I cannot agree that it would be a pity to raise the general standard of excellence, and to help the average person to achieve, as a task of great effort and constant care, very much the same result that the genius achieves without any such effort or care, and by a kind of instinct. As it is now, too much thought is bestowed on the genius; too much is left for the other boys to do by themselves or not to do at all: it would be far better if these were coached and practised in the foundations and elements, and *then* left to themselves more and more.

One of the greatest faults of our School-system is that the genius is encouraged and pushed forward, while there is no methodical system for helping the plodder to rise to the standard of the genius, and by hard work and conscious perseverance, for which he deserves real praise and glory, to make up for what he lacks in correct instinct and in unconscious ability, for which natural gifts he himself deserves no praise or glory whatsoever.

APPENDIX. SOME USEFUL REFERENCE BOOKS.

THE following list might easily be trebled : but I have preferred to give few works beyond those which I myself have found most useful. I should be glad, however, if my readers would suggest others.

The Asterisk * marks a work as likely to be especially useful to *beginners*.

Articles: very numerous (in the "Athenæum", "Fortnightly", "Nineteenth Century", "North American Review", etc.).

Askew (J. B.).	.	*Pros and Cons* (Swan Sonnenschein).
Dawson (C. J.)	.	*Essay - Writing and Paraphrasing* (McDougall).
*Fowler (J. H.)	.	*Nineteenth Century Prose* (Black).
Froebel	.	*Educational Laws for All Teachers* (Edward Arnold).
Gibson (L. M.)	.	*Handbook for Literary and Debating Societies* (Hodder and Stoughton).
*Hartley	.	*How to Speak Well* (Drane).
Hinsdale (B. A.)	.	*Teaching the Language Arts* (Appleton)
(?)	.	*How to Write* (Walter Scott).
Kay .	.	*Memory* (Cambridge University Press).
Lamb (J. B.) .	.	*Practical Hints on Writing for the Press* (Bradbury, Agnew).
Lewes (G. H.)	.	*Principles of Success in Literature* (Scott).
Lobban (J. H.)	.	*English Essays* (Blackie).
Meiklejohn	.	*The Art of Writing English*, and *A Hundred Short Essays* (Holden).

Skipton (H.) . . *The Essay-Writer* (Crosby Lockwood).
Spencer (H.) . . *Sociology* (Kegan Paul).
Stout (G. F.) . . *Manual of Psychology* (Clive).
Wagner (L.) . . *How to Publish* (Redway).
*Wendell (Barrett) . *English Composition* (Scribner's Sons).
Miles (E. H.) . *How to Remember* (Warne: in the press).
Morrell . . *History of Mental Philosophy* (Stewart).
Pater (W.) . . *Appreciations* (Macmillan).
Raleigh (W.) . . *Style* (Edward Arnold).
Shaylor (J.) . . *The Pleasures of Literature.*
Saunterings in Bookland
(Wells, Gardner, Darton).

A few *general books* may be added :—

*Buckle (T.) . . *History of Civilisation in England.*
Cunningham (Dr. W.) *Western Civilisation in its Economic Aspects,* and other works.
*Guizot . . . *History of Civilisation.*
Ihering (R. von) . *Evolution of the Aryan*
(Swan Sonnenschein).
Motley . . *Netherlands.*
Prescott . . *Conquest of Mexico,* and *Conquest of Peru.*
Seeley (J. R.) . . *Expansion of England.*

INDEX

411

Works, etc., by Eustace Miles, M.A.,

10, St. Paul's Road, Cambridge.

A BOY'S CONTROL AND SELF-EXPRESSION.
About 600 pages, with 250 Figs. 6s. (Post-free, 6s. 4d.)
Published by the Author at Cambridge.

MUSCLE, BRAIN, AND DIET (Sonnenschein). 3s. 6d.
(Post-free, 3s. 10d.)

AVENUES TO HEALTH (Sonnenschein). 4s. 6d.
(Post-free, 4s. 10d.)

CASSELL'S PHYSICAL EDUCATOR. 9s.
(Post-free, 9s. 6d.)

LET'S PLAY THE GAME (Guilbert Pitman). 1s. net.
(Post-free, 1s. 2d.)

SOME OF MY RECIPES; GOOD DIGESTION;
ALPHABET OF ATHLETICS (Routledge).
1s. each. (Post-free, 1s. 2d. each.)

QUICKNESS; BREATHING (Gale and Polden). 1s. each.
(Post-free, 1s. 2d. each.)

THE E.M. MEM.-HOLDER AND MEMORY-HELPER.
Handsome Case, with Cards and Book of Instructions.
10s. 6d. (Packing and carriage, 9d. extra.)

CHARACTER-BUILDING AND MORAL MEMORY
TRAINING. Four Lessons, with Exercises. £3 3s.
Prospectus sent on application.

INDIVIDUAL HEALTH COURSES : including Advice
on Diet and Drink, Exercise, Breathing, Massage,
Water - Treatments, etc. £2 2s. Prospectus and
Question-Form sent on application.

In Eight Volumes. Crown 8vo. 6s. net each.
The Complete Set £2 8s. net.

PERIODS OF EUROPEAN HISTORY

General Editor—ARTHUR HASSALL, M.A.

Student of Christ Church, Oxford.

THE object of this Series is to present in separate Volumes a comprehensive and trustworthy account of the general development of European History, and to deal fully and carefully with the more prominent events in each century.

No such attempt to place the History of Europe before the English Public has previously been made, and the Series forms a valuable continuous History of Mediæval and Modern Europe.

LONDON: RIVINGTONS

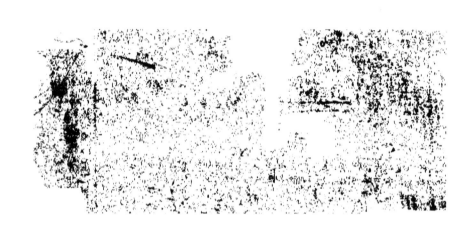

CPSIA information can be obtained
at www.ICGtesting.com
Printed in the USA
LVHW05s1444280918
591717LV00012B/656/P

9 781330 866528